AF652747

ESSAYS IN GOAN HISTORY

ESSAYS IN GOAN HISTORY

Edited by
Teotonio R. de Souza

CONCEPT PUBLISHING COMPANY, NEW DELHI-110059

ISBN 81-7022-263-X

First Published 1989
Reprinted 2002

© Teotonio **R. de Souza** (*b.* 1947)

Published and Printed by
Ashok Kumar Mittal
Concept Publishing Company
A/15-16, Commercial Block, Mohan Garden
New Delhi-110059 (India)
Phones: 5648039, 5649024
Fax: 091–(11)–5648053
E-mail: publishing@conceptpub.com

Dedicated to

THE PIONEERS

OF GOAN HISTORIOGRAPHY

PREFACE

One has to admit that a long period of political isolation and relative insignificance of Goa, added to little knowledge of Portuguese language and limited circulation of publications in that language, did not help to keep the interested academic and historical circles outside the territory sufficiently acquainted with the extent and nature of the available printed material on Goan history. It would be wrong to conclude from this that Goan historiography is so undeveloped or handicapped that it bears no comparison to developments in this line across the subcontinent. On the contrary, Goan historiography presents a challenge to the historians of this country to master the required languages and to acquaint themselves better with the wealth of archival and non-archival source-material available. Those who take up the challenge soon realize that they cannot dispense with the work done by J.H. da Cunha Rivara, F.N. Xavier, A.B. de Bragança Pereira, P.S.S. Pissurlencar and several others. We may be in a position today to dissent from their viewpoints, but it would not be correct to ignore their contribution. A glance at the footnotes in the essays included in this volume will testify to our indebtedness to the pioneers of Goan historiography. To them therefore we wish to dedicate this volume.

What is presented in this volume is a veritable mix of essays covering diverse themes and periods of Goan history. With few exceptions, most of these essays were presented in the form of a mimeographed volume on the occasion of the Golden Jubilee session of the Indian History Congress in Goa on November 5-7, 1987. All the essays have been contributed by scholars and students based in Goa. Not all may display a high degree of research excellence, but they certainly represent the enthusiasm of the new generation of post-liberation Goa to re-assess the past it has inherited, and to make it meaningful for its further growth. The introductory comments of Prof. Sheik Ali have expressed better these feelings. We are very grateful to him for his encouragement to Goan historiography, both through his personal inspiration and by creating structural facilities at the new Goa University. We are thankful to Dr. D.N. Jha, Secretary of the Indian History Congress for his prompt "no objection" to our publishing these essays which were originally submitted to the Indian History Congress. I wish to acknowledge also the expertise of Shri R.N. Naik of the Department of Archives, Archaeology and Museum (Goa), because he has enhanced the usefulness of this volume with a map of the territory. Our salute to Concept Publishing Company, which has by now contributed substantially to Goan historiography and Indo-Portuguese studies by publishing seven volumes of the Xavier Centre of Historical Research since 1979. Finally, we wish to express our abiding sense of gratitude towards the Calouste Gulbenkian Foundation (Lisbon) and others interested in the welfare and progress of the Xavier Centre of Historical Research (Goa) which enters its 10th year of existence.

Xavier Centre of Historical Research
Alto Porvorim, GOA
November 4, 1988

Teotonio R. de Souza
DIRECTOR

LIST OF OUR CONTRIBUTORS

B. Sheik Ali
M.A., Ph.D. (Aligarh), Ph.D. (London),
Vice-Chancellor of Goa University.

Nandakumar Kamat
M.Sc., Journalist, Research Scholar.

V.R. Mitragotri
M.A. (History), M.A. (Archaeology),
Asst. Superintending Archaeologist,
Directorate of Archives,
Archaeology and Museum, Panjim, Goa.

Carmo Azevedo
Journalist, Author.

R.R.S. Chauhan
Lecturer, Dept. of History,
Goa University, Goa.

B.S. Shastry
M.A., Ph.D., Head of the Department of History,
Goa University, Goa.

P.P. Shirodkar, van Goens
M.A., Ph.D., Director, Directorate of Archives,
Archaeology and Museum,
Panjim, Goa. Author.

Agnelo Fernandes
M.A., Ph.D., Research Scholar.
Charles J. Borges
M.A., Administrator,
Xavier Centre of Historical Research,

Porvorim, Goa.

Mira Mascarenhas
M.A., Research Scholar.

Pratima Kamat
M.A., Ph.D., Lecturer, Dept. of History,
Goa University, Goa.

T.R. de Souza
M.A., Ph.D., Director,
Xavier Centre of Historical Research,
Porvorim, Goa.

Joseph Barros
M.A., Ph.D., D. Litt., Secretary,
Institute Menezes Bragança, Panjim, Goa.

Mariano Dias
Research Scholar, Author.

S.K. Mhamai
M.A., Ph.D., Archivist (Management)
Directorate of Archives,
Archaeology and Museum,
Panjim, Goa. Author.

Carmo D'Souza
M.A., Research Scholar.

Sushila S. Mendes
M.A., Research Scholar.

Fatima Gracias
M.A., Research Scholar.

Archana Kakodkar
M.A., M. Lib., Assistant Librarian,
Goa University, Goa.

CONTENTS

INTRODUCTION

Prof. B. Sheik Ali
Vice-Chancellor. Goa University

If we believe in the dictum that a few pages of history give more insight into the human mind than all the metaphysical volumes ever published, we can ignore our past only at our peril. The present is the outcome of the past. Our faith, beliefs, morals, manners, ways of living and thinking, all sprout from our roots in the past. History is therefore far from being of mere academic interest. It is the living cell in our behaviour. We are Hindus, Muslims, Christians, Sikhs, Parsis, all because of the past. We are Bengalees, Madrasis, Punjabis or Goans, all because of the past. We are liberal, conservative, socialistic, humane or dogmatic, because past has a hold on us. Many of our problems are historical problems, and their solution rests on their correct understanding and interpretation. In Russia history is politics. History everywhere is a clue to existence whether you justify a legal code, explain a system of morals, examine the meaning of a religion or advocate the cause for reform or a revolutionary change.

Viewed from this standpoint history of Goa, so rich and fascinating in all sectors of human activity, is yet to catch the imagination of the people. This is because history has always been here in the process of making, and not of writing. Goa has been in the throes of a dynamic change, and has played a significant part in its own way in weaving the web of national life, but it did not find a Livy or Tacitus to project the events in the right perspective. Although in recent times it threw on the national stage a luminary of the order of D.D. Kosambi, he was of a different mettle, not meant to reconstruct the history of a tiny spot, however convulsive its record might have been. Therefore, we have yet to present a full, free, frank and scientific account of this region so as to help the people to judge of things past, to improve upon things present and to know what to follow, what to appreciate and what to avoid.

We are happy in the post-liberation era serious efforts were made to remove this lacuna. A number of scholars have concentrated their attention on this virgin soil, and have thrown light on many of its fascinating aspects. Yet a lot more remains to be done. It is only the colonial period that has been the focus of attention, and even here it is mostly the political, administrative and military details that have been examined to some extent. The socio-economic aspects, the art, faith, religion, morals, manners and customs of the people, the value system of the Goan society, the village communities, the land, labour, business, commerce, transport and industries, the inter-state and overseas relations, all need to be studied in depth in the light of the copious material now available to us. Moreover, not much has been done on the pre-colonial period. Excepting the work of Prof. George Moraes on *The Kadamba Kula* there is nothing else on our ancient and medieval period, although ever so many other dynasties such as the Satavahanas, the Chalukyas, the Rashtrakutas, the Vijayanagar rulers, the Bahamanis, the Bijapuris and the Marathas, had so much to do with Goa. It is for this purpose that Goa University has planned a five volume study on *Comprehensive History of Goa*. Hopefully, it may see the light of the day in the near future.

What one ought to be proud of in Goa is the availability of astonishingly rich archival material built over a long period of 450 years of Portuguese rule, and yet what distresses one most is the neglect and apathy with which this historical treasure is allowed to be heaped in the repositories without being properly utilised. A Mommsen, a Ranke, a Niebuhr has not yet emerged here to scan the material to project a correct picture of our history, nor has there been a Rajwade, a Parasnis, or a Sardesai to edit and publish this material, so that scholars in four corners of the world could draw the benefit of the wisdom and experience of the Goans. Not only the official records so painstakingly preserved over the centuries that would quench the thirst of inquisitive mind, but numerous other institutions as well, such as churches, the seminaries, the private houses, the temples, and the pre-historic sites, all possess so valuable a data that assiduous research of hundreds of scholars for decades would not be able to do justice to the mine of information that lies unexplored here.

It is to apprise our historians at the national level of the colossal quantity of our records here in Goa that a nascent University, two years old, undertook the difficult task of hosting the Golden Jubilee Year Session of the Indian History Congress in Goa in November 1987, when as many as 18 good papers on Goan History were presented. Although this was a solid gain to Goa, yet these papers needed thorough revision, much addition and extensive editing to form the substance of a monograph. This arduous job was done by Rev. Dr. Teotonio R. de Souza, Director of the Xavier Centre of Historical Research (Goa), who very graciously undertook the more important task of publishing them in a book form. We are indeed very grateful to him.

The papers presented here form only a grain or two of the vast historical past of Goa. These papers do not by any means conform to any set pattern or design. They are just an effort of Goan scholars and is reflective of the intense interest each one of them has to launch upon an exploration into the thick jungle of Goan history. Naturally, it is an assorted package including temple art, political, social and cultural affairs, inter-state relations, naval warfare, liberation struggle, international trade, religious and economic conditions, Goan historiography, and the nature of archival material in Goa. Needless to add, it is an anthology of varied thought-process, a bush of different colours, and a tapestry of different designs, all converging to project what Goa was. We are happy to have taken the first step in the long journey to reconstruct the history of this beautiful region, verily a piece of heaven on earth gifted to Goans, and the credit for this effort goes to the dynamic Director of the Xavier Centre of Historical Research, who has spared no pains to make this volume presentable.

4th July, 1988

Goa University
Bambolim, Goa

1

CULTURAL RELATIONS OF GOA WITH GUJARAT

Nandakumar Kamat

The western coastline of India, from the Gulf of Kutch to Cochin has an unique cultural ecology shaped by the events of thousands of years of history. Goa is not excluded from this intra-coastal cultural setting. Goa with its three ancient city-ports, namely Chandrapur (modern Chandor), Gopaka or Gopakapattana (modern Goa Velha) and the less known Revatidwuipa (Reddi on Goa's northern border) and many small entreports on the rivers Mandovi and Zuvari was a great attraction to sailors, fishermen, merchants, Buddhist monks and Jain shramanas, and intercontinental traders in spices, textiles, ivory and slaves.[1] The coastal Gujarat with its ports like Dwaraka and Lothal, Veraval and Somnathpatan, Surat and Bhadoch always had a flourishing trade with the Persian Gulf, Saudi Arabia, Egypt and Ethiopia and with the friendly port-cities on the western coast.[2] The coastal land-route running parallel to the western ghats and reaching as far as Malabar in the south and the Gulf of Cambay in the north, was an important communications link probably established before the aryanisation of the south (2500-1600 B.C. This land-route connecting the coastal port-cities like Sristhanaka (Thana), Suparaka (Sopara), Chemulya (Chaul), Gopaka (Goa), Honavara, etc. developed with the advent of the Mauryan empire.[3] For the people of Goa and Gujarat both the routes were accessible and they made good use of them for trade, pilgrimages and other forms of cultural linkages down the ages.

The waves of Aryan colonisers as they moved southwards they moved also through Goa, just like the Kols, the original settlers of Goa who came via Gujarat. These "Koolies" were aborigines of Gujarat and the hills adjoining that province.[4] The legend of Parashurama has eternally bonded Goa and Gujarat together through the successive colonising strategies of axe-wielding Bhargava clans that shaped the pre-historic Goan society in a peaceful manner.[5]

The Bhargavas in Gujarat, just like the Saraswats in Goa, trace their origin to the Brighu clan.[6] A wave of Kusha people or the Harappans at Lothal probably migrated to Goa around 1600 B.C. to escape the submergence of their civilization which thrived on sea-trade. The Gurjaras, the Satwantas, the Chavadas also started settling in Goa during the time of western Kshatrapas, Guptas, Satavahanas and Chalukyas. The reflection of their cultures is still traceable in Goan folklore, customs, art and place-names. This paper seeks to discuss the development of cultural relations between Goa and Gujarat, specially from a local historian's point of view, through different periods of recorded and unrecorded history, from the pre-historic period to the advent of the Portuguese.

The Pre-Aryan Period

Before the first waves of Aryan colonizers reached south India, there were self-administered tribal settlements of Kharwas, Kols, Shabars, etc. along the west coast. Probably these people were involved in the practice of "burn-and-shift" cultivation with fishing and hunting as supplementary occupations. The Kols settled in Goa around 3500 B.C. and took to fishing and primitive mode of agriculture.[7] The iron implements were introduced by the megalithic tribes as late as 1000-1200 B.C. and till then, for almost 2000 years the Kols and Mundaris might have been using stone and wood implements.[8] The hills east of Gujarat are called "Kolwana" and according to Sir George Campbell this area seems to be the property of the Koolie tribe of Gujarat. These people have settled along the Konkan coast and also the hilly western tracts of Sahyadris.[9]

The Kols might have followed the route from northern Gujarat which runs through Lata-desha (south Gujarat) and then through northern Konkan, crossing the western Ghat on the east and the Deccan plateau. One of its branches running along the sea-shore goes to the south. This branch was an important communication link between Goa and Gujarat. The Kharavi caste of Goa from Kutch, Khambayat and Saurashtra came after Kols and lived on sea and river shores employing themselves in fishing and boating.

The pre-Aryan society of Goa was an admixture of Mhars, Asuras, Kols, Mundaris and Kharavis. The colonization of south Gujarat by adventurous Bhrigu clan of the Aryans changed this picture.

The Bhrigu clan and Gomanta

The Bhrigu clan of Vedic Aryans was a powerful clan always in search of new provinces and pastures for settlement. This clan was related to the mighty Phrygians in Asia Minor and the Brugians in the Thrace province of Europe. This Brahmin, warrior-pastoral clan worshippped "Kubele", the cow-goddess of Asia Minor. This worship was popularised by the Bhargavas who were champion archers.

After crossing the Vindhya mountain ranges Aryans had established their settlements in the Dandakaranya (Central Deccan) region around 1800 B.C., probably after the submergence of the Lothal-Ratanpur culture. The Bhargavas then established themselves in the present Bhadoch district. Even today a major part of Surat and Navasari district is called "Parashurama-Kshetra", named after the legendary figure of "Parashurama" who is associated with the creation of land of Goa from the sea.[10]

The Bhargavas may have started their sea expeditions before the Mahabharata war (c. 1400 B.C.). Their strategy was to create a chain of settlements along the comparatively thinly forested western coast from Surat to Malabar. The legend of Parashurama will have to be seen from this angle of proto-historic Aryan settlement technology. The Bhargavas were better equipped to apply this technology as they had all the qualities of pioneering colonisers, i.e. knowledge of coastline, probably acquired through their interaction with the descendants of Lothal culture [11] in the Sabarmati river area, and the local aborigenes like Kols and the Kharwas of Saurashtra and South

Gujarat. They may have been guided to the Konkan coast by the same tribals, as they had already been exposed to the navigational traditions of a great maritime culture of the Harappans who had prosperous ports like Lothal. The warrior like qualities of the Bhargavas and their reliance on the axe (*parashu*) along with the bow also contributed to their settlement plans. The axe was an important weapon-cum-tool to clear the marshy vegetation along the west coast. It may have also been a totemistic symbol of the Bhrigu clan which had inherited the spirit of inventions from the Vedic period. The legend associated with the sage Jamadagni which explains the discovery of sandals for the bare-footed and that of umbrella to ward off Sun, the sacrifice of sage Dadhichi to forge Indra's weapon, the *vajra*, from his bones,[12] the consumption of fish by the sage Saraswata to escape famine, etc. [13] all point in the direction of inventions of primitive technology in which the Bhrigu clan was actively involved. The Bhargavas must have prepared the first proto-type of iron axe which they developed after their contacts with the megalithic people, who also brought iron-smelting technology to Karnataka and Tamilnadu around 1200-1000 B.C. [14]

The first literary reference to Goa occurs in the Bhismaparva of *Mahabharata* as *Gomanta*, which means the region of cows.[15] Obviously this sanscritized name of Goa might have been given by the Bhargava colonisers before the Mahabharata war. As discussed above, cows were sacred to the Bhargavas and in Gujarat also they had taken to rearing of cows, a tradition continued even today in Saurashtra and Kathewad.

Influence of Parashurama Legend

The legend of Parashurama [16] occurs in Punjab, Gujarat and all along the west coast. This is related to the route and pattern of Aryan colonisation from Punjab to Gujarat and from Gujarat to Kerala. Parashurama was a common title adopted by the successive clan leaders who led various exploratory and settlement missions from around 1650 B.C.- 1400 B.C. and even later. All these expeditions might have been via the sea-route with help from expert navigators of Kharwa origin from Gujarat and mainly from the region of Gulf of Cambay. These sea-expeditions of Bhargavas armed with axes and bows must have left indelible impression on the primitive tribals who were still using crude stone and wood implements and tools. This impression was further exploited by the successive Aryan settlers and by the dominant priest-class by giving it a perfect mythical touch through the legend of Parashurama. This created a belief in the historic period in which the west coast was uninhabited, unreclaimed before the advent of Aryans and specially the sea-faring Bhargavas. But the tribal settlements of Mhars, Kols, Mundaris and the coastal settlements of Kharwas were definitely there on the west coast, including Goa. The axe-wielding Bhargavas may have enslaved these tribals and exploited them by taking away the surplus production. They may have reduced the tribal settlements into feudatories with administrative authority established at some important places like Sopara, Guhagar, Chiplun, Kutthali (Cortalim), Canacona, Cochin, etc. In the later epochs of coastal colonisations the Chitpavans, the Saraswats, the Nambudris are found to have settled in and around the same centres. All these earlier and later settlements were formed through south Gujarat as transit point with the Bhargavas in Surat-Navasari-Bhadoch area acting as guides and agents. In the first epoch before the Mahabharata period Brahmins belonging to Bhrigu clan must have enjoyed special privileges bestowed on them by the Bhargava middlemen. In the post-Mahabharata period Brahmins of other gotras were also accommodated in the coastal colonies.[17] A sociological and demographic analysis of Brahmin population along the west coast might reveal their point of origin and period of settlement. The influence of the legend of Parashurama on the population of the west coast is but a relic of the role played by the Bhargavas of Gujarat.

The subjugation of Dravidian culture and militant tribals (*rakshasas*) by the folk-hero Rama of Aryan kingdom of Ayodhya around 2000-1800 B.C. was a fact known to the adventurous Bhargavas. They emulated the Aryan war-hero Rama by naming their first powerful clan-head also as Rama, who subsequently came to be known as Parashurama, or Rama wielding the *parashu*. This title stuck to the successive clan leaders due to the pioneering exploits of the first *Parashu*-Rama. The practice of naming persons and places after war-heroes, events, weapons was popular among the Aryans.

The Mahabharata Period

As already mentioned Goa was known as *Gomanta* during the Mahabharata period. Arjuna's conquest of the south followed the route along the holy places of Gokarna (very close to Goa), Prabhas (in Saurashtra) and Dwaraka near Okha going towards Indraprastha. The place name Gokarna may have been given by the Bhargava settlers. It appears from the route that Dwarka, the capital of Yadavas, and Prabhas, the holy centre of Saurashtra, both were linked to Goa. The Mahabharata also mentions that Balarama on his pilgrimage passed through Gokarna, Suparaka, and Tapi.[18] Suparaka is modern Sopara on the west coast and known to have been an ancient harbour. Balarama's pilgrimage route also shows that an important pilgrimage centre of ancient Goa (or Gomanta) like Gokarna was known in Gujarat.

The recent excavations by the Marine Archaeology unit of the National Institute of Oceanography (Goa) at Bet-Dwaraka have established the historical authenticity of the port-city of Dwaraka mentioned in the Mahabharata.[19] Krishna had established this city after the exodus of Yadavas from Mathura on the ruins of Kushasthali.[20] The adjoining island called Shankodhana (the land of conch-shells) was a part of the citadel. According to the story of Samba the city was devoured by the sea after the fratricidal war between the Yadava clans. The story also tells of Samba's curse and the birth of a *mugdala* (*mussoll* in Konkani, meaning pounding pestle) which eventually destroyed the Yadava warriors through the stumps of grass growing on the seashore as weapons.[21] This story has connection with the traditional *mussoll* dance of Chandor in south Goa.[22] The cultural exchange between Goa and Gujarat is reflected in the place names around the narrow gulf of Marmagoa. The ancient name of Dwaraka is found in Kushasthali (Cortalim) on the Zuvari river. The village name Verna is corruption of the Sanskrit name Varenya or Varunapur (the village of the sea-god). The people migrating from the submerged city of Lothal might have given the name Lotli to another village on the Zuvari river. Similarly the origin of the village names like Sancoale, Cansaulim, Dabolim, Guirdolim, could be traced back to Shankavali (village of conches), Kaunshahari (the slayer of the tyrant Kaunsa, a title of Krishna), Darbhavali (a place full of Dharbha or sacrificial wild grass), Guiridronam (a bowl-shaped village surrounded by hills). These village names are influenced by the Mahabharata traditions and may have been given by the early batches of Yadavas fleeing from Dwaraka. These Kshatryia Yadavas who later on became rulers of Saurashtra as Chavadas [23] have also influenced Goa in various ways. The Bhojas who ruled over Goa for about 500 years belonged to the Yadava clan. They seem to have migrated via Malava and Gujarat to Goa after the Mahabharata war.[24]

The post-Mahabharata Period

In the context of Gujarat-Goa cultural relations this period may be divided into three broad epochs: 1. The pre-Mauryan era; 2. The pre-Western Chalukyan era; 3. The Chalukyan era.

We can only speculate about the impact of the Mahabharata war on the economy and politics of the entire Indian subcontinent, including Gujarat and Goa. Around 1200 B.C. a nomadic Megalithic tribe passed through India via Gujarat, Goa, Karnataka, Tamilnadu, Andhra Pradesh.[25] This tribe due to its semi-nomadic character and skill in art and industry might have educated societies en route in iron-smelting, building and engineering, new forms of pottery, earthenware, copperware, necklaces and jewelry, etc. The practice of erecting memorials for the dead during historic period might have been influenced by the burial practices of the megalithic tribes.

The period of 1000 B.C.-600 B.C. must have seen rise of autonomous republics governed by the tribal councils in Gujarat and Goa. The republics were slowly overtaken by the more enterprising Kshatriyas. Till the establishment and expansion of Mauryan empire with royal patronage to Buddhism, the pre-Mauryan era was a period of cross-cultural pollination, intra-cultural amalgamation and evolution of ruling class hierarchy, transition from aniconic forms of worship to iconic forms possibly because of trade contacts with Egypt, Sumer, Babylon, etc.[26] The expedition of Alexander opened India's doors to the Mediterranean cultures by land and sea routes. We can now move into the thousand years of pre-Chalukyan era with this background.

One Thousand Years of Cultural Development

The southern limits of the Mauryan empire had been extended to northern Karnataka or ancient Kuntala. Emperor Chandragupta himself came down to Karnataka after embracing Jainism. Both Goa and Gujarat were in the Mauryan empire and we have reasons to believe that the ancient town of Chandrapur could have been named after Chandragupta. The wooden fortification of Chandor area and the use made of wooden pillars in the temple construction follows a Mauryan tradition of architecture.[27] The ancestors of the ruling dynasty of Bhojas of Chandrapur could be the first settlers of that port-city. Kautiliya's *Arthashastra* gives a glimpse of the flourishing coastal trade.[28] Konkan region is mentioned for textiles, precious crystals, teakwood, etc.

The port-cities on the west coast might have prospered due to the overseas voyages of the Jain merchants and Buddhist monks. Buddhist monuments in Saurashtra and in Goa and on the entire west coast from Sopara to Mangalore show us the impact of Buddhism on cultural exchange.

Prabhas or Somnath and Dwaraka or Dwaravati were the famous ports of Saurashtra in this era. The post-Mauryan rulers of Gujarat, like the western Kshatrapas, Abhirs, Guptas, and Maitrakas were both land and sea powers. The sea-borne trade of Saurashtra flourished under the Kshatrapas. In the 3rd century A.D. ships from Gujarat used to visit east African ports, Arabia and Persia.[29] The Satavahanas were the emperors of south from the 2nd century B.C.-200 A.D. They were ruling Goa through their coastal feudatories, the Chutus of Karwar. Satavahana was an established maritime power and their contacts with the Roman empire were established due to the coastal trade from Sindh to Saurashtra, from Bhadoch to Sopara and to Goa, where Greek and Roman ships would halt during voyages.[30]

Bhojas belonging to the Yadava clans of Gujarat fortified themselves after the end of Satavahana empire. They ruled over Goa and the adjoining area almost unchallenged for 500 years. [31] Having come via sea route they had built up a naval reputation. These Bhojas functioned as local naval commanders of the western armada of the Satavahanas with their headquarters at Chandrapur. In my opinion the Christian caste of *Chaddos* in the Cansaulim-Betul belt could be the Chavadas that migrated from Saurashtra following the footsteps of their ancestors, the Bhojas, who had migrated earlier to south Goa. The Bhojas of Goa gave patronage to Buddhism and even employed Buddhist converts of Greek and Persian origin.[32]

The Chalukyan Era

The conquest of Goa by Chalukyas and the expansion of their empire till south of Narmada was a new chapter in the cultural and political history of Goa and Gujarat. The western Chalukyas ruling from Vatapi or Badami ruled Goa through their governors from 570 A.D. to 757 A.D. Avanijanasraya Pulakesi ruled over Lata or South Gujarat and the Chalukyas continued to govern different parts of Gujarat through different branches till 730 A.D.[33] The common rule of one single dynasty over Goa and Gujarat influenced the spheres of administration, commerce, colonisation and religion.[34]

The Chalukyas had established trade relations with the Sasanid empire, obviously attracted by the sturdy Persian horses. The Chalukyan period also brought the sun-worshippers of Saurashtra to Goa. The Chalukyan Sun-image found at Kudne corroborates the local traditions of a Gurjara settlement at a place called Gujirvaddo. Kudne is an ancient village in Bicholim taluka. It is mentioned as Kundivatka in a 7th century Chalukyan inscription.

The entire Kudne-Aravalem area formed a socio-religious and commercial complex during Chalukyan period. The Gurjaras might have erected the Sun temple at Kudne in the 7th century A.D. The cult of Skanda or Kartikeya was also popular in the region. The Sun-pillar at Kudne was used to fabricate the Aravalem cave lingas. One linga bears the Solar disk, a feature of the Skanda cult.[35] The Gurjaras may have continued at Kudne till the attack of iconoclast Bahamanis.

The Chavada people belonging to Diu started visiting Goa on their migration from Saurashtra to Jave and Cambodia. The Chavadas of Diu had set up their settlements at the main trading centres on the coast route to the east of Diu during 7th and 8th centuries.[36] A large exodus of Chavadas seems to have occurred after their kingdom was destroyed by the Arabs in 740 A.D. This coincided with the end of the rule of Badami-Chalukya, although they still had Goa in their hands till 757 A.D. which benefitted the Chavadas seeking shelter in Goa. The Kshatriay Chavadas who settled in south Goa and are today known as Chaddos, started the worship of Shiva by erecting a temple at Chandrapur. [37] They also popularised their ancenstral home deity Somnath and even prompted Guhaladeva I to undertake a voyage to Somnath from Chandrapur, where Guhala had founded the Goa Kadamba dynasty (980-1000 A.D.)[38] Even today the dancers belonging to the Chaddo caste invoke Ishwara or Lord Shiva, their ancestral deity.[39]

The Chalukya rule had developed the port of Reddi or Revatidvipa in north Goa and had a garrisoned fort for its protection. The port city of Chandrapur came to be called Sindabur by the Arab travellers, and it catered for the trade of south Goa and its hinterland. Both these ports must have prospered during the heyday of Pulakesi I and II.

Anahilwad Dynasty and the Goa Kadambas

By far the most important historical relationship during the post-Chalukyan period was Gujarat-Goa matrimonial relationship that had a far reaching effect on the history of both the provinces.[40] Mayamalladevi, called Miyanaldevi or Minaldevi by Jain chroniclers, was married to King Karna, the son of Bhima I of Anahilwad Chalukyan dynasty. Minaldevi became the mother of the illustrious Siddharaja Jayasimha, the most celebrated name in the history of Gujarat. After the death of King Karna, while Siddharaja was a minor, Minaldevi carried on the Government of Gujarat and Saurashtra with the help of ministers. She was also instrumental in remitting the tax levied on the pilgrims bound to Somnath. Siddharaja had a chief among his generals named Jagadeva, who was a cousin of Goa Kadamba King Vijayarka (A.D. 1100-1107) and a nephew of his mother Minaldevi. [41] Shivachitta Permadi, the Goa Kadamba king also gave his daughter in marriage to Ajayapala who succeeded Kumarapala for three years on the throne. Ajayapala was married to Naikadevi, daughter of Shivacitta and after her husband's death, when her son Mularaja II was still a minor, acted as regent.

Naikadevi, the brave daughter of Goa, defeated Mahamud Ghori, who had invaded Gujarat at that time. The defeat saved Gujarat from the Muslim domination for hundred years more and established the kingdom of Anahilwad.[42]

The Goa Kadambas had reached the zenith of their power during the reign of Jayakesi I and II. The marital relationships of Kadambas with the kings of Gujarat strengthened their maritime trade and navy. They organized long expeditions to Gujarat to worship Somnath. The Lord Somnath became a popular household deity in Goa. A temple dedicated to Somnath was built at Agasaim on the banks of Zuvari, forming an important feature of the Kadamba port city of Gopakapattana.[43]

Shasta II had defeated the north Konkan Silaharas and made them his feudatories. His sphere of influence had reached as far as Ganadevi port of Surat, where he built a market shade for the traders.[44]

The port of Somnath, called Somnathpatan, was a great place for trading between East Africa and China as recorded by Al-Beruni (1201 A.D.)[45] The Jats, Meds, Chavadas, Gurjars are recorded as fleet-owners and trans-oceanic sailors by various chroniclers. The Chavadas of Saurashtra used to travel as far as China. Rajput sailors led voyages from Somnath to China between 1200-1400 A.D.[46]

The Goa Kadambas who had trade relations with the littoral states of Persian Gulf, East Africa, Gujarat, Ceylon, Bengal, etc. might have employed these skilled navigators and sailors from Saurashtra and Gujarat.[47] An 11th century cosmopolitan trade port of Kadambas, like the well developed Gopaka port on the island of Tisvadi, must have been bustling with sailors, ship-builders and repairers, middlemen and shipping agents, godown-owners, stable-owners, money-exchangers, pilots and guides for further voyages and people engaged in numerous other occupations related to maritime trade. The shipping experience of Gurjaras, Chavadas, Kharwas, Medas, Arabs, Somalians must have immensely contributed to the prosperity of the port which lured the Bahamanis, the Vijayanagara rulers, the Adilshah and the Portuguese during the later period of Goa's history.

The Jain Influence

Jainism influenced Goa due to its proximity to important Jain pilgrimage centres in Karnataka, like the Sravanabelgola. The Ganga dynasty, the Kalachuris, the Rattas and the Halsi Kadambas patronised Jainism. The Jain trading community of Karnataka and Gujarat built *basadis* at places like Narva, Kothambi, Bandoda, Kudne, Chandor, etc.

The Jain temple dedicated to Adinatha excavated at Kudne and belonging to early medieval period is built in typical north Indian *sikhara* style.[48] This was erected by the Gurjara community some time before 1400 A.D. Such temples are common in Saurashtra and south Gujarat.[49]

The Jain *basadi* at Narve-Bicholim goes so far back as 1150 A.D. and seems to have been built by the same Gurjara community involved in mercantile trade.

Jain *sartavahas* or merchant groups from Gujarat had established trade links since the Satavahana period, but they may have received a boost due to the matrimonial alliances between Anahilwad Chalukya kings and the Goa Kadambas.

The Influence of Gujarat on Goa's Folk Traditions

The *Harivamsha*, religious and mythological account of the king of Dwaraka, Lord Krishna, describes in vivid detail Krishna's duel with Jarasandha, which occurred on the border of Goa, on the scenic hills near the Dudhsagar waterfall.[50]

As discussed above the *mussall* dance of Chandor is also influenced by the folklore of Saurashtra, tracing the ancestry of Chavadas or Chaddos. The *ghodemanni* folk-dance is a gift of north Gujarat and it shows the impact of horse-trade on dance forms.[51] Dances like *talagadi* and *gof* also remind one of the traditions of *garaba* and *ras* in Saurashtra and Kathewad.[52] The Kathewadi-type Rajput headgear of the Chandor dancers also supports my viewpoint of their Gujarati origin.[53]

After the Kadambas

The Kadamba dynasty of Goa came to an end by 1327 A.D. Goa had been plundered by the Delhi sultans in 1310. Muhamad Tughlaq completed the job of destroying the wealth of Goa in 1327.[54]

The port of Goa had become strategically and commercially important for the rising Bahamani and Vijayanagar powers in the 14th century. For the Bahamanis it was a boarding port for Haj pilgrimages and they needed it to check the sea piracy. The pirates had become active due to the anarchy prevailing along the west coast and absence of a maritime power along the west coast. The pirates on the coast of Sindh, Saurashtra and down till Honavar shared common interests.

After a short but terrifying spell of the Bahamanis who did not spare Hindus and Jains in Goa, the Vijayanagar kings annexed Goa in 1380. The Vaja kings were active in Saurashtra till 1406 and they carried intense commercial activity at the sea.[55] Vijayanagara kings might have had trade contacts with them by the sea through the port of Goa. The major item of export from Goa was the betelnut, and Vijayanagara rule encouraged the cultivation of orchards of betel trees as found in their *agrahara* grants. Horse-traders from Saurashtra and Surat were probably involved in import, purchase and sale of horses to the Vijayanagara kings, as they were intolerant towards the Arab middlemen.

The Bahamanis seized Goa by sending Muhmad Gawan in 1472. The sultanate of Gujarat had been established by then with a royal navy at the fort of Diu. The Gujarat sultans were the lords of the seas till 1500.[56] They had relations with the natives of Egypt and the Kalif of Basra. The muslim rulers of Goa might have sought their protection to continue the trade in Arabian horses and to guard the Mecca pilgrims from coastal pirates.

A significant event of this period was the revolt of Bahadur Khan Gilani, an officer of Sultan Muhamudshah of Bijapur. Gilani seized power in Goa, brought Konkan ports under his control in 1493 and looted a large number of ships carrying valuable cargo and Arabian horses belonging to the sultan of Gujarat. The angry sultan had to send a *farman* to Bijapur demanding severe action against Gilani. The sultan of Bijapur acted by sending a large army to punish Gilani. Gilani was defeated and forced to pay compensation to the Sultan of Gujarat, but his failure to do so led to his further defeat and death.[57]

Goa came under the rule of Yusuf Adilshah from 1501. Goa had become a natural entreport of the commerce of Asia.[58] Its fame attracted travellers like Covilhã, Varthema, Corsali, and Duarte Barbosa. Ships from Mecca, Aden, Hurmuz, Cambay and Malabar used to flock to its port.[59]

The Muslim rule in both Goa and Gujarat must have been beneficial in influencing the Goan architecture, shipbuilding, food, handicrafts, music and the slave trade. The Abyssinian and Somali slaves were brought by sea to Goa from the slave markets of Surat and Bhadoch .

Portuguese Conquest of Goa, Diu and Daman

The Island of Goa was conquered by the Portuguese in 1510, Diu in 1539 and Daman in 1560. This was a turning point in the history of Goa and Gujarat as the Portuguese rule in Goa severed the cultural links between the mainland of Gujarat and Goa. Although the trade links continued, the oppressive religious policy of the Portuguese alienated the native population. The Gujarati banias who were observed in Goa by Linschoten [60] had also disappeared and migrated elsewhere. The Kattechis and Memons came to Goa with serious commercial interest only in the beginning of the 19th century. There were only 1345 Gujarati speakers in Goa at the time of liberation as per the census of 1961.[61]

Overall Impact of Gujarat on Goan Society

The long historical relationship of Gujarat with Goa has been responsible for the evolution of a secular Goan society. The ethnological pieces of the Goan social mosaic are almost indistinguishable today. It is difficult to identify Kols, Kharwas, Yadavas, the Lothal migrants, etc. solely on historical and mythological basis. The impact of Gujarat on Goan society is multi-dimensional. It is still felt in customs, folk-lore, place-names, deities and cults, the tolerant and hospitable attitude of Goans exposed to all sorts of "culture shocks", their love of the sea, and an instinctive urge to migrate.

And what has Goa contributed to Gujarat in exchange? Great queens and great sons, an ever welcoming land of promise for hordes of colonisers, troubled people and lost tribes without their power and wealth, and a market for the goods of Gujarat with a guarantee for their safety.

The pioneering spirit of Parashurama is a grateful gesture of the coastal people which they have enshrined in the legend. New areas of research in archaeology, epigraphy, sociology, anthropology, numismatics, naval history, ethnography might reveal some new facts and throw light on the large gaps in the history of western India and on the cultural relations between Goa and Gujarat.

REFERENCES

1. Kamat, N., "Gopakapattana through the Ages", *Goan Society Through the Ages*, ed. B.S. Shastry, Delhi, 1986, pp. 217-232.
2. Gune, V.T., *Gazetteer of the Union Territory of Goa, Daman and Diu*, Part III: Diu, 1979, p.21; Janaki, V.A.,"Some Aspects of the historical geography of Surat", *Geography Research Papers Series No.7*, M.S. University of Baroda, 1974, pp.1-11,26-42; Saletore, B.A.,*Main Currents in the Ancient History of Gujarat*, M.S. University of Baroda, 1960, pp.1-32.
3. Motichandra, *Sartavaha (Ancient Indian Travel Routes)*, trans. M.K.Pardhi (Marathi), New Delhi, Sahitya Akademy, 1974, pp.30-74.
4. Quoted by Satoskar, B.D. in *Gomantak: Prakriti ani Sanskriti*, I, Pune, 1979, pp. 29-30.
5. *Ibid.*, pp.105-121.
6. Nayak, K.D., *Gomantakachi Sanskritik Ghadan* (in Marathi), Margão: Gomant Vidya Niketan, 1968, pp. 60-69.
7. Dhume, A.R.S., *The Cultural History of Goa*, Panaji, 1986, pp. 43-97.
8. Kosambi, D.D., *The Culture and Civilisation of Ancient India in Historical Outline*, New Delhi, 1982, pp.112, 139, 163.
9. Satoskar, *op. cit.*,,p. 30.
10. Nayak, *op. cit.*, pp. 60-69.
11. Motichandra, *op. cit.*, pp. 37-43.
12. Nayak, *op. cit.*, pp. 60-69.
13. Satoskar, *op. cit.*, pp. 124-125.
14. Kosambi, *op. cit.*, pp. 91, 139, 190.
15. Satoskar, B.D., *Gomantak: Prakriti ani Sanskriti*, II, Pune, 1982, pp. 20-21.
16. Satoskar, *op. cit.*, I, pp. 105-110.
17. Nayak, *op.cit.*, pp. 90-99.
18. Satoskar, *op.cit.*, II, pp. 65-73.

19. Rao, S.R., "Marine archaeological explorations off Dwaraka, Northwest Coast of India", *Indian Journal of Marine Sciences*, New Delhi, CSIR, Vol. 16, n.1, March 1987, pp.22-30.
20. Nayak, *op. cit.*, pp. 90-99.
21. *Ibid.*, pp. 36-37.
22. Gomes, O. J. F., *Village Goa*, New Delhi, 1987, pp. 320-27.
23. Gune, *op. cit.*, III, pp. 14-16.
24. Satoskar, II, 104-110; Nayak, *op. cit.*, pp. 37-42.
25. Kosambi, *op. cit.*, pp. 139, 190.
26. Motichandra, *op. cit.*, pp. 35-36.
27. Kosambi, *op. cit.*, p. 160; Gomes,*op. cit.*, pp. 33-35, 50-53.
28. Motichandra, *op. cit.*, pp. 97-108.
29. Gune, *op. cit.*, II, Part 3, pp. 12-13.
30. Motichandra, *op. cit.*, pp. 144-48.
31. Satoskar, II, pp. 104-110.
32. *Ibid.*, p. 106.
33. Saletore, *op. cit.*, p. 35.
34. *Ibid.*, p. 36.
35. Satoskar, II, pp. 128-45; Dhume, *op. cit.*, pp. 215-22.
36. Gune, *op. cit.*, pp. 14-15.
37. Gomes, *op. cit.*, pp. 16, 33-35.
38. Satoskar, II, pp. 218-19.
39. Gomes, *op. cit.*, pp. 321-22.
40. Saletore, *op. cit.*, pp. 40-41.
41. Gune, *op. cit.*, pp. 15-18; Saletore, *op. cit.*, pp. 40-42.
42. *Ibid.*, p. 16.
43. Satoskar, II, pp. 225-38.
44. *Ibid.*, p. 379.
45. Gune, *op. cit.*, p. 17.
46. *Ibid.*, pp. 17-18.
47. Satoskar,*op. cit.*, pp. 220-40.
48. Personal observations during and after the excavations at Gujirvado-Kudnem (Bicholim), Goa.
49. Sankalia, H.D., *The archaeology of Gujarat (including Kathiawar)*, Bombay, 1939, pp. 1-60.
50. Satoskar, II, pp. 68-9.
51. Dhume, *op. cit.*, pp. 225-26.
52. Personal observations of dance performances and oral history recordings.
53. Gomes, *op. cit.*, pp. 321-7.
54. Satoskar, II, pp. 284-5, 290-2.
55. Gune, *op. cit.*, pp. 18-19.
56. Gune, *op. cit.*, pp. 20-1.
57. Pereira, G.A., *An outline of pre-Portuguese history of Goa*, Vasco da Gama, 1973, pp. 83-4.
58. Fonseca, J.N.da, *An historical and archaeological sketch of the city of Goa*, New Delhi (reprint), 1986, p. 132.
59. *Ibid.*, pp. 132-3.
60. *Ibid.*, p. 157.
61. Satoskar, I, pp. 579-85.

2

TRIKUTACHALA TEMPLE OF AGAPUR

V.R. Mitragotri

The earliest archaeological evidence of the syncretistic aniconic representation from Goa is found in Aravalem and there we find Siva, Surya and Kartikeya.[1] According to Vasanta Madhava the Goans were the first to make compromise between Vaisnavism and Saivism by invoking Siva and Vishnu simultaneously as known from Dodavad inscription.[2] The recent studies have shown that *Skanda Purana* is not later than 1100 A.D.[3] Therefore we need not hesitate to rely upon the data available in this Purana. In Kamakshi Mahatmya of Sahyadrikhanda of *Skanda Purana* there is a reference to Hari and Hara. A Brahmin named Agnimukha from Raia surrendered to Hari and Hara after Mahishasur demon swallowed his son Gunamukha. Agnimukha surrendered to both Hari and Hara and he did not discriminate between Siva and Visnu. Both Hari and Hara advised him to go to Kamakshi.[4] Therefore even here we find syncretistic trend.

The tradition of trikutachala temple in Goa was found in Rasaim in Salcete taluka on the banks of Aganasini (Zuvari) river.[5] There this trikuta is composed of Trivikrama, Narayana and Ishwar. This temple was destroyed by the Portuguese in the 16th century along with other Hindu shrines in the three talukas of old conquest of Goa, namely Salcete, Tiswadi and Bardez.[6] The Hindus were shocked to see their temples being destroyed, and it took them considerable time to recover. After nearly one and half centuries in the middle of the 18th century the devotees constructed the *trikutachala* shrine in Agapur in Ponda taluka which is opposite to Rasaim on the right bank of Aganasini (Zuvari). The tradition of **trikuta** could survive during this intervening period. However, this changed composition of it into Madhav, Govind and Rameshwar. It may be noted at Rasaim that the first two deities are Vaishnavite namely Trivikrama and Narayana, and in Agapur also the first two deities are Vaishnavite namely Madhav and Govind. In the case of the third deity also we notice that Ishwar is changed into Rameshwar at Agapur.

The unique syncretistic temple of Madhav, Govind and Rameshwar located in Agapur of Ponda taluka has been mentioned in Marg volume devoted to Goa in an article of the well-known German archaeologist Mitterwalner.[7] A year after the publication of the above article two professional architects from Goa wrote on Mahadeo temple of Agapur in the *Purabilekha-Puratatva*.[8] Dr. Mitterwallner had no scope in her article to discuss at length about this unique syncretistic temple of Agapur as it is a general paper devoted to the ancient medieval sculpture and architecture of Goa. However, the authors referred to later had an opportunity to discuss the various aspects of the said temple in greater detail. In order to furnish additional data available with me, I wish to take up this temple again for study.

The place name of Agapur according to traditions current is connected with the visit of the sage Agatsya to the South of Vindhyas. According to another tradition it is derived from Agnipura and Agni. Hence in the abode of peace on the bank of the river Aganasini the sages performed sacrifices. There are some who believe that Agrapur became Agapur. This village is about 34 kms. from Panjim. The temple of Madhav, Govind and Rameshwar was constructed in the midst of hillocks and is not easily accessible. In the mountainous parts of Goa there were no good roads connecting villages and towns. According to Fonseca the total length of the road network during this period was only 128 miles.[9] These were merely cart roads, and as ox-carts or horse carriages were scarcely used in Goa, the principal means of conveyance consisted of palanquins of various types.

It is interesting to note that we rarely encounter a hero-stone depicting cattle-raid scene. This is so because the cattle population in Goa region is meagre as compared with the neighbouring Deccan. Moreover the bullocks are not strong enough to carry the load in this difficult terrain as they get exhausted. Even for ploughing we often see buffaloes used in the Konkan. Due to these factors the people in Goa had to depend upon the river transportation. There were regular ferries sailing between Sakhali and Panji, Madkai and Kutthali, Mapsa and Sirganv, Durbhat and Panji, Savorde and Panji. This list is not exhaustive, but it gives an idea of the role played by the two rivers Zuvari and Mandovi in the economic and cultural life of Goa. There were regular ferries on the routes mentioned above right up to 1950. The journey by such a ferry caught the imagination of a local Marathi poet who has described it in a poem he published more than five decades ago.[10] The town of Ponda which is the headquarter of the taluka bearing the same name came into prominence only after the construction of metal roads and the introduction of automobiles. Earlier the headquarters of Ponda taluka (ancient Antruz) was Badarigram or Bori which is on the bank of river Zuvari.[11] Due to the above factors the people of Goa constructed their shrines in the villages which were not far from the river. The important temples like Mhalsa at Veranyapur, Mangueshi at Kushastali, Shantadurga at Kelxi, Narasinha at Sankval, the ancient Saptakoteswar temple of Divadi, Ramnath of Lottli, were all located on the banks of rivers. Nagesh temple and Mahalakshmi temple of Bandivade are also similarly located. Mhalsa temple or Shantadurga temple are recent constructions and were undertaken after the destruction of the temples by the Portuguese.[12] The village of Agapur provided shelter for the continuance of *trikutachala* temple tradition in Goa even after the destruction of *trikutachala* at Rasaim and it is the only such shrine in the territory of Goa.

It is not at all surprising to find Madhav and Govind (both being the epithets of Vishnu) together in Antruz. This Antruz is known as Anant Urjadesh, the land of infinite energy, and it may be also interpreted as Anant Uragapur. Vishnu is referred to as Anantshayana. Therefore, the locality came to be called Antruz. The taluka of

Ponda has four shrines of Vishnu and these were worshipped in the respective villages right from the Kadamba period. These four shrines are in Keri, Kunkaliem, Savaiverem and Priyol. They are dedicated to Narayan in the first two localities, the Anant temple is in Savaiverem, and the Keshav temple in Priyol. Alongside with the Vaishnavite deities there were also Shiva temples in the region. In Priyol itself there is Nagesh temple mentioned in a Kadamba inscription.[13] There is a Nagesh temple in Nageshi, and a temple of Ramnath in Ramnathi. Both these shrines are also in the Ponda taluka. All this goes to indicate mutual tolerance among the devotees of Vishnu and Shiva.

While the entrance is on the western side, the other three sides of the temple are surrounded by hills. The entire building of the Agapur temple is constructed with a locally available laterite. Only for the door jambs schist has been used. The three shrines are rectangular and built next to each other in a row. Each shrine is topped by a laterite dome and they have roofs covered with Mangalore tiles. The shrines share a common platform. The probings of the two above mentioned architects have revealed that earlier each deity had its own independent platform. It was only at later date that they all came to share a common platform. That completed the process of syncretisation.

The Portuguese took Ponda, Kankon and Sanguem from Sunda in 1763. However, their policy of religious persecution officially continued till the suppression of the Inquisition in 1820. It is easy therefore to understand why a secure and secluded location was chosen for the construction of the three shrines in the midst of the hilly area. It would be reasonable to fix the date of the construction of the temple to the middle of the 18th century.

We find the image of Madhava in the shrine on the extreme left. It has a rather disproportionately long chin and thick lips. This is not the classical style and belongs to c.1800 A.D. There is no image of Govind, but he is represented aniconically, which is not uncommon in Goa. The linga of Rameshwar is housed in the third shrine. Damodar is worshipped in Goa in the form of linga at Jambavali in Kepem taluka and Ravalnath is also worshipped in the form of linga in some Goan villages. This again goes to indicate the harmony that prevailed among the Vaishnavites and the Shaivites. The former were not reluctant to worship Vishnu in the form of linga.

The Dwarapalakas (the door keepers) housed in the niches at the entrance of Rameshwar temple are damaged on account of fire (as reported by the priest of the temple). However, only the outline of the *dwarapalaka* figures and the crowns adorning their heads have remained. These traces reveal that they belong to the middle of the 18th century. The crowns of the *dwarapalakas*, the style of sculpture resemble the Madhukeshwara *parivar devata* shrines housed in the *prakara* of the temple in Banavasi. This resemblance enables us to date the temple of Agapur to the middle of the 18th century.

It is stated that the earliest Indian domes are Buddhist in origin and pre-muslim.[14] The Buddhist stupas or relic shrines were almost hemispherical in shape and built of solid brick work, but later images of Buddha began to be placed under domed canopies supported by columns as seen in Ajanta. However, it may be noted that the dome is necessarily a structural one and being so would be constructed in Magadha country with ribs of bamboo bent in the shape of lotus leaf or bulbous shape. One can find such eight-ribbed structural domes at Mamallapur and Kulugamalai.[15] The stupas of rock-cut caves do not bear any load and no challenges of construction are involved. And to recall the definition of architecture by Percy Brown it implies good construction truthfully expressed.[16] This definition cannot be applied strictly to the rock-cut caves. They are expert achievements but involve no constructional principles. Their columns signify no adjustment of support to load, the arches carry no weight, nor do their counteract any thrust, and in the whole operation no structural intelligibility is required. In brief, rock-architecture is not architecture but sculpture on a grand and magnificent scale.[17] This makes it clear to us that the theory of Havell regarding the dome is not convincing and acceptable. On the contrary, Mitterwallner has rightly pointed out that the impact of Muslim art and culture on Goa is demonstrated by the triple shrines at Agastipura. The three temples placed on a common platform and dedicated to Madhava Deva, Govind Purusa, and Rameshwara are roofed by typical Muslim domes.[18]

The tradition current in the area of Agapur ascribes the temple to the period of Jnaneshwar. However, the evidence we have leads us to place the temple in the Portuguese period. Hence, the tradition is devoid of historical basis. It is an important relic of *trikutachala* tradition with Islamic architectural influence.

REFERENCES

1. K.V. Soundara Rajan, *Cave Temples of Deccan*, New Delhi, 1981, p.4.
2. K.G. Vasanta Madhava, "Gove-Karnataka Cultural Contacts from 1000-1600 A.D.",*Goa: Cultural Trends*, ed. P.P. Shirodkar, Panaji, 1988,p.28.
3. A.B.L. Awasthi, *Studies in Skanda Furana*, Lucknow, 1965.
4. *Sri Skandapurana-Sahyadrikhand* with translation in Marathi by Gaytonde Gajanan Shastri, Bombay, 1971.
5. Rui Gomes Pereira, *Hindu Temples and Deities*, Panjim, 1979, p.105.
6. V.R. Mitragotri, "Influence of Western Architecture on Hindu Temple of Goa (18th century to 20th century),*Rangavallli* (S.R. Rao Felicitation Volume), New Delhi, 1983, pp. 279-284.
7. Grittli v. Mittelwallner, "Hindu Past: Sculpture", *Goa: Cultural Patterns*, ed. S.V. Doshi, Bombay, 1983, p.37.
8. K.D. Sadhale and Raj Desai, "Mahadeo Temple of Agapur", *Purabhileka-Puratatva*, II,n.2, Panaji, 1984, pp. 101- 118.
9. J.N. da Fonseca, *An Historical and Archaeological Sketch of the City of Goa*, New Delhi, 1986 (reprint),p.33.
10. R.P. Vaidya," Hoditale Svapna", *Kavyakunja*, ed. Shiva Phatu Pai Angle, Panjim, 1930, p.67.
11. A.R.S. Dhume, *The Cultural History of Goa*, Panjim, 1986, p.193.
12. V.R. Mitragotri,*op.cit.*,pp.279-284. Cf.also *Goa: Cultural Patterns*,pp.53-60.
13. *Gazetteer of the Union Territory of Goa, Daman and Diu*, Panjim, 1979, p.62.
14. E.B. Havell, *Indian Architecture*, New Delhi,p.93.
15. *Ibid.*, p.19.
16. Percy Brown, *Indian Architecture*, Bombay, 1971, p.19.
17. *Loc. cit.*
18. Mitterwalner, *op.cit.*,p.37.

3

TIMMAYYA: A QUISLING?

Carmo Azevedo

It is sufficiently well known to those who are conversant with the history of India that an Indian native called Timmayya (*Timoja* of the Portuguese chroniclers) greatly helped the Portuguese. He not only prompted Afonso de Albuquerque to launch an attack on Goa (then under the sultans of Bijapur and a base where the Turks and Egyptians were building ships in the Portuguese fashion under his very nose) rather than sailing all the way to the Red Sea to destroy the fleet of the Sultan of Egypt, but also actively assisted the Portuguese Governor in the capture and recapture of Goa in 1510. The same Timmayya had earlier served as a mediator in peace-negotiations when D. Francisco de Almeida, the first Portuguese viceroy, was at war with the king of Gersoppa in 1505. The latter and himself subsequently became vassals of the king of Portugal.

Several scholars have in the last fifty years or so dwelt on the subject of Timmayya's relationship with the Portuguese. To begin with, Panduronga S. S. Pissurlencar published an article entitled "Colaboradores Hindus de Afonso de Albuquerque" in 1941 in which Timmayya holds a prominent place.[1] Joseph Barros presented a paper entitled "Local collaborators of Albuquerque" at an international seminar in Goa in 1983, and Timmayya also figured there very prominently.[2] But by far the most comprehensive account of

Timmayya's relations with the Portuguese is an article by B. S. Shastry, first published in a journal in Udipi and later incorporated in a book, covering as it does the entire period from the discovery of a sea route by Vasco da Gama (1498) to Albuquerque's grant, on Timmayya's death, of a pension to his family for the services rendered to the Portuguese (1513).[3]

Who was Timmayya who played a leading role in the conquest of Goa? I am not concerned here with Timmayya's "nationality", as Shastry puts it, whether he was a Maratha, as Longworth Dames[4] and V. T. Gune[5] think he was, or a Kannadiga, as his name seems to suggest[6], or even a Goan, as could be inferred from the fact that he had a brother in Goa, Chidambara by name, who had driven him out of the place, after not only having deprived him of his due share in the family estate, but also taken his wife and killed a son.[7] Nor am I concerned here with his religion, whether he was a Hindu, as the word *gentio* used by most of the Portuguese chroniclers would imply,[8] or a Jain, as could be deduced from the name of his brother as well as from the fact of his marriage to a princess of Gersoppa,[9] or even a Muslim, as at least one Portuguese chronicler asserts.[10] Yet a third question of no concern to me now is Timmayya's status in the society, his regular profession and/or his rank in the hierarchy of the Vijayanagar administration, whether he was a man of low birth[11], or a pirate[12], or a leader of robbers [13], or a high-ranking officer of the Vijayanagar emperors.[14] All these issues have been competently tackled by Shastry, except for the possibility, very remote indeed, of Timmayya being a Mohammedan and the ommission of his actually holding the post of Admiral and Governor of Honavar in the Vijayanagar empire.[15]

My only purpose in the present essay is to assess as objectively as possible Timmayya's role in the Indian history as far as the Portuguese are concerned, that is, whether it was right or wrong on his part to assist the foreign Portuguese intruders. The questions I am asking here could be formulated as : Was Timmayya just a good man as Albuquerque thought he was,[16] a man of high standing and great ambitions, eager for some reason or other to befriend or ingratiate himself with the Portuguese,[17] a dedicated friend of theirs,[18] a loyal servant of their king,[19] a self-proclaimed vassal,[20] a willing collaborator, as both Pissurlencar and Barros would seem to indicate by the very titles of their studies,[21] a real quisling, as Tristão de Bragança-Cunha, the Father of Goan Nationalism, and later Evagrio George, also a freedom-fighter dubbed him?[22]

While making an attempt at a value judgement on Timmayya in order to pronounce a final verdict on him, one must examine the whole question from all possible angles, taking into due consideration the peculiar circumstances then obtaining in India.

To start with, one must consider that at the time of the Portuguese arrival India was a distinct and clear-cut geographical entity, but it was not a nation in the modern sense of the term. It was an odd assortment of a multitude of kingdoms or principalities, big and small, fighting among themselves for survival or domination.[23] Moreover, some of the chieftains were Hindus (and a few Jains or Buddhists), while some others were Muslims. The Hindu and the Muslim rulers were at loggerheads with one another. With special regard to Vijayanagar, it must be borne in mind that this Hindu empire actually had come into being as a bulwark against the Muslim expansionism in the South,[24] and its emperors regarded the neighbouring Muslim rulers as sworn enemies. On the other hand, it must not be overlooked that the Portuguese also bore a fierce hatred for the Moors since the days of their occupation of the Iberian peninsula for over seven centuries (712-1492). This explains why the Portuguese were inclined to be friendly towards the Hindus, and actually developed intimate ties with the Vijayanagara emperors.[25]

Another factor to be taken into account is that Goa had belonged to Vijayanagar for over 100 years, namely from 1366 when Madhava Mantri, a general of Bukka I captured it, till 1469 when it fell to Mohamed Gawan, the minister of the Bahamani ruler Mohamed Shah III.[26] Following the break-up of the Bahamani empire and the emergence of the five sultanates of the Deccan, Goa fell naturally to the lot of the nearest of them, namely Bijapur. It was under the Adilshahi that Goa grew further in importance overshadowing both Honavar and Bhatkal, the two most important harbours of Vijayanagar on the west coast. Having thus lost two important bases for lucrative trade, it was but natural that the Rayas of Vijayanagar short of recapturing Goa should have minimised their loss by preventing the merchant ships from sailing up to Goa bypassing either Bhatkal or Honavar. In fact, it was under specific instructions from Krishna Deva Raya (the *Crisnarao* of the Portuguese chroniclers) that Timmayya was forcing the ships to avoid Goa in favour of Honavar and Bhatkal, and on their refusal, would attack and loot them.[26] Timmayya cannot be considered as a pirate since he was acting on the orders of his emperor and fulfilling his duties of an admiral of Vijayanagar. Vasco da Gama was doing the same for his king. Moreover piracy was the order of the day in those far-off times, and whoever felt strong enough indulged in it.

Timmayya also had personal reasons to prevail upon Afonso de Albuquerque to capture Goa.[27] As the chronicler Barros mentions more than once, Timmayya had not till then succeeded in his efforts in this direction.[28] Besides, dispossessed of his inheritance by his brother, he hoped that it would be restored to him by Albuquerque in case Goa was captured. As the Portuguese under Almeida appeared interested only in securing the mastery of the seas with a chain of factories and fortresses along the coast, and seemed to have no territorial ambitions, Timmayya was hopeful that in the event of Goa being freed from the Muslim control he would be made its governor or at least obtain it as a *jagir* in lieu of a fixed amount payable monthly or yearly.[29] It never entered his head that Albuquerque would reverse his predecessor's "blue water" policy and embark on an empire building venture, deciding on Goa as its headquarters. In Timmayya's view, with Goa restored to Vijayanagar, an alliance could be forged with Portugal, beneficial to both.[30]

In fact, in the political climate of India in those times, Timmayya cannot and should not be deemed to have behaved in an anti-national or unpatriotic manner. As an admiral of Vijayanagar he acted in the best interests of his sovereign by seeking Portuguese aid against a common enemy. If things did not work out the way he wanted or expect is a different story. A striking parallel could be found in the case of Ambhi the ruler of the region between Indus and its tributary Hydaspes (Jhelum). He had supplied 4, 000 men to Alexander the Great to defeat Porus in 327 B. C.[31] I may quote Rapson's apt comment in this respect:"It may be that the idea of a common Indian nationality, in whose cause he and his brother kings must stand together, did not even occur to him. India ws too large and too disunited for the mind to embrace it as a unit.... His policy

(Ambhi's) was largely governed by his antagonism to the rival prince of the Paurava house, who ruled on the other side of Hydaspes".[32] The same would also apply to Timmayya helping Albuquerque against the sultan of Bijapur. Seen in this light Timmayya cannot be judged to be a traitor to India, a collaborator, a quisling.

REFERENCES

1. Pissurlencar, P. S. S., "Colaboradores hindus de Afonso de Albuquerque", *Boletim do Instituto Vasco da Gama*, Nova Goa, n. 49, pp. 22-4.
2. Barros, J., "Local collaborators of Albuquerque". Paper presented at the 3rd International Seminar on Indo-Portuguese History, Goa (28-31 Jan. 1983), mimeographed pp. 1-6.
3. Shastry, B. S., "Timmayya and his relations with the Portuguese", *Journal of the Institute of Indian Studies*, Udipi, I, n. 2, Jan. 1979, pp. 34-55; *Studies in Indo-Portuguese History*, Bangalore, 1981, pp. 52-121.
4. Dames, Longworth, *The Book of Duarte Barbosa*, London, 1918, as quoted by Shastry, p. 118.
5. Shastry, *op. cit.,* n. 83, pp. 120-1.
6. *Ibid.,* p. 95. It is curious to note that while Damião de Gois says in his *Chronica do Felicissimo Rey Dom Manuel* (Lisboa, 1926, Pt. I, Cap. LIII, p. 95) that Timmayya was a native of Honavar, for Fernão Lopes de Castanheda (*Historia do Descobrimento e Conquista da India*, Coimbra, 1924-33, IV, Liv. I, Cap. VI, p. 65) he was only a resident of that locality. As Shastry rightly remarks, Timmayya is a typical Kanarese name.
7. Barros, João de, *Da Asia*, Dec. II, Liv. IV, Cap. V, p. 431.
8. Albuquerque, Braz de, *Commentarios do Grande Albuquerque*, Lisboa, 1774, Pt. I, p. 100; Castanheda, *op. cit.,* Vol. IV, Liv. I, Cap. VI, p. 65, Barros, *op. cit.,* Dec. I, Liv. V, Cap. IV, p. 427. It is significant, however, that with the messianic sense with which the Portuguese were imbued at the time Barros should say that Albuquerque felt that Timoja's words were not of a 'gentio' but from a messenger of the Holy Spirit. *Cf.* Barros, *op. cit.,* p. 429.
9. Shastry, *op. cit.,* p. 95.
10. Correia, G., *Lendas da India*, Lisboa, 1865, Tomo I, Liv. 2, Pt. II, Cap. V, p. 289.
11. Albuquerque, B. de, *op. cit.* , *loc. cit.*
12. Barros, *op. cit.* , *loc. cit.* ; Castanheda, *op. cit.* , *loc. cit.* ; Faria y Sousa, M. de, *Asia Portuguesa*, Porto, 1962, Vol. I, Cap. V, p. 271. Faria y Sousa refers to Timmayya earlier as "capitão governador da cidade" (p. 191), and later as "Capitão Timoja" (p. 292).
13. Castanheda, *op. cit.* , *loc. cit.* ; Correia, *op cit.* , *loc. cit.*
14. Shastry, *op. cit.,* pp. 92-121.
15. Panniker, K. M., *Malabar and the Portuguese*, Bombay, 1926, p. 77.
16. *Cartas* of Afonso de Albuquerque as quoted by R. S. Whiteway, pp. 148, 175.
17. Barros, *Dec.* II, Liv. IV, Cap. V, p. 427.
18. Goes, *op. cit.,* Pt. I, Cap. LIII, p. 75.
19. Albuquerque, B. de, *op. cit.* , *loc. cit.*
20. Barros. *op. cit.,* p. 277.

21. *Cf. supra*, nn. 1 & 2.
22. Both T. B. -Cunha and E. George branded Timmayya a "quisling" in their speeches and writings (Cf. *Free Goa*, and *Azad Goem, passim*). They need to be understood in the context of their involvement in Goa's freedom struggle, when pro-Indian and anti-Portuguese feelings were running high.
23. Panikker, *op. cit.,* p. 204: He pointedly remarks that "politically, the most important result of this Portuguese establishment in Malabar was that it checked the development of Malabar into a single confederacy under the Zamorin, because the Raja of Cochin with the help of the Portuguese stemmed the tide of the expanding power of the Zamorin".
24. Sewell, R. A., *A Forgotten Empire*, New Delhi, 1962.
25. Couto, D. de, *Decada* VIII, Cap. XV, pp. 93-94.
26. Barros, *op. cit.* , *loc. cit.*
27. It would be wrong to think that it was Timmayya who planted the idea of capturing Goa into Albuquerque's mind. This is denied by Albuquerque himself when he wrote to his king: " I took Goa because Your Highness ordered me to do so, and the Marshall (Fernando Coutinho) brought the order among your instructions" (Letter of 30 Nov. 1510). Timmayya played a decisive part only in the timing of the attack (Cf. Shastry, *op. cit.,* p. 127).
28. Barros, *op. cit.,* Dec. I, p. 384, II, p. 187 as quoted by Shastry.
29. Pissurlencar, *op. cit.,* p. 31.
30. Shastry, *op. cit.,* p. 98.
31. Rapson, E. J., *The Cambridge History of India* (Indian Reprint, 1968), Vol. I, p. 324; Simth, V. A., *The Oxford History of India*, Oxford, 1920, pp. 59, 63.
32. Rapson, *op. cit.,* pp. 312-13.

4

KUNJALI'S NAVAL CHALLENGE TO THE PORTUGUESE

R. R. S. Chauhan

Though the first Portuguese viceroy D. Francisco de Almeida had established his foothold in Indian waters in 1509, the Portuguese had not yet succeeded in controlling the sea fully. The main reason was that the Zamorin was rarely on good terms with them. The attempts made by the Indian seamen to drive away the Portuguese naval forces in 1536, 1545 and 1546 with the help of the Egyptian fleet had failed.[1] The most stiff and courageous attempt to oust the Portuguese navy was made by the Muslim admirals of the Zamorin, better known as Kunjali Marakkars. Their unending war against the Portuguese at sea lasted for 1000 years,[2] and though it ended in favour of the Portuguese, the credit for beginning the process of curtailing the Portuguese naval supremacy must go to the Kunjalis.

No sooner the Portuguese came to India they started calling themselves the Lords of the Seas. The Portuguese king and his viceroys also adopted the titles of the King of India and viceroys and governors of India respectively. However, it was not possible for Indian naval warriors to accept their lordship at sea.

The Kunjalis hailed from Pantalayani Kollan. Later, due to the harassment of the Portuguese they shifted to Ponnani, the southernmost harbour in the jurisdiction of the Zamorin.[3] In course of time they spread to Koltahkal, Tanur and other parts of the west coast. When Almeida attacked and destroyed their ships at Ponnani, they shifted to Agalpula and vowed to take revenge. The Zamorim who admired their courage and loyalty had conferred on the family the title of *Marakkar* with the right to wear silk turban.[4]

Till the signing of the first treaty between the Portuguese and the Zamorin in 1540, the Kunjalis fought several wars with the Portuguese and sometimes their fleets were totally destroyed. But the war was never given up and not a single man of this family ever surrendered to the Portuguese. Time and again the undaunted Zamorin provided them with new fleets and they were the first Indian naval warriors the Portuguese hated most. Firstly because they were Muslims, and next because they were the only native naval power that could confront them on seas. Without going into the details of wars, it will suffice here to say that till 1540 the Portuguese often defeated them, looted their richly laden ships, killed many of them and enslaved some. In return, the Kunjalis showed the Portuguese the efficiency of their guerilla tactics at sea and inflicted severe losses in ships, goods and men. The Kunjalis moved about with their lighter *paros* with ease, attacked speedily and escaped. It is a fact that their flags on these *paros* kept flying from Colombo to Kutch and from Calicut to the Red Sea in near complete defiance of the Portuguese *cartazes*.[5]

The naval warfare had exhausted the treasury of the Zamorin and affected the Portuguese badly as the latter had to equip fleets annually to meet the menace of the Kunjalis. In order to end the war the Zamorin was compelled to sign a peace treaty with the Portuguese on 6th January 1540. The Zamorin agreed to accept the Portuguese *cartazes* and to maintain peaceful relations with the raja of Cochin, a friend of the Portuguese. He had also to give in to the conditions of selling all his pepper and ginger to the Portuguese at a reasonable price.[6]

However, the peace did not last long as the Portuguese were too difficult to be satisfied. They tried to loot some Hindu temples of South India, including the temple of Conjeevaram, during the viceroyalty of Martim Affonso de Souza (1542-45). It was then that Abu Bakr Ali, a nephew of Mamali Marakkar, who belonged to the richest family of Cannanore, was murdered by a Portuguese. The Kunjali retaliated by destroying Portuguese merchantships. He managed to avoid pitched wars with the powerful navy of the Portuguese. According to F. C. Danvers, D. Francisco de Mascarenhas attacked 3 *paros* of Kunjali and boarded the biggest one with his flotilla of 15 units in 1564. It is interesting to note that the two other *paros* not only rescued the *paro* under attack, but forced the Portuguese to defend their own ships and men.[7] The viceroy first complained to the Zamorin, and as he received no satisfactory response, a fleet under Diogo de Mesquitta was sent to punish him. Kunjali lost 24 vessels and nearly 2000 of his men were captured and beheaded. The Zamorin regarded this as termination of the 1540 treaty and declared war. In a joint action the Zamorin and the king of Cannanore destroyed the Portuguese fort at Cannanore and Kunjali burnt down many Portuguese vessels found in that harbour. The Portuguese followed up the hostilities with another raid by D. Diogo de Menezes who carried fire and sword to the entire coast of Malabar, devastating the towns of Pontalayani Kollan, Irkkoti, Ponnani, etc., and killed or enslaved more than 1, 000 men.[8] These cruel deeds and particularly the sight of floating bodies in the sea and on the beaches along the coast had deeply hurt their feelings, and a more serious challenge to the Portuguese came in 1570, when the combined forces of Bijapur, Ahmednagar and Calicut tried to oust them from India. The strategy failed, but the Portuguese realized that they should give up their expansion with sword. They were under heavy pressure from the men of the Zamorin at Chaliyam in 1571. The siege of the fort was so effective that the Portuguese had to subsist on animals. Later the old captain D. Jorge de Castro who surrendered the fort due to unavoidable situation was beheaded publicly by the authorities in Goa.[9]

Both the Kunjalis and the Portuguese acted and reacted with matching barbarity. Dom Gil Eanes Mascarenhas was cruising off the Malabar coast in 1582 and he opened fire on Calicut, Ponnani, Calegate, Daruh, etc. and slaughtered a large number of inhabitants. As he went further down the river he captured a vessel lying there, but in this campaign 6 Portuguese were captured and one of them was slain by the Kunjali himself with a single blow of his sword.[10] This sadistic desire of chopping the enemy heads with a single blow is also recorded by the French traveller Pyrard de Laval.[11]

Earlier, in 1581, Mathias de Albuquerque had followed Kunjali's ships seriously and then proceeded into the territory of the Zamorin. Tired of the war and on demand from his subjects the Zamorin sued for peace. The Portuguese exploited the situation and demanded a site for erecting a fort at Ponnani. The Zamorin delayed a decision as long as he could and tried offering alternative sites, but ultimately he had to yield in 1582. An agreement was signed to this effect and it also envisaged mutual exchange of the prisoners of war.[12] The Portuguese were most happy with their victory which would now permit them to check the Zamorin and to wipe out the Kunjali, who warned their king about this danger in vain. The Kunjali then built a fort at the mouth of the Kotta river towards the north of Calicut to counteract the Portuguese move with due permission of the Zamorin. But he died in 1585 and was succeeded by Mohammed Kunjali Marakkar, who proved more determined to face the new danger. He quickly enlarged and strengthened the fort of Kotta with heavy guns and opened the offensive against the Portuguese. By his expert guerilla tactics he captured their many vessels on the Coromandel coast, and when the Portuguese retaliated his exploits fetched him some notable prizes, thereby almost paralyzing the Portuguese trade on the western coast.[13] On the other hand the Portuguese were not inactive and we learn from a letter of the Portuguese crown that they had compelled the Zamorin to hand over hostages to be kept either at Cochin or at Goa as a guarantee to maintain the latest peace contract. The Portuguese king hoped also that the Portuguese garrison at Ponnani would try its best to destroy the fort of Kunjali and would not permit its reconstruction. However, Kunjali had infused new life in Kotta. This fort was protected on two sides by water, and on the third side by a swampy salty marsh. It commanded the bar of the river. When Kunjali sensed that the Portuguese meant his annihilation, he cut a deep ditch with a double wall of 7 feet thickness on the land side and on this he erected towers at regular distances armed with cannon. He also built a strong wall between the two creeks and lined the whole sea-shore with bastions, one of which was mounted with heavy cannon to defend the harbour which was further guarded with masts chained strongly to each other.[15]

The Portuguese viceroy kept his king informed about these developments. The king wrote back in 1589 to say that "as the fort of Kunjali was armed with various galliots and there were many other corsairs who pounce upon my ships resulting in many deaths, you should remind the Zamorin that as per the peace contract he was bound to destroy the fort of Kunjali".[16] Thus, we can conclude that the peace accord was arranged secretly with the Zamorin and pressure was brought against his admiral. The honour of the Portuguese crown was at stake in the ensuing battle. It disapproved the erection of the fort at Ponnani and instructed the viceroy to utilize the funds for raising a fleet to combat the corsairs whose ships were still sailing to Mecca without Portuguese *cartazes*. It was also repeated that the Zamorin was expected to join the Portuguese efforts to curb the activities of Kunjali.[17]

The Portuguese took time and waited for a suitable opportunity. This came in the form of the changed attitude of Kunjali towards the Zamorin. He had taken measures to protect himself not only against the Portuguese but also against his own king. He had backed the rani of Ullal against the Portuguese, but annoyed his king and a large number of Hindus by violating the honour of a noble lady. In 1596 the Portuguese sent Alvaro de Abranches to conclude a fresh treaty with the Zamorin. The latter had his feelings hurt by the Kunjali who had cut the tail of his elephant. The Zamorin entered into an agreement with the Portuguese in 1597,[18] whereby he freed Portuguese prisoners including the priest D. Pedro Fernando Lobo and agreed to give site to the Portuguese and Christians to erect churches in Calicut and Ponnani.[19] This was a sure sign of his good intention and the Portuguese started their offensive soon thereafter.

While the Zamorin was to attack on land, the Portuguese would attack on sea. The indomitable Kunjali repulsed 10,000 men brought by the Zamorin. Such were his preparations that Dom Luis de Gama, viceroy's brother, met the same fate on sea. His armada of 4 galleys, 35 smaller vessels, and 2 large barks plus 10 other ships came under intense fire of Kunjali's galliots. The Zamorin sought help from the Portuguese and Belchior Ferreira went to his assiatance with 600 men, but lost 28 of them and had to withdraw. Luis da Silva, who had earlier captured some ships of Kunjali at Chaul and in Chapora river, tried to land his 500 men from 60 boats under his command. Bento Correa, the first man to land was shot dead and Luis da Silva fell similarly. The new commander Francisco Pereira followed suit and many noblemen only added to the list of fatal casualties. The viceroy's brother then jumped into water with a drawn sword and called his men to follow him. In this attempt another 300 lost their lives. Those who landed killed a large number of Kunjali's men, but had to withdraw. Luis da Gama retired to Cochin leaving D. Francisco da Gama to guard the entrance of the river.[20]

The news of the disaster stunned the inhabitants of Goa and they crowded in front of the viceroy's palace to know about their relatives and friends. The Portuguese authorities put the blame on the untrained recruits for the defeat, but this appears incorrect if one goes through the list of *fidalgos* who died in the action.

The next expedition in 1599 was led by a hero of many naval encounters, Andre Furtado. The Kunjali had assumed the titles of *defender of the island*, *protector of the Muslims*, and *expeller of the Portuguese*. Furtado's force consisted of well-equipped and well-manned 3 galleys, and 54 other vessels besides 2 galleys, 11 ships and 21 other ships with 790 men that had recently arrived from Portugal. He successfully persuaded the queen of Ullal and the raja of Mangalore to give up the cause of Kunjali, and he concluded a new treaty with the Zamorin, who agreed to provide a force of 1, 000 labourers at his cost. His contribution to the siege would also include 15 elephants and timber required for the operation, in addition to 5,000 nayars duly armed. The fort of Kunjali was to be razed after the war and his ships, goods and treasury would be equally divided. The Zamorin was also given the chiefs of Ponnani, Pudure and Tolape Nair in addition to his nephews as hostages and they were to be kept at Cochin during the war. He was also required to provide 4 *manchuas* and 30 *jangadas* (rafts) with seamen and lascars to keep watch over the river. The Portuguese were also to keep hostages with the Zamorin, and these were Pedro de Noronha, Jeronimo Botelho, Captain Antonil Matoso and two priests.[21]

Furtado first surveyed the enemy's defence and then controlled the river by attacking the obstacles placed by Kunjali with many batteries. His arrangements were very effective and he was in a position to bombard the fort itself. The Kunjali himself came to reinforce the defence and expelled the Portuguese. Andre Furtado, however, was not the man to give up so easily and personally led his men and dislodged Kunjali's men with heavy losses. He kept up the bombardment for 5 days and pressed Kunjali so hard that he had to give up by March 1600. He surrendered to Zamorin on the condition that his life would be spared. As he threw himself at the feet of the Zamorin, Furtado pulled him away. The treachery resulted into a tumult among the nayars who threw themselves against the Portuguese but were overpowered. Kunjali's fort was razed to the ground and he along with his 40 followers were brought to Goa. The victorious fleet of Furtado was welcomed in Goa with gaiety and celebrations. When 4 or 5 prisoners disembarked they were stoned to death. Due to this Kunjali was led secretly to the *tronco* (=State prison). Within a few days the judges completed the legal formalities and sentenced him to death ignoring the condition of his surrender. A team of priests tried their best to convert him to Christianity in his last moments, but it was in vain. He was beheaded on a special French type of guillotine in front of viceroy's palace in the presence of a vast crowd comprising of common men, fidalgos, noble ladies, merchants, etc. His body was then quartered and limbs were exhibited on the beaches of Panjim and Bardez. Later his head was salted and conveyed to Cannanore with a view to strike terror.[22]

By the turn of the century the Portuguese had to face their new adversaries, the Dutch and the English. It is on record that during 1601-1608 more than one-third of their ships coming from Portugal were either burnt, wrecked or captured by the Dutch.[23] As early as 1603 the Zamorin was found to be in league with the Dutch to oust the Portuguese from Cochin.[24] And even though the Kunjali was no longer around, it appeared as if his ghost was still haunting the Portuguese. A cousin of Kunjali, whose Christian name was Dom Pedro Rodrigues, harassed the Portuguese relentlessly, looted their ships frequently, and was feared by them even in Ceylon.[25] When he was a boy of 13 he was captured by Andre Furtado during one of the battles off Cardiva, and was subsequently brought to Goa. Pyrard saw a young man in 1608 in the galleys of Goa. It is interesting to note that he was named Dom Pedro Rodrigues. The young man of about 30 looked somewhat unique to Pyrard as he introduced himself as a Spaniard and not a Portuguese.[26] The man seemed none other than the cousin of Kunjali, who was baptised in Goa and later married to a Portuguese orphan.[27] He must have known of the fate of his cousin. All we know about him is that one fine day or night he fled from Goa and managed to reach his old place safely. Nothing is known about how and when he slipped away from the Portuguese custody. He gathered followers in Calicut and arranged 5 *paros*. With these he crossed the Cape Comorin and passed through Ceylon to the Tanadiva island. He entered the beach of S. João and there he punished the Franciscans who had baptised him in Goa. At the quay of elephants in the island of *Forcados* he took possession of all the cattle.[28] One can conclude that in spite of having been a Christian for over 20 years he retained all his hatred against the Portuguese and he continued his spree of plundering their ships whenever possible. There are reasons to believe that he had established contacts with the Dutch.

The Portuguese viceroy in India was instructed from home that all the vessels should sail heavily armed and as far as possible under cover of *cafila*. The viceroy expressed his inability to provide convoy on every occasion, but he would do what he could about punishing the Malabari corsairs whose number was increasing and endangering the reputation of the Portuguese arms.[29] We get some idea of the daring exploits of Dom Pedro from the official correspondence addressed by various captains to the viceroy in Goa. Thus for instance Constantino de Sa wrote from Ceylon in March 1618 saying that the renegade Dom Pedro had indulged in plunder and caused incalculable damage to the Portuguese on the coast of Manar only with his 5 *paros*. He stated further that the same Dom Pedro had plans to do more harm at the request of Changali who wished to be reinstated as the Lord of Jaffna. The viceroy discussed this information in his State Council in May 1619 and it was decided that no ships could be sent to counter the situation due to lack of funds and because the monsoon would set in soon.[30]

There is also a letter of the chief captain Felippe de Oliveira dated 8th June 1619, stating that 5 paros entered the coast of Manar at the instance of Changali and committed countless acts of thefts. The Malabaris disembarked in other islands and when the captain of Manar sought help from the sea to drive away the enemy, Constantino de Sa sent 2 galliots with many men, apart from 40 Portuguese vessels commanded by Vitorio de Abreu. Dom Pedro won a total victory on this occasion and the Portuguese were discredited (Felippe de Oliveira put the blame for the defeat on sins,) disorderly movement of the Portuguese forces, and contrary winds.[31] He failed to give any credit to Dom Pedro, who had attacked the *cais dos elefantes* first and deliberately. This had forced the captain of Manar out of the fort in pursuit of his *paros* with 1 galliot and *tones*. Dom Pedro and his men who were on land boarded their *paros* and killed 500 men, including some Portuguese that were in the *tones*.[32] The exploit becomes remarkable when we see that his *paros* were all safe. Another letter of Constantino de Sa, dated 7th May 1619, tells us that Dom Pedro's men had occupied the *ilha das vacas* and seized its fort.[33] From here he was impeding the Portuguese navigation and intercepting t' eir trade. The Portuguese also feared Dom Pedro entering Ceylon and acted quickly by sending a force under Filippe de Oliveira to Jaffna.[34] However, Dom Pedro succeeded in capturing 12 out of the 18 *tones* under command of Vitorio de Abreu. He killed 300 men in the action and enslaved the rest, including Abreu himself.[35] According to Danvers, Dom Pedro attacked one more Portuguese fleet, which was under convoy of a squadron and captured a ship without any appreciable resistance. The aggressiveness of Dom Pedro scared the Portuguese to such an extent that the captains of the convoy shamelessly refused even to try recovering the lost ship.[36] Dom Pedro then sailed back with impunity to Maldives with his grand booty that included men, women and money like a real pirate, quite different from his forefathers.

REFERENCES

1. Gune, V. T., *A Guide to the collection of records from the Goa Archives*, Panaji, 1973, pp. 1-3.
2. Nambiar, O. K., *Portuguese Pirates and Indian Seamen*, Bangalore, 1955, pp. 105-29.
3. George Chalakkal, "Portuguese versus the Malabar Seamen". Paper presented at the 3rd International Seminar on Indo-Portuguese History, Goa, Jan. 28-31, 1983.
4. Padmanabha Menon, K. P., *History of Kerala*, Asian Education Services, Vol. II, New Delhi, 1983, p. 186. Cf. also Krishna Ayyar, K. V., *The Zamorin of Calicut*, Calicut, 1938, pp. 210-11.
5. Nambiar, *op. cit.*, pp. 106-38.
6. *Subsidios para a historia da India Portuguesa*, ed. Rodrigo Jose de Lima Felner, Part II, Lisboa, 1868, pp. 251-2.
7. Danvers, F. C., *The Portuguese in India*, I, London, 1966, p. 256.
8. Padmanabha Menon, *op. cit.*, p. 152.
9. Panikkar, K. M., *Malabar and the Portuguese*, Bombay, 1929, p. 131; Danvers, *op. cit.*, II, p. 8.
10. Danvers, *op. cit.*, p. 51.

11. *Viagem de Francisco Pyrard de Laval*, I, ed. J. H. da Cunha Rivara, 1862, pp. 251-52.
12. Padmanabha Menon, *op. cit.*, p. 157.
13. Panikkar, *op. cit.*, p. 159.
14. *Monções do Reino* (Manuscript of Historical Archives of Goa. Henceforth referred to as **M. R.**), No. 3-A, fls. 125-26.
15. Nambiar, *op. cit.*, p. 156; Padmanabha, *op. cit.*, p. 186.
16. **M. R.** , No. 3-A, fl. 327.
17. *Ibid.*, fls. 352-3.
18. Danvers, *op. cit.* , p. 112.
19. **M. R.** , No. 2-B, fls. 489-502.
20. Danvers, *op. cit.*, pp. 115-6.
21. *Tratados de Pazes*, ed. J. P. I. Biker, Tomo I, Lisboa, 1881, pp. 186-8.
22. Nambiar, *op. cit.*, pp. 178-99; Danvers, *op. cit.*, p. 188.
23. Disney, A. R., *Twilight of the Pepper Empire*, London, 1978, p. 64.
24. Poonem, T. I., *A Survey of the rise of the Dutch power in Malabar, 1600-78*, Travancore, 1948, p. 45.
25. Fernão de Queiroz, *Temporal and Spiritual Conquest of Ceylon*, trans. by S. G. Pereira, Colombo, 1930, p. 628.
26. *Viagem de Pyrard*, II, p. 24.
27. Nambiar, *op. cit.*, pp. 200-201.
28. Fernão de Queiroz, *op. cit.*, pp. 627-9.
29. Souza, A. B. de, *Subsidios para a Historia Militar*, 1618-1638, III, Lisboa, 1953, pp. 16-18.
30. *Assentos dos Conselho do Estado*, No. 1 (HAG: Ms. 9530)fl. 22.
31. *Assentos do Conselho da Fazenda*, HAG: Ms. 1159, fls. 147-51.
32. Souza, A. B. de, *op. cit.*, p. 64.
33. Pissurlencar (ed.)*Assentos do Conselho do Estado*, I, Bastora, 1953, p. 52.
34. *Ibid.* , fls. 58-60.
35. Souza, A. B. de, *op. cit.*, pp. 73-4.
36. Danvers, *op. cit.*, II, p. 203.

5

THE PORTUGUESE COMMERCIAL RELATIONS WITH BIJAPUR IN THE SEVENTEENTH CENTURY

B. S. Shastry

Close Neighbourhood

At the opening of the 17th century the Adil Shahi sultanate of Bijapur included Konkan coast from Domel to Sadashivgad, excluding Portuguese-controlled Goa. In the 1630's the Adil Shahi coastline was extended from Sadashivgad down to Basur, excluding again the Portuguese pockets therein, when the king of Keladi recognized the sovereignty of Bijapur. Further addition to the coastline was made in 1636 when Shah Jahan condeded to the Adil Shah the coastal region from Domel to upper Chaul, excluding the Portuguese lower Chaul. Thus by 1636 the Adil Shah had a shoreline of about 300 kms. from the upper Chaul down to Basrur, excluding the Portuguese possessions along the line -- lower Chaul, Goa, Honawar, Gangolli and Basrur. This shoreline remained with him until Shivaji began to make inroads into it in the 1660's. The Adil Shah made much profit from the commercial transactions at the ports in the coastline, namely at Upper Chaul, Dabhol, Rajapur, Vengurla, Sadashivgad and Basrur. Dabhol was the most important among these.

In 1675 the Portuguese and the Adil Shah ceased to have common borders as Shivaji took over the entire coastline belonging to the Adil Shah by then. In coastal Karnataka the lands of Keladi formed a sort of a buffer state between the Portuguese possessions of Honavar, Gangolli and Basrur, and the territories of the Adil Shah. While discussing therefore the commercial policy of the Portuguese towards Bijapur one should bear in mind that the Adil Shahi coastline changed from time to time in the 17th century and also that the entire Adil Shahi kingdom itself came to an end in 1686 when it was annexed to the Mughal empire by Aurangzeb.

The Foundation of Commercial Policy

The treaties signed between the Portuguese and the Adil Shahi were indicative of the commercial policy of the former with the latter. The treaty of 22nd October 1576 continued to be valid throughout the period covered by this paper (1600-1686). The very first clause of this treaty was a grand concession to the Adil Shah and his subjects. A ship with a Portuguese *cartaz* was not to be molested, detained or subjected to extraction of bribes, presents or slaves on board. If the ship was suspected of violating any provision of the *cartaz*, it was to be taken to Goa or any other Portuguese port for inspection. It was subject to confiscation or to some other punishment as per the treaty, if found guilty. The Portuguese captains, who were responsible to bring the ship were also subject to punishment of losing their captaincies and other benefits if found guilty of bribe or unlawful detention of the ship.

The second article of the treaty indicates that the Adil Shah requested the Portuguese not to collect the recently imposed additional one percent tax from his merchants while leaving Goa, nor to take away their usual arms, wives, children or slaves, but to allow them to return freely, provided that they paid the usual dues. The Portuguese agreed to all these, except that the additional one percent would be collected on the goods taken by sea. It was a tax meant to help the cost of maintaining the naval guard of the coast which benefitted the Adil Shah also.

He was granted another significant concession under article 3. His vessels were permitted to load at Hurmuz without being subjected to bribes or presents, or obligation to purchase horses or other commodities or to surrender of slaves. In case the captain of Hurmuz did not observe this provision, he was liable to be dismissed from his captaincy and sent back to Portugal. Besides, compensation was to be given for the vessel for any damage.

Under article 6 the Portuguese agreed to supply sulphur, lead and copper to the Adil Shah on demand. He in turn would supply them timber for constructing ships, saltpetre for gunpowder manufacture, steel, iron and mariners for the fleets, stone cannon balls and ballasts for the ships, meat, wheat, rice, firewood and coal, apparently for general consumption, pulses for horses, straw, vegetables, fruits, and numerous other articles.

The Mecca ships were to be allowed to sail into Old Goa as before with merchandise and to sail away without being deprived of slaves on board provided the customary dues were paid (article 14).

Lastly, the goods on board the enemy vessels which entered the Adil Shahi ports and were captured by the Portuguese without the help of the Adil Shahi men were to be divided equally between the signatories (article 15).

This treaty of 1576 and another of 1582 which we shall discuss later, were re-affirmed in 1633 and 1655.[1] Both occasions of re-affirmation arose from mutual complaints of violation of the treaty provisions and hostile actions.

The Cartaz System

We shall now proceed to consider some issues of commercial policy. Article 1 of the 1576 treaty contained a provision regarding *cartazes*. In this connection it must be noted that there were some specific provisions in an earlier treaty[2] (13th December 1571). These earlier terms were valid in the 17th century and the Portuguese had a definite policy with regard to their *cartaz* system.[3]

The treaty of 1571 provided for a Portuguese factor at Dabhol, who was to issue *cartazes* to the merchants of the Bijapur kingdom for the coastal trade and for sailing to Hurmuz (art. 11). Besides, six free *cartazes* were to be granted to the Adil Shah every year on his request for ships sailing to any part (art. 12). Further, the Portuguese factor of Dabhol was to farm out the dues levied on the vessels entering the port with *cartazes* (art. 13). The royal ships of Bijapur with free *cartazes* were exempted from the dues (art. 14). The captain of the city of Old Goa was to issue *cartazes* to the royal ships if the viceroy was absent (art. 15). One of the six royal vessels could bring horses from Hurmuz to Dabhol (art. 19). This was a special concession as the trade in horses was a royal monopoly of Portugal and ordinarily no Indian ship was allowed to carry horses on board. One of the conditions in any *cartaz* issued to any Indian ship was that it should not carry or trade in horses.

Apart from the conditions laid down in the treaties, there used to be several other conditions stipulated in the *cartazes* themselves. For instance, the following conditions were specified in the *cartaz* of 9th August 1613 issued to the Adil Shah:[4] The vessel should sail from Dabhol to Jeddah and return to Dabhol without taking or bringing anything that was banned, namely Rumes, Turks, Abyssinians, cinnamon from Ceylon, timber, pepper, ginger, iron, steel, copper, lead, lime, brass, wood, planks, coir, saltpetre, sulphur, bamboo, mules (*machos*?). There was a ban also on carrying any Portuguese national, horses (except those officially purchased) and slaves (except Muslim ones). If there was any doubt that some of the slaves were Christians or children of Christians, an inquiry was to be conducted by the factor of Dabhol before the vessel sailed away. The factor was to certify regarding the slaves on board.

Because of these conditions and others, such as that a *cartaz* was issued for one year only, or that a vessel should possess a *cartaz* for coastal voyage even if it was sailing to Goa to obtain a *cartaz* there, or that varying fees had to be paid for *cartazes* depending on their destination, and that it should not sail into enemy ports, easily led to misunderstandings and skirmishes. Besides, the Portuguese were not always ready to issue a *cartaz*, even to a royal vessel of Bijapur. For instance, in 1618 the first request of the Adil Shah did not yield any *cartaz*, but the second request accompanied by some pressure got him one.[5] The pressure adopted was in the form of detention of some Portuguese vessels at Dabhol. In those days the Portuguese were not in a position to displease the Adil Shah too much as the Dutch were already hindering Goa and were in contact with the Adil

Shah.

Occasionally the Adil Shah used to seek more *cartazes* than what was specified in the treaty. The Portuguese were unwilling to consider such requests.[6] Apparently the issue of *cartazes* was subject to some other material considerations, rather than only the usual fee. It is clear from a document dated 11th September 1621 that the Portuguese were reluctant to issue the usual *cartazes* because the customary annual presents to the king of Portugal had not been offered that year. The *cartazes* materialised as soon as the envoy of Bijapur turned up with a cash present of 300 *xerafins*.

Sometimes the Portuguese preferred to be lenient towards Bijapur in order to maintain it friendly, or at least neutral, in the face of Dutch hostility. In 1625, for example, a *cartaz*-less vessel belonging to a grandee of Bijapur was taken at Rajapur. The envoy of Adil Shah sought its restoration. After much initial fuss and quoting of rules the vessel was released.[8] There was another case of leniency in 1642. The vessel was captured at Rajapur and burnt. However, following an Adil Shahi threat to break peace, it was decided to restore the value of the ship and to promise that the officials involved in burning the ship would receive punishment.[9] Again in 1644 another vessel was captured at Hurmuz for not carrying a *cartaz*. It belonged to an important person of Bijapur and the Adil Shah recommended its restoration with its cargo on the grounds of prevailing peaceful relations. The request was granted.[10]

There were instances in which religious considerations prevailed in the enforcement of the *cartaz* requirements. Usually every *cartaz* contained a clause that no Christian slave or children of Christian slaves should be carried on board a vessel. In 1632 the Portuguese detained 3 Adil Shahi vessels on the grounds that the maid-servant of a Portuguese medical practitioner who had gone to Bijapur to treat the Adil Shah was detained even after the death of the doctor. The Portuguese authorities insisted that the maid should be brought to Bicholim where the Portuguese missionaries would make sure whether she was a Christian or Muslim. Her release would be demanded if she wished to remain Christian. The Adil Shah did not accept the demand.[11]

In 1636 the Portuguese captured an Adil Shahi vessel at Sind and refused to return it even when Bijapur threatened to break peace. The Portuguese justified the confiscation saying that the captain of the ship had fired at the Portuguese when ordered to slow down for inspection. And on inspection it was found carrying pepper and other prohibited articles of trade.[12]

When Shivaji appeared along the Konkan coast after 1657, the Portuguese became friendly with the Adil Shahi. The latter were told that *cartazes* would be issued ast Dabhol, Chaul, etc. for the asking. The Portuguese were satisfied by merely telling the rulers of Bijapur that *cartazes* were necessary for their ships and that no vessel should sail out of any port of Bijapur to Arabia, Persia and Mecca without a *cartaz*. Even when vessels without *cartazes* were captured, they were returned when requested to do so.[13]

Dabhol

The Portuguese always had their eye on Dabhol, which was the most busy port of the Adil Shahi. They had established a factory there by 1535, but it was often attacked by the Adil Shahi men, whenever there were hostilities or misunderstandings. In 1582 a definite treaty[14] was concluded with regard to Dabhol. Under the treaty the Adil Shah agreed to destroy his fortress of Dabhol, hand over all its artillery to the Portuguese, return detained vessels, pay all dues such as those on horses, and make all merchantmen to sail to Goa for trade. Hostages were retained in Goa until the provisions of the treaty were implemented.

The factor at Dabhol was responsible for issuing *cartazes* and regulating trade there as per the treaty of 1576. For instance, a viceregal order of 3rd April 1613 required him to take over all ships that came from Hurmuz and other ports of western India and send them with their crew and cargo to Goa or Chaul for trial and disposal as per the treaty.[15]

In 1652 three Arab ships which entered the port of Dabhol were captured and burnt by the Portuguese. Any Adil Shahi objection or protest was to be overruled.[16]

The Dutch Factor

Exclusion of the Dutch from the Konkan trade was a major policy issue before the Portuguese from the second decade of the 17th century when the European rivals commenced their operations for obtaining some trade concessions, including the establishment of a factory. Strangely enough none of the treaties between the Portuguese and the Adil Shahis contains any provision regarding the exclusion of the Dutch. The Portuguese seem to have preferred to take ad-hoc steps to block the Dutch moves. They succeeded in the initial stages in persuading Bijapur not to grant any trade concessions to their European rivals, including permission to set up a factory.[17]

It is evident that during the third decade of the 17th century the Dutch developed friendly ties with the Adil Shah, whom they encouraged to confront the Portuguese. The latter had captured an Adil Shahi vessel with horses on board at Chaul some time in 1628-29. Emboldened by the Dutch, the Adil Shah ordered his officials not only to hinder the Portuguese trade along the coast, but also to take into custody any Portuguese found at his ports. Besides, he also threatened to invade Bardez and Salcete if the vessel was not returned.[18] He in fact refused them commerce at his ports and captured some of their vessels at Rajapur and Ankola. He prepared to invade Bardez and Salcete in spite of the efforts of the Portuguese to appease him.[19] However, good relations were soon restored as his vessel was restored and the treaty of 1576 was re-affirmed in 1633, as already noted.

The Dutch did not give up their efforts at obtaining commercial concessions from Bijapur. In 1637 we find them negotiating successfully, getting permission to establish a factory at Vengurla and urging the Adil Shah to attack Goa by land while they would attack by sea.[20] It is known from the correspondence of the Portuguese viceroy [21] that the Dutch commenced building their factory at Vengurla by September 1638. However, at the instance of the Portuguese the Adil Shah got the Dutch to suspend their work.[22] This turned out to be only a temporary suspension. The work was resumed and the factory was completed by 1640. There was even an agreement between the Dutch and the Adil Shah to attack Goa jointly. The plan was not realized because the Portuguese paid a heavy compensation for the vessels they had confiscated. The Portuguese also went out of their way to appease the Adil Shah on instructions from the home government in Portugal.[23] Heavy bribes or gifts were given to the Adil Shah and his men in an attempt to get the Dutch out of Vengurla in vain.[24]

There was a party hostile to the Portuguese at the Bijapur court. It was led by the Queen Mother and Abdulla Hakim who invaded the Portuguese lands of Goa in 1654. It had the backing of the Dutch, who instigated the attack. The Portuguese however repulsed the attack and Bijapur was forced to re-affirm the treaty of friendship in 1655.[25]

Hakim intruded into some land of Goa in 1659 also. He was again repulsed with loss of 400 to 500 men.[26] Shivaji took Upper Chaul in 1659, Dabhol in 1660 and other parts of the Konkan in the subsequent years. With the fall of the Adil Shahi coastline into Shivaji's control the Dutch factor in Adil Shahi-Portuguese relations ceased to be.

We have already noted the articles of trade exchanged between the Portuguese and Bijapur as per the treaty of 1576.[27] Regular transactions took place both by land and sea whenever the relations between them were cordial. However, there used to be disruptions whenever the relations were strained. The Adil Shahi would then issue orders to his port officials and *tanadars* not to supply any article, but to prevent or even take into custody such Portuguese vessels and merchants who happened to enter his ports and lands.[28]

The Portuguese seemed to depend heavily on the Adil Shahi supplies of certain items like mariners and saltpetre. Mariners were recruited mainly from Ponda, Banda and Kudal, which were under the Adil Shahi *havaldar* of Konkan. The Portuguese used to appoint a number of agents under a Chief Agent to procure mariners. The Chief was paid liberally and he had the power to make advance payments to the recruits, some of whom never turned up in Goa after receiving the advances.[29] Whenever the relations with Bijapur were not friendly it was hard for the Portuguese to obtain mariners. In fact the Portuguese agents were ill-treated and even imprisoned on such occasions.[30]

Much of the saltpetre needed by the Portuguese seems to have come from the lands of Bijapur. Some quantitites were procured from Sind and Kanyakumari. Out of whatever was collected in 1631 the Portuguese sent 500 quintals to Portugal.[31] The rest was apparently meant for the arsenal at Old Goa.

Resident Envoys

The treaty of 1576 had provided for an Adil Shahi resident envoy in Goa. One of the grievances of the Portuguese against such envoys was that the latter preferred to reside in Bicholim or Ponda, just outside the Portuguese borders, violating thereby the treaty requirement. What was more offensive to the Portuguese was that the envoys used to take undue advantage of the provision of diplomatic immunity to smuggle articles of trade during the course of their visits to Goa. Complaints were frequently lodged at Bijapur against such practices, but they drew little attention. The Portuguese then issued specific orders that such envoys should live in Goa, and informed the Adil Shah that he would otherwise be treated as an ordinary merchant with his goods subject to inspection and taxation.[32] This firm stand did not prevent the envoys from absenting themselves from Goa for months under some excuse of illness or alleged non-cooperation of the Portuguese authorities.[33] A stage came when the Portuguese thought that the resident envoys served no purpose. As a result, when the envoy in 1645 requested the viceroy to permit him to go to Bijapur because he had not received his salary for long, he was granted permission promptly and willingly.[34]

REFERENCES

1. Biker, J. F. J. (ed.), *Colleção de Tratados e Concertos de Pazes*, (14 vols., Lisboa, 1881-1887), I, pp. 170-80, 293-9, II, 232-8.
2. *Ibid.,* I, pp. 160-7.
3. Shastry, B. S., "The System of Cartazes", *Journal of Indian History*, LI (1973), pp. 297-300.
4. Pissurlencar, P. S. S. (ed.), *Assentos do Conselho do Estado*, (5 vols., Bastora, 1953-7, and a Supplementary Volume, I, Pt. II, 1972), I, pp. 6-7.
5. *Ibid.,* I, pp. 5-8.
6. *Ibid.,* p. 115.
7. Historical Archives of Goa (= HAG), *Assentos do Conselho da Fazenda*, No. 1, fls. 185-6.
8. *Assentos*, I, Pt. II, p. 73.
9. *Ibid.,* II, pp. 374-5.

10. *Ibid.*, III, pp. 30-1.
11. *Ibid.*, I, pp. 470 ff.
12. *Ibid.*, II, pp. 94-5.
13. *Ibid.*, III, pp. 611-2, IV, pp. 236-7.
14. Biker, *op. cit.*, I, pp. 184-6.
15. Cunha Rivara, J. H. da (ed.), *Archivo Portuguez-Oriental* (=APO) 10 vols., Nova Goa, 1857-1876, VI, pp. 943-4.
16. *Assentos*, III, pp. 194-5.
17. *Boletim da Filmoteca Ultramarina Portuguesa*, IV, p. 854; HAG: *Monções*, No. 12, fl. 299v.
18. *Assentos*, I, pp. 240-2.
19. *Ibid.*, I, pp. 314-6, 316-23, 334-40.
20. *Ibid.*, III, pp. 666; Joshi, P. M., "The Adil Shahis and the Bardis", *History of Medieval Deccan*, ed. by H. K. Sherwani and P. M. Joshi, I, Hyderabad, 1975, pp. 369-70, n. 289.
21. *Assentos*, III, p. 647; Fosters, W., *The English Factories in India*, 1665-1660, p. 234.
22. *Assentos*, II, pp. 166-7, 182-4, 238, 549-55; Biker, II, pp. 88-98.
23. *Assentos*, II, pp. 312-7.
24. *Ibid.*, II, pp. 317-21, III, p. 658.
25. *Ibid.*, III, pp. 500-1.
26. *Ibid.*, IV, p. 62; *English Factories in India*, 1655-60, p. 249.
27. Cf. *supra* n. 3.
28. *Assentos*, I, pp. 240-2, 314-6, 334-40.
29. *Ibid.*, I, p. 558.
30. *Ibid.*, pp. 170-80, 195-6.
31. *Ibid.*, p. 531.
32. *Ibid.*, I, pp. 498-500, I, Pt. II, pp. 4-5, 124.
33. *Ibid.*, I, pp. 236-8, 334-40; *Chronista de Tissuary*, Nova Goa, No. 2, pp. 40-3.
34. *Assentos*, III, p. 90.

6

DUTCH-PORTUGUESE RELATIONS IN THE EAST (1663-1795) VIS-A-VIS INDIAN PENINSULA

P. P. Shirodkar,

van Goens

With the fall of Cochin and Cannanore, the last stronghold of the Portuguese on the Malabar coast in early 1663, the Portuguese had received such a severe blow to their empire-building efforts in the East that they could not bear it. They therefore continued their efforts for retrieval and signed a peace treaty to that effect in Europe on 14th December 1662. Presumably, as a result of this patch-up the viceroy in Goa deputed an envoy to Batavia in March 1664 to plead forcefully for the restoration of Cochin and Cannanore on the basis of the aforesaid treaty. However, the Dutch contended that though the treaty was ratified on 14th December 1662, it was enforced in the East as per its article 6 only three months after ratification.

Nevertheless, Portugal continued to pursue the claim in Europe and we find it doing so even two years later, but the Dutch refused to consider their demand seriously. Before considering the ultimate fate of this claim, Portugal signed a treaty with France on 31st March 1667. It stipulated that the king of Portugal would strive to secure Cochin and Cannanore from the Dutch. The claim was ultimately rejected when Netherlands signed a treaty with Portugal on 30th July 1669 stating explicitly that Cochin and Cannanore would remain with the Dutch East India Company till the payment of the war indemnity stipulated in the earlier treaty of 1661 had been settled, besides the defraying of special indemnity towards all the operations and the cost of the company fleet which had conquered them.[1]

Soon after the conquest of Cochin the Dutch tried to consolidate their position, thereby adopting certain far-sighted measures. Besides developing the town, they destroyed the churches, monasteries and seminaries as well as colleges and a library of the Jesuits. Being Calvinists the Dutch were sworn enemies of the Catholic Church. To do away with another source of irritation they expelled all the European priests from there.[2]

The Portuguese who had already lost all their trading contacts with Kanara since 1650s, when the Nayak of Ikkeri expelled them from there,[3] now they lost all hopes of continuing to trade on the Malabar coast, first with the fall of Cochin, and then with the signing of the treaty by the Dutch East Indian Company with the ruler of Travancore on 2nd March 1664. This treaty specified that none should be allowed to export pepper or cinnamon out of Travancore or to sell these spices to any party except the Dutch, and the Dutch East India Company would have the monopoly of exporting, selling or exchanging opium.[4]

Be that as it may, the fear of the British and the Portuguese attacks was still haunting the Dutch and therefore Van Goes had been empowered to be prepared for any eventuality with a strong war fleet.[5] Their anxiety was not at all unfounded, because Holland and England were at war in Europe in 1665, and even France had joined Holland against the British the next year.[6] But this did not deter them from consolidating their power in South India. Obviously, they signed two more treaties with the king of Travancore, one in April 1665 and the other in August 1666. The latter pertained to regulations regarding religious issues such as expulsion of the Roman priests permanently from the kingdom, while the former treaty referred to the commercial and political interests in Travancore. This latter treaty stipulated amity and peace between the Dutch East India Company and the king of Travancore. Both were to come to each other's assistance in the eventuality of a war with any belligerent power. Besides, the king of Travancore was not to permit the nationals of any of the above mentioned European countries to reside or carry out trade negotiations in his territories. Only the Dutch Company was authorised to take away all the pepper produced there and was also allowed to import opium by sea. The responsibility of controlling the smuggling was left to the king of Travancore. These and other treaties with other local princes helped them monopolize with ease their political, commercial and religious authority to such an extent that by 1667 they already had their complete sway over Quilon, Kayamkulam, Purakkad, Karunagapally and Tengapatanam.[7]

By 1680s Portugal was better informed of the developments in the East and started dispatching ships to regain the lost ground. This is discernible from dispatches of the Portuguese authorities in Goa and Lisbon. For instance, in 1680 there was a demand to send to Goa by January 1681 eleven big ships of 1400 tons, two frigates and two galliots with 3, 500 men and 200, 000 xerafins in addition to daily expenses, because it was presumed that many of them were likely to be lost in that year itself. Lisbon was also informed that the Portuguese had very inadequately armed forces in Goa and Ceylon. This situation could not be allowed to continue in the context of alarming reports from Batavia, and in view of requests of many Indian provinces that wanted the Portuguese to wage a war against the Dutch in India. But for understandable reasons, it was believed by the Portuguese that such a step was not advisable as it would disturb its commerce in the East.[8]

The Dutch on the other hand were forging ahead militarily as well as in trade. Their overseas trade in 1699 had touched the limit it had attained five decades earlier during the period of the treaty of Münster.[9] Within a span of 8 years, from 1689-97, they were in a position to set sail 100 warships with 2, 400 men besides a multitude of privateers and thousands of seamen who crossed the seas with or without convoy.[10] In 1689 they had succeeded in making Natal their colony.

As a matter of fact they had consolidated also their position in Bengal and were obstructing Portuguese shipping. The situation can be gauged from the complaints received from the Augustinian fathers who had gone from Goa to Bandel. They had reported on 30th December 1693 that they had sought an audience with the official in charge of the Mughal area to apprise him of the violent behaviour of the Dutch in preventing their ship from going out of Bengal. They informed that the captain of their ship, Cosme Gomes, had made the purchases as per the orders of the Portuguese viceroy, D. Pedro Antonio de Noronha, Count of Villa Verde, and with much efforts had loaded the ship with saltpetre and other costly materials and had paid the required customs duties. The captain also informed that the Portuguese viceroy had requested the Great Mughal to order the Dutch not to put any obstacles as they were friends of the Great Mughal and were living in his lands and were serving him in various ways, such as providing gun-powder and other necessities. The official assured them that he would call for the Dutch attorney, but when they approached him a second time they were told that the Dutch were in control over the area and not the Mughal. They received the same reply when they called upon Ibrahim Khan, the Mughal governor.[11]

The Dutch maintained that they dominated the Indian seas and that the Portuguese should be happy with 15 ships in the bar of Lisbon.[12] Obviously, it was a sad commentary on the Portuguese state of affairs in the East. The situation was not very much favourable to the Portuguese elsewhere in India despite some show of bravery on the part of the Portuguese. Thus, for instance, the Portuguese Captain of the Sea and War, Bento Pereira da Almeida, burnt a big ship, forced another to run aground another two vessels, including one which the Dutch alleged to be belonging to an influential trader of the South, Baba Parbu Pathare. This happened at Panane in the territory of the Zamorin. During the war against the Dutch in Cochin this Baba Parbu had conspired against the Portuguese and had been instrumental in handing over Cochin to the Dutch. But subsequently he severed his relations with the Dutch, escaped from Cochin and settled with his family in Panane under Zamorin, whom he had helped in his fight against the Dutch. But at the time of the incident of burning the vessel, Panane was in the possession of the king of Cochin who was at war with the Dutch. His property in Cochin had been seized by the Dutch company because he owed them a huge sum. Now the Dutch tried to exploit the situation and asserted that three ships burned by the Portuguese belonged to Baba Parbu and that he was their factor and associated with their trade. But Captain Bento Pereira da Almeida made the Dutch confess that what they claimed as their goods were neither theirs nor they had any vested interests in them and that they belonged to none other than the Mohammedans. Captain Almeida averred that if the owner had hoisted the Dutch flag on the ship and had informed him about the damage caused to it by the Captain-in-chief of the South, Francisco Pereira da Silva, some days before the incident, the said ship could have been freed. He maintained that neither he had indulged in any hostility by not allowing the hiding Dutch to get out of the ship and take away the Dutch flag, which they had unfurled before while plying, thereby appeasing the Portuguese Governor of Cochin. He averred that it was not expected from Holland, with which Portugal was then on peaceful terms, that it should help the ships of the enemies of Portugal to dodge in this manner. In fact, as confirmed on oath by a Franciscan Friar Antonio de Pesos, a missionary stationed in South India since 1683, the two ships which were burnt by the Captain-in-chief, Francisco Pereira de Silva belonged to a Muslim named Xheque Marca, an enemy of the Portuguese, and the other two ships set ablaze by the Captain of the Sea and War, were owned by Baba Parbu.[13]

Another significant incident occurred after three years. A Portuguese ship *Fatemura* captained by Fernão Manoel was coming from Bengal to Daman with French goods. It was seized enroute by a Dutch commander Honton and was taken to Cannanore under suspicion that it had abroad a French pilot and three Frenchmen, and hence maintained that the goods too belonged to the French. The Portuguese in fact were in a very embarrassing position because the Governor of Daman had exceeded his powers in issuing the credit card (*carta de crença*) and the neutrality which they maintained in the recent past vis-a-vis the French and the Dutch was almost on the brink.[14] But they saved themselves from the discomfiture by forgoing the claim of the seized goods as they proved to be French beyond doubt and opting for the neutrality with the Dutch.[15]

It can be undoubtedly concluded from the aforesaid episodes that the Portuguese were lying low at the end of the 17th century and did not desire at all to enter into any serious conflict with the growing Dutch power in the East. The Dutch had virtually monopolised the pepper trade there since they had captured Bantam, a strategically important centre in Java.[16]

On the western coast of India, the Dutch enterprise in the beginning of the 18th century was the acquisition of certain privileges and a plot of land at Surat.[17] They as well as the Arabs had also started in 1708-9 the intrigues in the Persian court against the Portuguese.[18] They lost Mauritius to the French in 1710. Now they were more interested in their settlements in Malabar because the pepper which fetched rich profits in European trade could be collected there. Given the practical problems, they were convinced that they required considerable manpower to safeguard their interests there. Consequently Batavia sent there 1, 573 men in September 1715, followed by another batch of 1, 500 in September 1716.[19]

In 1715 the Portuguese had no doubts that the Dutch would succeed in case of any possible military operation they might mount against Calicut or other ports of the Zamorin. These fears were clearly expressed by the viceroy Vasco Francisco Cezar de Menezes to his factor at Mangalore.[20] By the beginning of 1716 the Zamorin lost Chitica and the viceroy surmised that the Dutch would continue to make progress since they found themselves wielding considerable power.[21] Quite obviously the viceroy replied cordially to the Dutch factor at Barcelor, Daniel France Exipeel, in response to his letter reminding him of the amity existing between the Portuguese and Dutch monarchs.[22]

In the following years the Portuguese were found augmenting their missionary activities in Malabar. The viceroy Count of Ericeira praised the efforts of Fr. Antonio Dias, provincial of Malabar, and promised to write to the king of Tannur recommending him to have more missionaries for more conversions, and also to construct a stone memorial at the entry of the Christian street and to finance the Church of Tannur with 200 fanões. He was not surprised about the reports of persecution of the missionaries.[23] He therefore cautioned Pedro da Costa Coelho, the factor of Calicut in Tannur not to have any dealings with the Dutch and to be careful with the Zamorin and other coastal princes to prevent disastrous consequences to the Portuguese State and the religion.[24] In fact, the unbearable obstacles put by the Dutch in the way of the Portuguese missionaries in Malabar prompted the viceroy to write to his king early next year urging him to use his good offices through the Portuguese ambassador in Holland. The Dutch crown ought to be asked to instruct its subjects in Malabar not to perturb the missionaries who did not interfere with their trade.[25]

Interestingly in 1721 the Portuguese on the western coast seemed to be in good books with the Dutch as well as the British. This is perceived from the letters addressed by the viceroy Francisco Joseph de Sampaio e Castro to the Dutch factors in the port of Barcelor, Exipeel and Roos, as well as to R. Courtney, the English captain and factor in Karwar.[26]

In contrast, when the Dutch occupied a port south of Mozambique, the British tried to take possession of the port of Mozambique. The Portuguese king then instructed the viceroy to dispatch forthwith one frigate with necessary men and ammunition to expel the Dutch from there and to establish a colony in the bay. He also desired another frigate to be sent against the British, in order not only to safeguard the reputation of the Portuguese crown, but also to avoid serious damage to the Portuguese trade in general and that of Mozambique in particular.[27] Within a week the king wrote to him once again informing about the efforts made by him to stop the British from their activities in Mozambique in view of the existing treaties. The viceroy was given instructions as how to proceed in case the British ignored the Portuguese pleas.[28]

Three years later, there were reports from Cochin that the Dutch were making preparations for a major combat.[29] The next year they were masters of the bay of Loureno Marques and had erected a fortification there. The Portuguese viceroy had entrusted to Antonio Cardim Froes the task of instigating the Africans there to continue their conflict against the Dutch.[30]

While Portugal lost Mombasa to the Arabs in 1729, in western India the rule of the Dutch East India company was waning and it has even been termed as their "black period". It was beset with large-scale corruption.[31] Constant wars, specially with Zamorin involved a considerable expense for the Dutch, so much so that holding on to Malabar was no longer a profitable proposition.

In their attempts to penetrate the North the Dutch had caused enough damage to the Portuguese fort at Surat by the end of 1731. To counter their menace the Portuguese viceroy João de Saldanha da Gama had recommended to the crown that it should ask the Mughal court to keep its representative as a stand-by in the said fort to deal with them. The crown turned down this suggestion as impractical and instead advised the succeeding viceroy Count of Sandomil to cultivate the friendship of the Mughal in whatever way possible and block the construction of the fortress there by the Dutch.[32]

It is worth noting that after three years the Dutch had established their trade in Surat so formidably that the Portuguese viceroy wrote to his envoy there to procure the ammunition and the cloth in that port from the Dutch.[33] And in contrast, when they were establishing their trade in the Cape in Africa, the Portuguese monarch D. João had instructed his viceroy in Goa to embarrass the Dutch trade there as it would cause a great loss to their overall commerce in Mozambique.[34]

With so much ill-will, in 1745 the Dutch who had a strong factory at Surat tried to play a ruse on the Government of Daman. On pretext of relaxing in the pleasant countryside of Daman, the Dutch Director arrived on the shore of Daman and sought the permission of its governor to enter the place. The Governor was suspicious of the true motives of the visitor, but was still willing to let him in. But Fr. Eusebio de Mattos, administrator in Daman, and a Surat-based French merchant cautioned him about the Dutch malice. Following the advice the governor refused permission to the Dutch director, who had to go away with all his accompanying officers, clerks and armed entourage.[35]

In the Far East the Dutch increasingly subjected the Portuguese shipping there to unbearable insults. They tried to seize the Portuguese vessels carrying opium and approaching Macao. They would lie there in wait with large fleets, check the cargo and tow the ships off to Malacca branding the goods as contraband. Their absolute power in the Far Eastern waters enabled the Dutch to treat cavalierly the Danes and the English as well. Aware of their weakness, the Portuguese preferred to resort to diplomacy in absence of force.[36] When the viceroy Marquis of Alorna received complaints of

Dutch ill-treatment from the captains of the ships *Piedade* and *S. Catarina* plying in the eastern seas, he drew the attention of the Dutch governor at Malacca to the breach of propriety and violation of the freedom of trade.[37] A similar note of complaint and protest was sent to the Governor at Batavia detailing the damages and loss caused to the Portuguese ships in Malacca and requested him to restore the goods to the rightful owners.[38] In the meantime Marquis of Alorna was entertaining hopes of capturing the Dutch factory at Vengurla. This had been established following the 8-month blockade of Goa in 1638.[39] At the same time we find the Dutch factor of Cannanore thanking the Portuguese viceroy for helping his father-in-law, captain of a brigantine, to recover his ships back from the ruler of Melondim (Malwan) who had intercepted them in front of the fortress of Rarim, off north Goa.[40]

Another seeming contradiction is that though the English and the Dutch were keeping the Portuguese in good humour, they did not hesitate to subject the Portuguese to insults whenever their interests were seriously affected by the Portuguese activities. The Portuguese presence was not wanted on the Coromandel coast, and this was irritating the Marquis of Alorna no end. He seems to have vowed to restore the Portuguese trading presence at S. Thome.[41] As a matter of fact, by the time Marquis of Alorna returned to Portugal in October 1750, he was convinced that the Dutch were still not ready to reconcile with whatever remained of the Portuguese presence. After making two attempts to drive the Portuguese out of Daman, they were lately confabulating with the Marathas to obtain a foothold in the Portuguese territories in the north. The British had also been hostile. Only the French had shown positive feelings and had even offered help in need.[42]

Given this background, the Portuguese received disturbing reports at the end of 1754 that the Dutch and the Marathas had signed a convention whereby Captain Colig Prie had proceeded to demarcate and establish a factory in the jurisdiction of Bassein. The aim of this activity seems to have been to secure Daman. The Portuguese viceroy Count of Alva reacted to this situation by alerting the Governor of Daman and by impressing upon the crown at home the urgency of rushing naval help to meet the crisis and of re-establishing the naval yard in Goa to restore its lost prestige and power.[43]

What helped to defuse the situation was the third treaty that the English signed with the Marathas on 12th October 1756. It stipulated among other things that "the Maratha Government will never permit the Dutch to settle or come into their dominions, but on the contrary, will issue express orders to prevent their carrying on any trade therein". Another clause stated that the Dutch goods would not be permitted to be landed at Rajapur nor their trade suffered to be carried on there.[44]

It is not out place to record that the rise of English influence in Hindustan since 1755 had a very deleterious effect on the Dutch holdings in India in general: A Dutch expedition to Bengal in 1757 was a failure and Bengal fell in the hands of the British. The next year the Dutch surrendered Chinsura. The same year they signed the treaty of peace with the Zamorin. While they tried to concentrate more in the East, they were engaged in war with the king of Kandia (in Ceylon) who was backed by the English since 1761. The war continued till 1764 and was concluded with a peace treaty. In the meantime Hyder Ali could entrench himself in Mysore and contributed to further weakening the Dutch presence near Tuticorin and in the profitable pearl fisheries there.

However, the Dutch continued to exercise their muscle power in Malacca, where they harassed the Portuguese vessels to maximum extent possible, extorting heavy anchorage duties of about 4000 xerafins in violation of the existing treaty agreements.[45]

The Dutch decadence had well set in on the Indian coasts. It resulted into fall in their trade with Ceylon, Malabar, Coromandel, Bengal and Japan in 1780. Worse still, the next year the English seized their settlement at Negapatam in Madras. One year later they captured the Dutch holdings in Malabar, Coromandel and the Bay of Bengal. Trinquimale went into English hands early in 1782, but the Dutch succeeded in recovering it with French aid. Under such dire circumstances the Dutch had no option but to sign a treaty with England on 20th May 1784 conceding to England navigational rights in the Indian seas. The Dutch position was further weakened with the Revolution of 18th January 1795 in the Netherlands and the escape of the Prince Stadtholder Wiliam V to England.

It is not surprising that the British took advantage of the situation and captured the Dutch settlements in Ceylon, Malabar, Coromandel, Bengal, Malacca, Molluccas and even in the Cape of Good Hope. The Dutch Indian Company's Government was formally closed once for all and their dominance in the East for 157 years and in India for 138 years came to an end. With the fall of the two European powers, namely the Portuguese and the Dutch, it was now the turn of the third power to dominate the Indian scene for the next 152 years.

REFERENCES

1. Galleti, A., *The Dutch in Malabar*, Madras: Government Press, 1911, pp. 18-9. For earlier relations, see P. P. Shirodkar, "Dutch-Portuguese Relations in the East (1560-1663) vis-a-vis Indian Peninsula" (Paper presented at the IV International Seminar on Indo-Portuguese History, Lisbon, 1985).
2. Menon, A. S. (ed), *Kerala District Gazetteer, Ernakulam*, Trivandrum: Govt. Press, 1965, pp. 154-5.
3. Disney, A. R., *Twilight of the Pepper Empire*, Harvard University Press, 1978, p. 154.
4. Menon, A. S., *Kerala District Gazetteer, Quilon*, Trivandrum: Govt. Press, 1964, p. 122.
5. Batavia Diary for the 4th November 1665 as quoted by Poonen, *Survey of the Rise of Dutch power in Malabar (1603-1678)*, p. 204.
6. Lyall, Sir Alfred, *The Rise and Expansion of the British Dominion in India*. London: John Murray, 1916, p. 35.
7. *Vide supra* n. 4, pp. 126-7.
8. Historical Archives of Goa (henceforth *HAG*): *Monções do Reino*(henceforth *MR*), No. 22, fl. 354.
9. Boxer, C. R., *The Dutch Seaborne Empire 1600-1800*, New York:Alfred A. Knoff, 1965, p. 105.
10. *Ibid.,* p. 275.
11. *HAG:MR*, No. 58, fl. 309 (15 Jan. 1694).
12. *Ibid.,* fls. 307-307v (18 Jan. 1694)
13. *MR*, No. 58, fls. 303-304v, 311, 311.
14. *MR*, No. 61, fl. 289 as quoted by Pissurlencar, *Assentos do Conselho do Estado*, V, pp. 46-7. *Cf. Ibid.,* p. 55.
15. Pissurlencar, *op. cit.,* pp. 54-5.
16. Kasturi, N., *History of the British Occupation of India*, Calcutta, n. d., p. 55.
17. Raj, N. R. (ed.), *Dutch Activities in the East*, Calcutta, 1945, App. p. 55.
18. Pissurlencar, *op. cit.,* , pp. 247-92.
19. *Vice supra* n. 1, p. 20.
20. *HAG*: *Canara*, No. 1, fl. 116.
21. *MR*, No. 8, fl. 216.
22. *HAG:Reis Vizinhos*, No. 8, fl. 32.
23. *Ibid.,* fl. 67v.

24. *Loc. cit.*
25. *MR*, No. 84-B, fl. 432.
26. *Reis Vizinhos*, No. 8, fl. 103v.
27. *MR*, No. 89-B, fl. 300.
28. *Ibid.,* fls. 301-301v.
29. *MR*, No. 90, fl. 170.
30. *MR*, No. 92, fls. 307-307v.
31. *Vide supra* n. 1, p. 25.
32. *MR*, No. 102-A, fl. 31.
33. *Marathyanchea Itihasachi Sadhane*, I, P. 3, ed. S. S. Desai, Bombay: Maharashtra Rajya Sahitya Sanskriti Mandal, p. 443.
34. *MR*, No. 108-109, fl. 50.
35. Overseas Historical Archives (Lisbon), Cod. 448, fl. 71.
36. *MR*, No. 122, fls. 114-114v, 161-161v, 195-195v.
37. *Ibid.,* fls. 159-60.
38. *Ibid.,* fls. 163-64.
39. *MR*, No. 75, fls. 390 ff.
40. Overseas Historical Archives (Lisbon), Cod. 448, fls. 111.
41. *Ibid.,* , fls. 101v ff.
42. Overseas Historical Archives (Lisbon), Cod. 449, fls. 188 ff.
43. *MR*, No. 127-A, fls. 108-108v.
44. Aitchison, C. V. (ed.), *A collection of treaties, engagements and sanads relating to India and neighbouring countries*, vol. I, Delhi, pp. 14, 16.
45. *MR*, No. 152, fls. 63v, 632.

7

GOA IN THE INTERNATIONAL TRADE: (16TH-17TH CENTURIES)

Agnelo Fernandes

Introduction

Goa has been since long a great centre of trade on the western coast of India. During the Portuguese domination it became the metropolis of the *Estado da India* and the hub of a widespread trading network. Here I shall briefly analyse their *cartazes* system and briefly present the network of trade voyages from Goa, attempting to bring out the significant role Goa played as an interlink with the international centres of Indian Ocean trade.

Goa around 1500 A. D.

Immediately before its conquest by the Portuguese the territory of Goa was ruled by the Adilshah of Bijapur. Describing this Muslim city Duarte Barbosa wrote: "The city was inhabited by Moors, respectable men and foreigners and rich merchants; there were also many great gentile merchants and other gentlemen, cultivators and men at arms. It was a place of great trade. It has a very good port to which flock many ships from Mecca, Aden, Hormuz, Cambay and Malabar Country.... The town was very large with good edifices and handsome streets surrounded by walls and towers. [1] Tome Pires, writing in the 1511, also describes the greatness of Goa in above tune. He points out that Goa was a great centre of trade where the inland trade from the different States from the interior, conducted through long cattle-caravans, met the sea trade, run "through many Naos which sail to many parts and the Naos of Goa were esteemed and favoured in all parts. " The duties which were collected in Goa were worth 400, 000 *pardaos* annually.[2] Goa was a place which was capable of leisurely undertaking voyages in one year which the Muslims in Suez were not undertaking in 20 years.[3] M. N. Pearson feels that the above description of Goa by the two Portuguese writers is influenced by a desire to push up the importance of the Portuguese conquest of Goa.[4] However, there are other records which support the statements of those Portuguese writers. According to Ferishta, when the news of the conquest of Goa in 1472 reached the ears of the Bahamani sultan Muhammad Shah, he was so jubilant that he held a grand celebration of the victory lasting over seven days.[5] Goa had provided the Bahamanis an access to the west and a great position in the sea trade, with direct link to the Gulf and Arabia. This gave them an edge over the other Deccani kingdoms.

The reference to cattle caravans pouring merchandise from the mainland interior into Goa is not to be underestimated. Francisco da Costa in his *Relatorio sobre of trato da pimenta* points out how the cattle caravans from Malabar would treck to the Mughal empire and go upto Bengal and also Masulipatnam and to Negapatnam.[6] When Sambhaji attacked Goa in 1683 the cattle caravans of the main merchant of Bardez consisted of 3, 000 cattle heads, which made yearly 5 to 6 journeys across the Ghats.[7]

Goa was an important trade centre before the Portuguese conquered it. It was connected also through the coastal fleets and ocean-borne vessels. The horse-trade, so vital in the times when cavalry was the backbone of a State's armed strength, dominated the commerce of Goa. It is said that in order to encourage this trade several concessions were made to traders in this item. The Portuguese continued the trade and the concessions. Whenever *cartazes* were issued to ships going to Hormuz to fetch horses, they were required to keep sureties to guarantee that they would return to Goa with their precious cargoes.[8]

The Cartaz system

Vasco de Gama's arrival in India in 1498 resulted in the first direct contact of the Christian Europe with the countries of the Indian Ocean littoral. It initiated the era of colonisation of the Indian Ocean countries. The Portuguese came to believe that they were the exclusive masters of the Ocean by right of discovery and conquest. It was a claim further justified by their philosophy based on the principle that the Indian Ocean countries were non-Christian. The king of Portugal proclaimed himself "the Lord of conquest, commerce and navigation of Ethiopia, Arabia, and India." The Portuguese began to subject all the indigenous powers who sailed in the Indian Ocean to their laws. This gave rise to the *cartaz* system backed by the Portuguese roving fleets.

The subject has been treated recently by M. N. Pearson.[9] A brief outline is given here to highlight the role of Goa in its functioning. It was one source of revenue tapped by the Portuguese to run their newly founded empire. It was so devised that it did not only uphold Portuguese sovereignty over the seas, but also brought goods into the Portuguese customs. The written permit which the indigenous ships had to buy from the Portuguese to enable them to sail safely in the sea was called *cartaz*. The name of the ship, the particulars of the crew, the route of the voyage, and the rules to be observed were stated in the permit. These rules excluded transportation of certain commodities, which were regarded as monopoly or banned for reasons of security or religion. Any ship sailing without a *cartaz* or in contravention of the rules of the system was liable to be searched and captured as booty or sunk in case of resistance. Only the large ships, sailing in individual capacity, had also to possess a *cartaz*.

Goa was the central *cartaz* issuing counter. Merchants or their agents on the west coast of India visited Goa to buy the permits for their ships. The ships sailing overseas had to obtain their permits directly from Goa,[10] while those sailing along the coast could get them from the nearest Portuguese fortified settlement. In order to check the functioning of the system, the Portuguese organized different *armadas*. The chief armadas were: The high sea armada, the Red Sea armada, the Gulf armada, the armada of Malacca, the northern and the southern armadas sailing along the northern and southern coasts of western India, and several other local armadas covering the coast of Diu, Cambay, etc. If any vessel was caught transgressing this permit system, it was liable to be seized and brought to Goa where the case was brought before justice. It would be set free if it was not found guilty. Otherwise it was auctioned along with its cargo.

Generally speaking the rulers and merchants of the Indian subcontinent accepted this Portuguese imposition as an unavoidable evil. The obedience to the Portuguese thalassocracy became a way of life to them and gave the Portuguese a sense of pride and power to see even mighty land powers of the subcontinent seek their *cartazes*. This, however, did not mean that there was no evasion, but the obedience was more obvious than the defiance.

C. R. Boxer's remark that no one should maintain that the Portuguese 16th century thalassocracy in the Indian Ocean was always and everywhere completely effective is very correct.[11] It is known that Malabar and Atjeh were successfully bypassing the Portuguese controls and supplying spices to the Red Sea areas. There were other violators as well. But while all this was so, no country had challenged the Portuguese claims of sovereignty over the seas. However, neither the limited resources of the sovereign permitted to exercise any full-proof checks. And barring the first few decades of the 16th century the Portuguese could not monopolise the export of the spices to Europe.[12] Of course, with the entry of the North Europeans in the eastern trade and later the rise of the Omanis completely destroyed the Portuguese claim of spice monopoly.

The indigenous powers who entered into political treaties with the Portuguese and accepted the *cartaz* system openly were often granted some concessions. However, as years passed the evasion tactics increased and were often beyond detection by the Portuguese fleets. However, the system survived well into the 18th century.

Goa-based Maritime Trade

The Goa-based maritime trade, which was considerable during the pre-Portuguese times, rose to greater heights as Goa became the metropolis of the Portuguese *Estado da India*. By 1519 the city of

Goa, which was endowed with the privileges of the Lisbon municipality,[14] had become a hub of a widespread network of trade voyages. Merchants arrived from Arabia, Armenia, Persia, Cambay, Bengal, Pegu, Siam, Malacca, Java, Moluccas, China, etc.[15] The visible effect of this affluence and wealth was the emergence of "Golden Goa". Goa was at the climax of its glory during the viceroyalties of D. João de Castro and D. Luis de Athaide.

The Portuguese economy in the East was organized in Goa and it was based on the trading voyages, reinforced by the imposition of the *cartaz* system. There were three types of trading voyages conducted by the Portuguese from Goa. The *carreira da India* (Goa-Lisbon and return voyages), the *cafilas*, and the interport voyages. These voyages were responsible to bringing Goa in contact with most of the known centres of the Indian Ocean trade. A comprehensive discussion of these voyages is yet to be attempted, though C. R. Boxer, M. N. Pearson, M. A. P. Meilink-Roelofsz, V. Magalhães-Godinho, K. S. Mathew and some others have made rich contributions to this subject. These voyages not only received direction from Goa as per standing orders of the crown, but they also contributed fixed percentage of taxes to Goa.

Carreira was the first category of organized trade voyage of the Portuguese to the East, and these first voyages can be considered as unmatched feats achieved by the Portuguese. They marked a revolution in the knowledge of geography. And the oceanic link with the East shattered the monopoly of the overland route via the Italian countries. The Portuguese succeeded in breaking this monopoly at least during the first few decades of the 16th century.[16]

The carreira ships were generally loaded at Goa from the time Goa became the metropolis of Portuguese India. Mozambique was the main stop enroute to Lisbon and back. There the ships and passengers rested and were re-provisioned.[17] Very often the captains carried orders not to touch any other ports than those mentioned on their sailing instructions.[18] With the regularity of the *carreira* Goa had the trading agents based there.[19]

Spices constituted the staple of the *carreira* trade during the 16th century. In the 17th century the arrival of the North European powers destroyed the Portuguese monopoly over spices. This forced the Portuguese to go in for additional trading items, such as saltpetre, diamonds, textiles, musk, etc.[20] These goods were brought to Goa by the cafilas and the interport voyages.

We mentioned local armadas that complemented the services rendered by the usual cafilas and interport voyages. Thus, for instance, a special armada would be sent to the ports of Canara coast to gather pepper in case the regular cafilas were delayed or obstructed. So also in the 17th century merchants were encouraged to go to Bengal and bring supplies of saltpetre.

A quick glance of the interport voyages can be obtained in the accounts left by Pedro Barreto Rezende and Antonio Bocarro.[21] However, the subject is awaiting further research and there is no dearth of archival information. The interport voyages were organized regularly from Goa after the headquarters were shifted thither in 1530. These voyages were conducted by convoys of ships, and need to be distinguished from the voyages granted to some individuals as *mercês* (grants). However, in either case the ships involved in this intra-Asiatic trading network had to follow instructions issued by the Goa authorities.

The interport trade voyages linked Goa with Mozambique and the East African *swahili* ports, with Hormuz till Basra in the Persian gulf region, and with Sindh in the western side.[22] On the eastern side Goa was linked with Malacca, China, Manila, etc. In the 17th century these voyages were far more profitable than the *carreira*.[23] The benefits through customs helped the local administration in Goa raise revenues for its various works.[24] But above all, the benefits accrued to the private purses of the officials involved in this trade and the administration directly linked with it.[25] With the loss of access to many of these trading centres in the second half of the 17th century, Goa began experiencing the effects very visibly. The situation was only partially remedied with revival of trade voyages to East Africa by adopting fresh methods.[26]

Finally, there were also the small ships of the indigenous merchants. According to a State proclamation no indigenous ships of small capacity could sail independently. They had to seek shelter of convoys and fleets.[27] The ships thus convoyed were not required to obtain a *cartaz*, but they were required to follow all the rules of that system.[28] During the halcyon days of Portuguese Goa the number of ships that gathered in the river to form a convoy sometimes exceeded 500.[29] However, by the close of the 17th century Goa became a shadow of its past. It had ceased to be what it was, a centre of maritime trade.

REFERENCES

1. Duarte Barboza, *A Description of the Coast of East Africa and Malabar in the Beginning of the 16th Century* (Transl. by H. E. J. Stanley), London, 1866, p. 74 as quoted by J. N. da Fonseca, *An Historical and Archaeological Sketch of the City of Goa*, Bombay, 1878, p. 132.
2. *A Suma Oriental de Tome Pires*, ed. A. Cortesão, London, 1944, pp. 215-7.
3. *Ibid.*, p. 214.
4. Pearson, M. N., *Coastal Western India*, New Delhi, 1981, p. 69.
5. M. K. Ferishta, *History of the Rise of the Mohamedan Power in India* (Transl. by Briggs), Calcutta, 1909, Vol. II, p. 485; Fonseca, *op. cit.*, pp. 127-35.
6. Silva Rego, A. da (ed.), *Documentação Ultramarina Portuguesa*, III, Lisboa, 1963, pp. 295-379.
7. Ajuda Library (Lisbon), Cod. 51-VII-23, fl. 296; Goa Historical Archives (=HAG), *Conselho de Fazenda*, Ms. 1127, fl. 154.
8. *HAG*: Ms. 3027, fl. 20-20v.
9. Pearson, M. N., *Merchants and Rulers of Gujarat*, Delhi, 1976, Ch. II. *Cf.* My Ph. D. thesis on *Portuguese and the Mughals, 1627-1707*, University of Bombay, 1987 (Ch. 2).
10. Fernandes, A. P., "Rustom Manock and the Portuguese at Surat". Paper submitted to the Indian History Congress (1981), cf. *Proceedings of the Indian History Congress*, pp. 224-32.
11. Boxer, C. R., "A note on Portuguese reactions to the revival of the Red Sea spice trade and the rise of Atjeh, 1540-1600", *Journal of South East Asian History*, 1969, p. 415.
12. *Ibid.*, pp. 415-28; Das Gupta, A., "Gujarati Merchants and the Red Sea Trade", *Age of Partnership: Europeans in Asia before Dominion*, eds. Bling and Pearson, Honolulu, 1979.
13. *HAG*:, Ms. 1363 (Livro de Cartazes); Meilink-Roelofsz. M. A. P., "The structures of trade in Asia in the 16th and 17th centuries", *Mare Luso-Indicum*, IV, Paris, 1980, p. 5.
14. Brito, R. S. de, *Goa e as praças do Norte*, Lisboa, 1966, p. 96.
15. Lopes, D., *Expansão da lingua portuguesa no Oriente nos sculos XVI, XVI, e XVII*, Lisboa (2nd ed.). n. d., p. 6; Meilink-Roelofsz, *Asian Trade and European Influence in the Indonesian Arhipelago between 1500 and 1630*, The Hague, 1962, p. 185.
16. Godinho, V. M., *op. cit.*, III, pp. 81-110; Mathew, K. S., *Portuguese Trade with India in Sixteenth Century*, New Delhi, 1983, pp. 200-25.
17. Boxer, C. R., "Moçambique island and the carreira da India", *Studia*, VIII, Lisboa, 1961, pp. 95-132; "Moçambique as a way-station for Portuguese East-Indiamen", *Mariner's Mirror*, XLVIII, London, 1962, pp. 3-18. Some-

times the *carreira* ships also halted in Angola and Brazil; Aquivo Historico Ultramarino (Lisboa), Cod. 1221, fl. 297v.

18. *HAG*: Livro dos Segredos. This has been calendared in the *Boletim da Filmoteca Ultramarina Portuguesa*, Lisboa, n. 6; Iria, A., *Da Navegação Portuguesa no Indico no Seculo XVII*, Lisboa, 1973, pp. 53-8.
19. Mathew, K. S., *op. cit.,* pp. 157-69.
20. Steensgaard, N., "The return cargoes of the Carreira in the early 16th century", *Indo-Portuguese History: Old Issues, New Questions*, ed. Teotonio R. de Souza, New Delhi, 1985, pp. 13-31.
21. Biblioteca Nacional (Lisboa): Ms. 140; Antonio Bocarro, "Livro das plantas de todas as fortalezas", in A. B. Bragança Pereira, ed., *Arquivo Portugues Oriental*, Bk. IV, Vol. 2, Pt. 1-3; T. R. de Souza, "Goa-based Portuguese Seaborne Trade in the early Seventeenth Century", *The Indian Economic and Social History Review*, XII, 1976, pp. 433-42; C. R. Boxer, *Portuguese India in the Mid-Seventeenth Century*, Delhi, 1980, pp. 43-46.
22. Habib, I., *The Atlas of the Mughal Empire*, Delhi, 1982, p. 16.
23. Boxer, *op. cit.,* p. 42.
24. Biblioteca da Academia das Ciencias (Lisboa), Ms. A-98, fls. 9v-10; HAG: Ms. 7747, fl. 4; Ms. 832, fl. 30v.
25. *HAG*: Ms. 7865, fl. 61v; Boxer, C. R., and Azevedo C., *A Fortaleza de Jesus e os Portugueses em Mombaça*, Lisboa, 1960, p. 51.
26. Axelson, E., *Portuguese in South East Africa, 1600-1700*, Johannesburg, 1860, p. 145; A. P. Fernandes, "Portuguese Trading Company and its Impact on Diu-Mozambique Trade, 1694-99", *Purabilekha-Puratatva*, V, 1986, p. 16.
27. The annual expenditure on the armada conducting the cafila to Canara and back was about 20, 000 xerafins.
28. Pearson, *Merchants and Rulers of Gujarat*, pp. 45-7. I have included a discussion on the subject in Ch. VII of my thesis.
29. National Archives (Lisbon), Ms. *Tomo III E*, fl. 21. In 1670 the cafila of the north consisted of 100 vessels. Cf. Biblioteca da Academia de Ciencias (Lisboa), Ms. A-500 (2nd Jan. 1670)- Folios not numbered.

8

FOREIGN JESUITS AND NATIVE RESISTANCE IN GOA 1542-1759

Charles J. Borges

Some author contributors to this volume have discussed the impact of Christianity on Goan society. The role of some Goan priests has been analysed as well, to find out if their reactions can be classified as a freedom struggle against the Portuguese colonialism. One writer seems to conclude that they were only reacting to their personal frustrations. But where does colonialism show itself if not in the lives of individuals? And if some of these individuals are conscious of the real causes of their frustrations and openly say so through their words and deeds, it would be futile to deny their contribution to the building up of the resistance movement. It is not only those who finally join the final onslaught that deserve the credit of being called freedom-fighters. The resistance began to build up right from the early times of the conquest. It was not restricted only to those who preferred to keep away from the pale of the new dispensation. Those who accepted Christianity were not exempted from experiencing the discrimination. Rather, being closer to the new order they experienced the frustration all the more and developed the consciousness faster. This paper seeks to trace some aspects of this discrimination in the behaviour and attitudes of the European Jesuits in Goa. This is not a new theme and it may almost be considered a hackneyed theme. What is new is some fresh information from the archives and perhaps some fresh insights.

The Religious in Goa

The Franciscans were the first religious order to come to Goa, followed by the Dominicans (1548), the Jesuits (1542), the Augustinians (1572), the Carmelites (1607), and the Theatines. There was an air of militancy in their activities, a fact that suited well the colonial designs of the Portuguese and the more determined efforts of King John III to establish effectively the Portuguese colonial presence in the new empire.[1]

Numbers were necessary in order to keep the religious-colonial control over the missionary enterprise, yet there were fears that too many were joining the religious houses thus proving a drain on the Crown economy.[2] It was in response to frequent complaints of this nature that several orders were issued to control the establishment of new Religious institutions and to check the acquisition of more land properties by the established ones.[3] The latter propensity had created religious feudalism and the bankruptcy of the village communities leading to the maintaining of a baroque style of worship that did not suit the modest economy of the Goan villages.[4] But the checks and official restrictions were often a result of the inner contradictions and conflicts of interests among the white settlers themselves.[5] Village lands had been appropriated in a number of ways to provide foundations for the religious colleges and convents, and to procure funds for foreign missions. The Jesuits alone were said to have possessed half the income of the Public Treasury. They were absolute masters of a great part of the island of Goa, and the property they had in Salcete was considered to be sufficient to maintain all the religious houses in Goa.[6]

Despite their growing numbers, the foreign missionaries could not entirely do without native assistance and native labour. But they had to contend with their social organization and their expectations. At the Seminary of Santa Fe and later the College of St. Paul, native boys were trained as interpreters to the priests in their missionary work. Some of them eventually became secular priests. While the principles of equality were being preached, the caste system was retained, a fact that was to cause immense harm to the Church of

Goa in the long term.[7] Only brahmins were admitted to the priesthood since to do otherwise would lower the greatness of the priesthood in the eyes of the lower castes. The Church Provincial Councils[8] held this point of view with varying insistence in its deliberations. Many of those who became priests were soon disillusioned. Their hopes of being treated as equals along with the religious remained a dream. The religious clergy kept them lower on various fronts to guarantee for themselves permanently higher positions.[9]

The Jesuits patronised the natives to the extent they were required to fulfill unavoidable subsidiary roles. They used the Brahmins and later the Chardos, following the lead of Francis Xavier, to function as interpreters in their parishes and missions. Yet when these natives were proving to be troublesome, lower castes seem to have been inducted into the priesthood to offset the increasing hostility of the higher caste clerics. There is little publicised information of such induction, but one comes across in Baião's study of the Inquisition that at least three Goan *shudra* priests trained by the Jesuits and favourites of Jesuits were condemned by the Inquisition in 1736.[10] The concern the Jesuits frequently voiced for the handicaps they noticed in the lives of the native brahmin clergy, does not seem to have worried them when it came to members of the lower castes whom they had prepared for the priesthood. It was not without cause that the Marquis of Pombal accused them of fomenting dissensions between the members of the various castes in order to serve their ends, much to the detriment of the Crown and the State.[11] A Belgian Jesuit, François de Rougemont (1601-76), working in South East Asia, was frank in admitting the tendency of the European missionaries to perpetuate their authority over the natives. He seems to have remarked : "Are we more concerned with maintaining our authority than with maintaining and spreading the Faith"?. This clinging formed the latent basis of their objections to devolve authority to the native clergy.[12]

Resentment had been growing within the native clergy against the discriminatory methods of the religious, and Dom Mateus de Castro[13] spear-headed a revolt against their machinations. He did so especially against those of the Jesuits. It was not the cry of a lonely heart hindered as he was in his personal ambitions, but the voice of one who spoke for many. They drew up a memorial to the King in

1646, in which they listed the grievances they were suffering at the hands of the Jesuits.[14]

The Grievances

The brahmin clergy accused the Jesuits of persecuting them, and of being ignorant of the local language while teaching the faith. They claimed that confessions were heard only once a year, though the people would have liked to confess oftener, that interpreters were used in the confessionals, and that the brahmin priests were prevented from hearing confessions in their own parishes. The other charges were that the missionaries were hard on the people who had to flee to escape their violence, that they owned vast property which they retained by every possible means at their disposal. They lacked the fear of God and uttered many calumnies against the brahmin priests, especially against Mateus de Castro who had to escape to Rome as a result. They prevented the general assembly (*camara geral*) of Salcete village communities from meeting and arrested its members and the chief *ganvkars*.

The Jesuit Viewpoint

The Jesuit Provincial, Fr. Manuel de Mendonça, differed in his reply of December 24, 1646, to the King, wherein he delineated the work his men were doing vis-a-vis the brahmin clergy. His group taught brahmin children to count and sing, to read and write, to dance and play musical instruments. They taught Latin, philosophy, theology, morals as well right up to the time they became priests and said mass, sustaining them at the cost of the Seminary and the colleges of Santa Fe, Rachol and Bassein. Those who could not study, were given paid jobs in the colleges and were helped to look after themselves.

The priests of the Society claimed that they knew the vernacular well enough to teach with courage and erudition. They had composed several books, and during the present year alone they had printed the following: Two booklets (*cartilhas*), two grammars, one *Flos Sanctorum*, four *Puranas* in which they dealt with the errors of paganism and described the mysteries of the faith in very noble terms which very few of the brahmins understood. They were expecting Crown help in having others which were in manuscript form, printed : A *Flos Sanctorum* in verse, three vocabularies, a book of examples, a book on God Triune and One, on the immortality of the soul, the mysteries of the faith, two *Puranas* in verse, a book on the Gospels for the year, the life of Peter and other matters of the faith, a book of explanations for all the Gospels and feasts of the year, and a booklet of hymns. No native brahmin had done anything comparable. Besides, it was rare for any brahmin to preach, while the Jesuits did so in much better terms. They claimed further that many of the parishioners came to them for confession on several occasions, and were better disposed than the Europeans. This was the result of the training they had received as students at school where they used to confess every month. The confraternities and brotherhoods set up by the Fathers, all recommended frequent confession. This was unlike the case in the parishes of the brahmin clergy where the parishioners were slow in the faith. In Jua, they continued to worship idols although they had been baptised, and were punished by the Inquisition. The parishioners and the natives would come to the Fathers of the Society, their parish priests, to have their quarrels attended to or to seek help for their orphans and the widows. They never approached their own priests who were dark-skinned and poor like them and for whom they had no respect. The Jesuits maintained that they did not hear confessions through interpreters, and only those who were new to the job sought the help of these. They did not prevent the native clergy from this job if they were approved and known for their good behaviour. The brahmin women did not approach the native priests for the sacrament, a fact that hurt them, but went instead to the priests of the Society.

The Jesuits claimed they rarely had property enough to sustain their colleges and residences in India. The power they enjoyed was that of good example and virtue, and of being respected by all on account of the good they did. They had little money and even that was sent off to Portugal to pay off loans they had taken in India. They had never persecuted the native clergy but had raised them to the level they were then at. If at all Mateus de Castro had to escape, he had to do so to escape the might of the Count of Aveiras, who wanted him arrested and sent to Portugal for his seditious behaviour in inviting the Dutch to take over Goa and Salcete. Moreover, they had never arrested the *ganvkars* of Salcete as alleged or interfered in their village affairs except when asked for assistance or guidance. They suggested that it would be good to have a Jesuit priest at every village meeting to follow the proceedings. They could then inform the King of any treachery that the villagers were said to have been plotting all the time.

Counter-points

The native brahmin clergy dismissed the above, maintaining that Mateus de Castro was always a faithful subject of the Crown.

In his zeal for souls he went to Bijapur, to the court of Adil Shah to preach the Gospel in his territory and built a church at Bicholim. Thus at long last the Christians were cared for by the native brahmins. The Jesuits had obtained a brief of His Holiness withdrawing the native priests from the churches they were serving, terming Castro anti-national and friendly to the Dutch. They informed the Crown that their churches were clean and well equipped with silver and other ornaments for the services. They had schools for reading and writing and taught the playing of the organ and other musical instruments. They instructed the faithful under their care better than those under the religious, teaching them in their mother tongue (*lingua materna*) which they better understood. They had converted many to the faith and spent much of their own salaries and property for this cause. Besides, they had discovered many errors of paganism and even the Inquisitors had sought their help in this work.

The Jesuits accepted nothing of this. They termed Mateus de Castro a traitor and described how suspect his activities were in Bijapur. The church he claimed to have built was literally a hut (*palhota*). He lived in it like a criminal to evade the many crimes he had committed. A woman he called his relative kept him company in it, and this caused much scandal to the Christians as well as to the Hindus. He had been admonished by a fellow native, the parish priest of Chorão, Bernardo Coutinho.

Bishop Castro had illegally ordained some to the priesthood who were later suspended. There existed no Christian faith in Bicholim or in the Muslim lands. On a number of occasions, the Jesuit priests went to Bijapur and could do no more than hear confessions and assist the slaves of the Portuguese. The Provincial, too, went there, as well as to Karwar, to see the church of Mateus de Castro, but did not find more than a hut, twenty spans in length and twelve in height. Within was a bench on which he noticed things like eatables, rice, cereals, etc. being sold by a non-Christian. Some of the Christian masons who worked for the Governor of this place, mentioned that the bench served as the altar. Two native clerics used to visit the place twice a year for a period of eight days, during which time the seller vacated his spot. In Goa, however, it was described as a sumptuous church. The English who had a factory thereabouts, were scandalised by this state of affairs and requested the authorities to put a stop to it. This could hardly be something the priests of the Society were said to be jealous of.

The Jesuits had no brief from His Holiness as was wrongly mentioned. The churches of the native priests were neither clean nor adorned with silverware. As religious, the Jesuits could own no private wealth. All they had was by sheer industry and the alms received in their churches. Yet no parish was without its income, its cross and thurible, its cruets and candelabras, gilded retables, its rich ornamentation and valuable pieces. All this was due to the zeal of the Provincial and parish priests of the Society. The churches of the natives had no foot of the altar, their salaries were paid by the Crown, and they collected much.

Children were better educated in the schools run by the religious and the natives did not mind if their children were punished, but would not hear of the native priests doing the same since they were dark-skinned like themselves. The faith lagged behind, a fact due to the priests' ignorance of Latin and of Portuguese. Few of them could preach, yet made such mistakes in matters of faith that the parishioners did not approve of it. The Fathers of the Society were more sought after since they were better educated and trained in theology. They picked up the local language within two months and preached in it, something the native priests could not rival. As a result there were very few native preachers and the few that did preach, repeated the sermons of the Jesuits.

The native priests had not converted a single person while the brothers and priests of St. Paul went out every year all over Goa looking out for orphans and catechumens for baptism, an event celebrated with great pomp on the feast of the conversion of St. Paul. If the native priests were asked to help, they did so with much reluctance and in the hope of receiving gifts like holy pictures, reliquaries, rosaries, crosses, etc. The errors they detected were the ones they came across when they served as interpreters to the Inquisitors. The Jesuits, on the other hand, had learnt the language and had written grammars and vocabularies in it. They kept the native clergy away from their parishes not because they were ignorant of the language, but to prevent them from plotting against the State as they had once done only to be discovered. That was the reason why the King of Spain warned against the priests of the Society leaving Salcete, convinced as he was that each priest was a captain in a fortress, seeing to the safety of the lands and the genuine interests of the State.

The natives had no respect for the brahmin clergy, who were dark-skinned like themselves, and from whom they received neither alms nor favours. Their priests had their own self-interests and exploited the poor while they received bribes from the rich. It was not without reason that King John III had written to Fr Francis Xavier to have the brahmins evicted from their lands, for they were idle, troublesome, and bent on destroying religious peace and the faith.

To crown his self-defence the Jesuit provincial had to go to lengths that seem to have clouded his reasoning, unless he was truly convinced of the historical discoveries he had made about the origin of the brahmins of Salcete. He describes these descendants of Brahma as descendants of Abraham, and as such as being Jewish in origin and belonging to the lost tribe of Israel. He also states that the *chardo* majority of Salcete are the good-natured and rightful inhabitants, while the brahmins were the intruders and troublemakers. It appears that the Jesuit was deliberately introducing antisemitic and caste elements in his story in order to make the brahmins easier targets for the hostility of the European and other native sections respectively.

Missionary ethnic and colonial superiority?

The above letter of the Provincial, Fr. Manuel de Mendonça

shows the despicable way in which the religious held the native clergy. Linguistic inadequacies seem to have been covered up by the more adequate doctrinal training of the foreign missionaries, which they could always cite against the natives as a permanent shortcoming.[15] Frequent references were made to the fact that the clergy was dark-skinned and that the parishioners had no respect for them as a result. The Jesuits were not alone in this attitude and the Franciscans too rivalled them in their feelings against the native clergy. A Franciscan Frei Antonio de Encarnação, parish priest at the Church of Colvale, excommunicated for striking his native assistant, wrote a virulent attack on the native clergy. He called them *negros chamados curas* (=blacks called curates) and termed them perverse and insolent.[16] This was at a time when the archbishop of Goa Fr. Ignacio de Santa Theresa had greater regard for the native clerics than for the religious whom he regarded as insolent and overbearing.[17] The Franciscans seem to have gone out of their way at this time to expand on the viceregal decree of 1606 regarding making the natives illiterates in their own mother tongue and literates or half-literates in Portuguese to qualify for the sacraments.[18] Though the Jesuits made many attempts to learn the local language, some of the accusations of the native clergy against them on this score were justified. Their Visitor had insisted on a proper language foundation and brothers spent time at their language school in Margão studying along with the natives and in six months could write and speak the language perfectly.[19] The Crown had been informed about the impediment of ignorance of the local language (*lingua da terra*) in the work of conversion and the matter was asked to be remedied.[20] The people felt the want of priests who could speak to them in their own tongue, and if they knew one they went to great lengths to get his help. The Jesuits secured the services of one such in 1556 for Chorão who was of the soil and the son of a Portuguese settler. Ten years later there were two Konkani-speaking priests on the Goa islands.[21] Fr. Diogo de Borba, the cathedral preacher, used to go to Banastarim on Sundays with a boy from St. Paul's to instruct the people in their own language. Students at the college had helped in drawing up catechisms in their respective languages.[22] It was true that more was wanting in the study of the local language and at a consultation at Chorão which the Visitor Alessandro Valignano[23] convened on December 6, 1575, it was decided to ask the General of the Order to issue a letter to the whole Indian province urging all to a study of the language and to zeal for the missions. He had suggested that classes in philosophy and theology be suspended to free students for language study, but it was not carried through.[24] Many were the compositions to further the language[25] but it was the work of a few and the same could not be said of the vast majority of Jesuits who manned the parishes in Salcete. If the religious had better churches with richer ornamentation, it was due to the many alms and endowments they received from the faithful. The native clergy worked under more difficult odds due to a lack of cohesion often using their own resources in the service of the faith. Besides, they worked in frontier territory which made their efforts the more creditable, Mateus de Castro having established chapels in Bicholim, Banda and Vengurla.[26] The work of Fr. Joseph Vaz and of his band of native followers in this respect was particularly significant. He received encouragement and approval from the Jesuits because their judgement was not in this case vitiated by any threats to their interests nearer at home. The distrust by the Crown and ecclesiastical authorities of the local people and of their priests was evident in that the parishes of Bardez and Salcete which had their boundaries in common with territories ruled by native rulers, were not thought fit to be given to the native clergy. Each religious parish priest was considered a captain of his fortress. The duel between the religious and the native clergy was certainly one-sided. The former had the backing of the government, a superior culture consciousness, immense funds and a network to amass more.[27] The latter lived with no hope of running their parishes the way they wished and were subject to the taunts and accusations of the powerful religious. It is difficult to believe that they sought curios like religious objects in return for services they rendered at the behest of the religious. Would they have stooped so low? The role and contribution of the native clergy and of the local Christians to the growth of the church in colonial times was largely belittled or ignored. The religious did not involve the local people sufficiently in the work of the faith and they appear usually as silent recipients of the Gospel. If they resisted the culture, morality and social system of the religious, it was dismissed as the work of the devil, and most of the religious saw no elements in the native culture worth emulating.[28] The native clergy played its part in initiating and furthering the freedom struggle against the ecclesiastical dominance of the religious. In this struggle, the native clerics were not functioning in isolation from the lay natives, a fact noticeable from a memorandum they drafted in 1642 on behalf of the village community of Salcete.[29] The so-called "Conspiracy of the Pintos" in the late 18th century was another clear instance of the native clerics and laymen plotting jointly against the Portuguese rule.[30] One can conclude safely that the impact of the frustrations of the native clerics was not without its effect in the building up of the atmosphere of resistance to the Portuguese colonial presence which used religion as an important pillar of its colonial policies.

REFERENCES

1. Souza, T. R. de, "A Response", Amaladass, A. (ed), *Jesuit Presence in Indian History*, Anand, Gujarat Sahitya Prakash, 1988, p. 38.
2. Disney, A., *Twilight of the Pepper Empire*, Cambridge, Harvard University Press, 1978, pp. 21-2. The Count of Linhares while Viceroy in the 1630's had asserted that there were twice as many clerics in India as there were Portuguese laymen.
3. Souza, T. R. de, "Foreign Elements in the Rural Economy of Goa during Sixteenth and Seventeenth centuries", in N. R. Ray, (ed), *Western Colonial Policy*, II, Calcutta, 1983, p. 280.
4. *Ibid.*, p. 278.
5. Souza, T. R. de, *Medieval Goa*, New Delhi, 1979, pp. 72-73
6. *Ibid.* p. 72. *Cf. Arquivo Portugues Oriental*, I, Pt. II, doc. 10; *AHU*(=Arquivo Historico Ultramarino, Lisbon), India: Caixa 15, doc. 110 (1643).
7. de Melo, C. M., *The Recruitment and Formation of the Native Clergy in India*, Lisboa, Agencia Geral do Ultramar, 1955, p. 140.
8. They were held between 1557 and 1606 in Goa and were the highest ecclesiastical body to deal with problems of the faith. *Cf. Bullarium Patronatus Portugalliae Regum in Ecclesiis Africae, Asiae atque Oceaniae*, I, Olisipone, 1868.
9. de Melo, C. M., *op. cit.* , p. 140. They were taught Latin and cases of conscience which would be good enough for them in their ministry as assistants.
10. Baião, A., *Inquisição de Goa*, I, Lisboa, Academia das Ciencias, 1949, pp. 285-6. The names of the thee priests are given as Fr George Pereira dos Remedios of Cortalim, Fr Constantino Rodrigues of Loutolim, and Fr Bartolomeu Dias of St. Mathias.
11. Barbuda, C. L. M. de, *Instrucções com que El-Rei D. Jose mandou passar ao Estado da India.... no anno de 1774*, Nova Goa, Imprensa Nacional, 1841, I, pp. 39-41;II, 9-11, 16-7;III, 15-20.
12. Boxer, C. R., *The Church Militant and Iberian Expansion, 1440-1770*, Baltimore, The Johns Hopkins University Press, 1978, pp. 95-6.
13. Was a christian of brahmin parents of Divar, Goa, ordained at Rome, November 30, 1635, and consecrated Bishop of Chrysopolis, in *partibus infidelium*, and came to India as Vicar Apostolic in 1637. A brilliant cleric, he gave much to the religious to think about.
14. *Archivum Historicum Societatis Iesu* (Rome): *Fondo Gesuitico*, 1443/9, file 23, *Memorial dos opprobrios pelos clerigos Bramanes de Goa aos Padres da Companhia de Jesus, etc.*
15. *AHU*: India: *maço* no. 62 (1750). The religious (Jesuits in Salcete and Fran-

ciscans in Bardez) were accused of being ignorant of the local language and of leaving the ministering of the sacraments to the native clerics. The latter were said to be better trained than their contemporaries in Portugal.

16. *AHU*:India, *maço* 35 (1729). In an audience with the Archbishop Ignacio de Santa Teresa whom he had earlier attacked in his letter, he sought pardon for writing what he wrote under duress and at the instigation of Frei Francisco de Spirito Santo, rector of the Church of Manapasser in the Northern province.
17. Rocha, L. da, *As Confrarias de Goa*, Lisboa, 1973, p. 452, n. 265.
18. *AHU*: India, *maço* 9 (January 18, 1729). The parishioners, mostly women and widows, paid fines to the Franciscans for not having learnt Portuguese. Those who could not pay had to mortgage their plants to effect the payments. The friars were accused of turning their churches into prisons, and charged four *tangas* for confessions. *AHU*: India, *maço* 62 (1750):The viceroy marquis of Castelo Novo informed the archbishop that it was an impediment to marry natives not knowing Portuguese language.
19. Souza, F. de, *Oriente Conquistado a Jesu Christo pelos padres da Companhia de Jesus*, II, Bombay, Examiner Press, 1886, p. 64.
20. *Documentos Remetidos da India*, I, Lisboa, 1880, doc. 121, Feb. 21, 1610, p. 359;doc. 24, Jan 17, 1607, p. 84. The *canarins* naturaes da terra (native Christians of Goa) were preferred in parishes since they knew the language.
21. D'Costa, A. *The Christianization of the Goa Islands*, Bombay, 1965, pp. 188-9. Held in 1567. At the Seminary in Goa, students below the age of thirteen were not accepted lest they would forget their mother tongue, and study-groups were formed to exercise it.
22. Schütte. J. F., *Valignano's Mission Principles for Japan*, Vol. I, Pt. I, Gujarat Sahitya Prakash, 1980, p. 173.
23. A native of Chieti, Italy, he was sent to India as Visitor and had the task of "visiting" the entire Indian province, and promoting its activities according to the picture he had formed of its spiritual and material state.
24. Schütte, J. F., *op. cit.* , pp. 156-7. Questions discussed at the consultation were the slave problem, the language school, the Thomas Christians, the spice and silk trade, the conversion work and its obstacles, etc.
25. Saldanha, M, "A primeira imprensa em Goa", *Boletim Instituto Vasco da Gama*, 1956, n. 73, pp. 102-3, lists 14 printed works for the sixteenth century and another 14 for the seventeenth. These included *Doutrina cristã*, *Conclusões da Filosofia*, *As conclusões pedagogicas*, *Coloquios* of Garcia de Orta (16th c.), and *O Purana*, *Gramatica Concani* of Thomas Stephens, and *Sermoes* of Miguel Almeida (17th c.)
26. Nazareth, C. C., *Mitras Lusitanas no Oriente*, Lisboa, 1897, p. 162.
27. *AHU*: India, *maço* 69 (1747). In Assolna the Jesuits did not pay the tobacco and arrack revenue when they took over their properties in 1744, thus causing the State a loss of 6000 *xerafins*. The *ganvkars* of Velim, Ambelim and Assolna in a representation to the king, bemoaned their misery and the ease with which the religious of the Society of Jesus moved the courts in their own favour. *Maço* 75 (1745) accuses the Jesuits of having more properties in the Goa islands than the State.
28. Amaladass, A. (ed), *op. cit.* , pp. 20, 38.
29. Souza, T. R. de, *op. cit.* , Appendix A-8, pp. 241-8. This representation to King John IV lists the financial burdens the people were undergoing at the hands of the fidalgos, the tobacco tax farmers and the Jesuits. The memorandum was signed by Frs. Antonio de Pinho and Estevão da Gama.
30. Cunha Rivara, J. H. de, *A Conjuração de 1787 em Goa*, Nova Goa, 1875.

9

THE CHURCH IN EIGHTEENTH CENTURY GOA

Mira Mascarenhas

Introduction

It is commonly believed that Goan Church history was really made only in the 16th century. Highlights of wonder and tragedy certainly filled that age. But "for us who live in a world which worships the pattern of a free church in a free state"[1] it is important to know that the foundations of today's "free church" of Goa were actually laid in the 18th century.

The 18th century was a century of transition, a period when medieval ideologies gradually gave way to modern ones. Dramatic events hastened this gradual process to radically mould the old outlook, which, basically identified the religion of the subjects with that of the ruler. Ashoka had taken the path of organized persuasion; certain Muslim rulers used violence and sword. The Portuguese in Goa followed a middle path of coercive measures and discriminatory legislation against those of other faiths. As a result of changed thinking in the 18th century, the official policy took a positive turn towards religious tolerance such as the one that had made the Portuguese originally welcome to the local Hindu population in 1510 and that marked the beginning of our basic freedoms today.

If we analyse the factors chiefly responsible for this change of ideology and attitude, we find that some were purely political, some social or economic, some cultural, and only a few strictly religious. Events like the acquisition of the "new conquests" of Goa were purely political, but even the expulsion of the Jesuits and the abolition of the Inquisition were politically motivated.

The emergence of a capable and confident indigenous clergy was strongly influenced by the socio-economic context of the time, as well as by the enlightened ideas blowing in from the West. Education was freed from the clerical moulds towards the end of the 18th century, and culturally speaking, we may say that Goan craftsmen came of age in this "last great age of Goan art".[2] It is sufficient to remember that most of the outstanding churches and chapels standing today in Goa were either built or rebuilt or completed in the 18th century or very close to it. In short, the 18th century is a landmark in Goa's religious history, and it well worth being looked into.

Structures

In all Portuguese territories the Roman Catholicism was the official religion, and since the latter half of the 16th century the open practice of other religions had come under increasing restrictions in Goa, which in 1700 A. D. comprised the "old conquests" of Tisvadi, Salcete and Bardez.[3] The Church in Goa was controlled by the Church and the State, the former being represented by the Archbishop and the latter by the viceroy or governor. Both were chosen by the crown of Portugal, the choice of the Archbishop being merely ratified by the Pope. This was a privilege conferred on Portuguese sovereigns two centuries earlier, in recognition of the yeoman service rendered by Portugal to expansion of Christianity. In addition the tithes due to the papal treasury (a 10% tax on all produce of Christian lands) were turned over to the Portuguese crown, to be spent on missionary work and on the upkeep of Christian clergy and institutions.[4] This meant that, through the royal purse-strings the crown and its viceroys exercised a definite control over the church and every religious institution in the Portuguese dominions.

The Archbishop was accorded a protocolar rank second only to the viceroy's, and like the latter, he lived at Panelim, the elite capital city's suburb. His see was at the Cathedral in the city of old Goa, and from there he governed the far-flung archdiocese that stretched from Africa to Japan, including parishes and mission stations in territories outside Portuguese control.[5] He also wielded considerable political power whenever he took over the reins of the secular government from an outgoing or absentee governor. He decided all clerical appointments, and his religious decrees affected the social and moral lives of thousands. During the course of the 18th century Goa had eight archbishops, and they took over the secular government also eight times in all.

The clergy was divided into two main bodies: The "secular" and the "regular". The secular priests lived singly or in groups, each on his own stipend or private income, except for higher-ranking dignitaries of the Cathedral Chapter who were mainly Goans in the 18th century. The regular clergy belonged to the monastic communities, known as religious orders or congregations. These shared a common life and income, and had strict rules to observe. Such were the great mendicant, preaching and teaching Orders: The Franciscans, Dominicans, Augustinians, Jesuits, Carmelites, Theatines, and Oratorians. Their huge convents in the city of Goa were centres of learning and training, from where members were sent out to man colleges, parishes, and mission stations all over the Portuguese *Estado da India*. In Goa proper, the Franciscans were running 24 parishes in Bardez, besides a couple of colleges and hospices. The Jesuits were in charge of about 60 parishes in Salcete, the famous St. Paul's "university" in Old Goa, the royal hospital and other institutions. The Dominicans and the Augustinians had colleges and parishes in Ilhas (Tisvadi). There was an Augustinian nunnery called Santa Monica, the only one in the archdiocese, and not far from it, there was a monastery of hospitaller lay Brothers. The all-Italian Carmelites and Theatines dwindled in numbers and favour with the government as they did not show willingness to take the required oath of loyalty to the Portuguese crown.[7]

All the regular clergy was European or Eurasian at the beginning of the 18th century and full-blooded Goans were not yet accepted in their ranks. As a result, a group of Goan priests decided to organize themselves into a religious congregation. They came to be known as

Oratorians and they did a splendid job in Ceylon where, after the Dutch conquest, the Catholics became victims of Calvinist and Buddhist persecutions. At the opening of the century Fr. Joseph Vaz, a daring pioneer of this missionary group, had already gained legendary fame for holiness, charity and inspiring service of the Church. He died there in 1711.[8]

By this time the bulk of Goa's population had converted to Christianity. According to a report of the viceroy in 1707 there were about 100, 000 Christians to 3000 Hindus in Salcete, and a roughly similar proportion in the other two talukas of Bardez and Tisvadi.[9] Most Hindus who had not become Christians had migrated to the mainland areas of Ponda, Bicholim, or Zambaulim, or still further afield. Only in the market city of Goa there was a majority of non-Christians, and many of these came from diverse and distant places and countries. According to a letter from a judge to the crown of Portugal in 1704 there were 30-40,000 non-Christians in the city of Goa.[10] Although the earlier figures of the viceroy were inaccurate in the light of subsequent census figures, there is no doubt that members of the Church formed the vast majority of the population in the countryside. A parish census in 1719 gives 67, 252 as total number of Christians.[11] It was probably not exhaustive, since the State census of 1750 lists 169,696 native Christians and 1,370 whites, as compared to 23,355 Hindus and 2,953 Muslims in a total population of 201,814.[12]

Christian Life

After conversion Goan Christians were expected to make a clean break with their Hindu past. Not only were the personal names changed, but food habits, social customs, and even dress had to conform to the way of living of the European Christians. Naturally, this was no easy task. We get to know about how the 18th century Goan Christians lived from the various Church decrees and prohibitions issued during this and earlier periods. An edict of the Inquisition in 1736, for instance, draws a detailed picture of practices which the Christians had to shun,[13] so as not to be confused with Hindu neighbours and their socio-religious customs. But since habits die hard, many ancestral customs that were not directly connected with Hindu worship still live on.

Several episcopal decrees were prompted by the age-old custom of child marriages and arranged marriages. Archbishop Santa Catarina (1784-1812) condemned the practice of getting 12-year-old girls married "before they were capable of evaluating the duties of marriage". He also condemned ostentatious and financially ruinous marriage celebrations, and marriages forced by parents on youngsters who scarcely knew their intended partners.[14] One decree ruled that the bride's face should be unveiled and clearly seen at the wedding ceremony and that her responses to the vital questions thereat be audible.[15]

Hindu superstitions connected with birth, death and marriage obviously persisted. Religious legislation warned against the belief that demons sought to enter the home on the 6th day after a child's birth, and should be kept away with all-night feasting and fireworks, the child being protected by a black wrap and a smoke-screen! Women were reproved for not going to church for 40 days "in manner of the Jews" after giving birth to a child. Loud lamentations and melodramatic scenes attended the presence of a corpse in a home. One superstition held that the administration of the last sacraments was a signal for the devil to enter and begin his last fight for the departing soul. As a result there was a very real fear of calling for a priest to administer the last rites.[16]

Several old Hindu practices were enhanced in their Christianized version. Thus, the place of honour given to the Hindu household deity was now given to the *oratorio*. The votive flame now burned before a crucifix or images of Christian saints. The *tulsi* plant pedestal gave way to the cross in front of a Christian home, and Christian prayers now accompanied such pre-marriage customs as ritual sweet-making or the coconut-juice bath. In the village *novem* (Konkani expression for the annual harvest procession), a Christian, instead of a Hindu priest, now carried on the traditional practice of blessing the first sheaves of paddy.[17]

Processions and feast days were very popular with the people, who were inclined to turn them into veritable *melas*. They were warned not to make the public spectacles of penance or dramatic performances of Lent and Christmastide into garish displays. Vending booths in the vicinity of the churches, as well as rowdy entertainments of *olly* and *zaqor* were banned time and again, with the threat of deterrent action against the whole village.[18] Interdicts and fines, however, have not fully succeeded in rooting out these practices.[19]

It is common fact that the wealthy and landed gentry has always tried to extend its influence over the Church. We come across injunctions against the celebration of baptisms in homes instead of in the church, against long funeral orations inside the church, and against additional display of liturgical paraphernalia at christenings and weddings of the influential laymen.[20] Bridal couples even went to the extent of announcing their arrival at, or departure from, their parishes with the pealing of church bells, a privilege that was reserved to archbishops and viceroys![21]

The parish priest was instructed to teach his flock sound Christian doctrine and morals regularly. He was also expected to encourage heads of families to repeat the traditional catechism lessons in song, a practice inherited from the time of St. Francis Xavier. The vicar was also enjoined to take an annual census of his parishioners, verifying numbers by personal visits to the families under his spiritual care. He was to see that there was silence and decorum in and around the church premises, and scrupulously observe the royal decree banning the unhealthy practice of burials inside the church building. For this purpose, airy cemeteries were ordered to be built on village hill-sides and isolated places.[23]

An important function of the parish priest was the running of the parish school. Though theoretically open to all the local Christian lads, it was frequented mostly by the sons of the Brahmin or land-owning families. The caste traditions continued after conversion, specially in the choice of professions and marriage partners. The boys were taught the "Three R's", and given quite a sound training in the basic harmony and singing of western music, as well as musical instruments like the violin and organ. This enabled them to take part in liturgical services, but also to earn livelihood.[24]

Girls were not admitted into the schools, but were often tutored at home. Although the position of women was considerably upgraded in society by the Christian concept of monogamy, by property laws that benefited the women converts, and by positive encouragement given to young widows to re-marry,[25] their place was still strictly in the home. After two and half centuries of Christianity, Europeans could still remark that "though all-powerful in the home, women are openly disparaged by their husbands -- a remnant of the Hindu tradition".[26]

Maintenance and repairs of the church buildings were, as in Hindu times, carried out by the village communities, known as *communidades* to the Portuguese. The State aided major works, and also paid stipends to the priests, often from taxes levied on the same *communidades*.[27] The administrative boards of the latter usually sat in the church premises, a practice handed down from the temple times, and along with committees of *confrarias* (pious confraternities) and *fabricas* (administrators of the church property) often made such a nuisance of themselves that vicars were repeatedly urged to stop all the meetings on church premises.[28] However, the practice carries on to this day.

Official Religious Policy

Several laws were in existence favouring conversion to Christianity, and discriminating against the practice of other religions.[29] These were periodically re-enacted, changed or abolished by the crown in Lisbon on recommendation of the viceroy, archbishop or important religious entities. Prominent in the latter category were the Jesuits, zealous promoters of faith, and the court of the Inquisition, dreaded custodian of the same. By the 18th century, for instance, no non-Catholic place of public worship was allowed. Those temples that had not been officially destroyed had fallen prey to time and weather conditions, since they could not be repaired. Goan Hindus and Muslims prayed in their homes, performed what rites they could without fanfare, or else attended ceremonies in the temples beyond the boundaries of the "old conquests".

In 1718 it had been decreed that orphaned children of non-Christian parents could be legally claimed for baptism or religious instruction in the Catholic faith by the *Pay dos Christãos* (=Father of the Christians) who was in charge of an institution called the *caza dos catechumenos*. The relatives who spirited such children away to the mainland were fined or punished. The decree was renewed in

1754. Three years later another law reversed an earlier liberal interpretation on the subject of taking away illegitimate children from non-Christian mothers and baptising them as Christians.[30]

In practice, however, these laws were scarcely obeyed. A tolerant attitude had already begun to creep into official policy in the 17th century, when viceroys and officials were covertly representing to the crown that religious discrimination was having an adverse effect on the commerce and general prosperity of Goa, since Hindus constituted the business community of Goa. In fact, it became the fashion to impute the decline of the whole Eastern empire of the Portuguese to this, though there were several other far more important causes for the decline.[31]

Indeed, we find the *pay dos christãos* regularly complaining to the king in the 18th century that officials were not carrying out the regal decrees meant to defend and care for new converts.[32] In 1735 he imputed the slow pace of Christianization to the great freedom and esteem which the Hindus enjoyed in the State, and to the general slack in observing laws and charters in favour of Christians. Years before, in 1712, another *pay* had described the contemporary scene in detail. Not only was he not consulted before public offices were given away to Hindus -- thereby depriving many a deserving convert -- but Hindus were allowed to live in Catholic Goa with privileges. They used money earned here to build and renew temples on the mainland, coming and going as they pleased. They enjoyed the honours of the palanquin, umbrella and horse-riding, which other rulers reserved only to a privileged few. They had obtained permission to bring their *bottos* (priests) and dancing girls into Goa for the celebration of marriages, and even took their dying (lest they should ask for baptism in their last hours) across to the mainland, where they had no home, doctor or hospital. They were adept at hiding children who had to be turned over to him for instruction, and for getting favourable interpretations from the authorities regarding property and other other laws. Finally, they treated relatives or acquaintances who had been converted so insultingly and badly that even the stoutest of heart would be deterred from taking that step.[33]

Goan Hindus were also quick to send formal protests to the Portuguese crown against their disabilities or any unjust treatment by an official.[34] It is significant that the Inquisition Edict of 1736 sought to counteract the tolerant tendencies evident in every section of society by tightening control over the social, rather than the religious habits of the Christians, since they provided the basis for ethnic identification and friendly co-existence between the two major religious communities in Goa.[35]

The first bold step towards a liberalisation of the official religious policy were taken by viceroy Alva (1754-56) and Ega (1758-65) when they tried to consolidate territorial gains outside the "old conquest". Pernem and Bicholim-Sanquelim had been reluctantly ceded by the Bhosles of Sawantwadi in 1754;[36] Ponda and Zambaulim were militarily wrested in 1763; Canacona was brought in by the raja of Sunda when he was under attack of Hyder Ali and sought refuge under the Portuguese in Goa in 1764.[37] Thereafter, the boundaries shifted more than once, but by the end of the century the "new conquests" had more than doubled Goa's original land extent. By cleverly treating the predominantly Hindu "new conquests" as if they were outside the pale of Christian Goa, these viceroys were able to promulgate decrees permitting their new subjects "the preservation of their temples, ministers, Brahmins, rites and customs".[38] Furthermore, this permission was offered as inducement to all Desais and Ranes who would voluntarily come forward to swear fidelity to the State.[39]

Governor de Melo (1768-74) went a step further, when he pleaded with Lisbon that non-Christians in Christian Daman be allowed to practice their faiths, just as their counterparts in Diu had been allowed to do.[40] His plea was granted. Obviously, the winds of change were blowing.

Much of this new boldness on the part of the Goa government authorities was due to the backing of the prime minister in Lisbon. This man, known as Marquis of Pombal, was a strange mixture of ruthless, dictatorial and liberal ways. He had been governing the Portuguese dominions under king Joseph I since 1750, and he did far more than any of his lieutenants in Goa could have dreamt of doing to change the official religious policy when he destroyed both the Jesuits and the Inquisition, the twin pillars of that policy in the Portuguese empire.[41]

The Expulsion of the Jesuits

The nobility and the Jesuits had enjoyed unlimited influence over the Portuguese royal court and the realm for generations. Both had snapped their fingers contemptuously at "upstart" Pombal's attempts to create a "new" Portugal. With hatred mounting in his heart, the king's minister bided his time, An attempted regicide in 1758 was his opportunity to strike. Leading noble families were accused and exterminated., The Jesuits were also accused, and by March 1759 royal decrees had expelled the whole "Society of Jesus" from the Portuguese dominions.[42]

The bombshell fell on Goa in September that year when the ships from the metropolis arrived. Within a day all institutions belonging to the Jesuits were surrounded by troops, and every Jesuit was under arrest.[43] Soon they were shut up in monasteries of the other religious Orders, and with the return sailing they were shipped off to Lisbon gaols. All Jesuit estates, rents, grants and other property were confiscated and declared crown property.[44] It was a busy time for both viceroy and archbishop, because the vacancies left by the Jesuits had to be filled. Missionaries had to be appointed from other religious Orders to substitute them in parishes and mission stations all over the Portuguese India. Needless to say, Jesuits outside Goa ignored the call to return and submit tamely to arrest warrant, and since they were held in high esteem by their Christian flocks, it was difficult to capture them even in the Portuguese fort settlements. Besides, the raw substitutes sent were no match for the well-trained Jesuits, who always studied the culture and learnt the vernaculars of the districts where they exercised their apostolate.[45]

Replacing Jesuit teachers and professors in their educational institutions was also just a difficult task. After several trials, it was found that the only ones who could do the work somewhat satisfactorily were the Oratorians, the congregation of the Goan priests.[46] But perhaps the greatest headache caused to the State by the expulsion order was an appreciable fall in commercial activity. All over the world the Jesuits had invested their vast resources to the maximum advantage, and it was "difficult to find some branch of economic activity in Portuguese Asia where they were not directly or indirectly involved", particularly shipping, building, trade and finance. They were also the trusted custodians of Crown funds, managers of Goa's royal hospital, and responsible for the upkeep of fortifications and minting of coins at some places. Their land-holdings had long been the subject of complaint by envious officials, but their defence was that far-flung missionary efforts could not be supported by crusading zeal alone.[47] The fact remained that the Jesuits' business acumen, educational excellence and missionary success found very poor successors when Jesuit concerns were taken over by the Church and State.[48]

The abolition of the Inquisition

When Pombal destroyed the Jesuits, he won for himself a host of voluble enemies and critics. But when he suppressed the Inquisition in 1774 everyone applauded. Both steps had been utterly unexpected. Both were effected with such dramatic speed and efficiency that the Christian world gasped in disbelief. But this time there was public relief and rejoicing.

Although it has been shown that every practice of the Inquisition commonly objected to had already figured in the Indian *dharmashastras* and in Roman law,[49] it is certain that average person greatly feared the Inquisition. Much of the dread was due to the ominous silence which surrounded its working methods, its trials, and daily treatment of the prisoners. There were vaguely whispered horrors and the frightening sights periodically provided by the *autos da fé*, at which the accused were either acquitted or publicly condemned and tortured. Various punishments were meted out to the public sinners, heretics, apostates and blasphemers among the Catholics, for whom this court functioned, but the greatest was the burning of the "impenitent" at the state.[50] During the 71 *autos da fé* held in Goa from 1600 to 1773 (practically during the entire life of the Inquisition in Goa) 121 out of 4046 men and women sentenced received this supreme punishment. Of these 121, 64 were already dead, so that only their bones and effigies were burnt at the stake.[51] Nevertheless, the Inquisition's potential for high-handed justice was very real, since any enemy could turn into a deadly informer under its protective veil of secrecy. Even non-Catholics could be denounced as preventing Catholics from practising their religion, or perverting them with evil practices and rituals. No wonder friend and foe alike praised Pombal for the abolition of this dreaded institution. When revived for a time after Pombal's downfall, it was a ghost of its former self, shorn of all its former power. It was suppressed for good in 1812.

The extinction of the Inquisition in Goa was formally decreed by the Cardinal Inquisitor-general and king in Lisbon. The decrees were executed by the chief justice of Goa in October 1774. Its 37 prisoners were released and 14 boxes of archived papers sent to Lisbon. These were ultimately destroyed in the final extinction of the "Holy Office". The State revenue department picked up a sizely amount in cash and securities of precious metals and stones, as well as immovable property. The three inquisitors and official clerk were retired with pensions.[53]

Indianisation of the Clergy

Whether or not Pombal expelled the Jesuits and abolished the Inquisition because he "could stomach no tyranny but his own",[54] he certainly contributed two landmarks to Goan Church History. They paved the way for an enlightened official religious policy in the coming centuries. A more significant achievement, however, concerned the Goan Catholic clergy. For more than a century and a half before his coming into power as Prime Minister, the native priests of Goa had been quietly proving their worth and efficiency in the parishes and missions assigned to them to work in. However, though the European religious hierarchy leaned heavily on them for language and manpower, they were loath to acknowledge them as their equals. As we mentioned already none of the Regulars admitted a pure native into their ranks. The cathedral chapter, vicarships and professorships in Goa were filled by Europeans, no matter how incompetent in comparison with Goans. Outside Goa, however, the Papal Congregation for the propagation of faith (better known as *propaganda fide*) was enthusiastic about the work of Goan priests. It had already appointed three Goan bishops in the 17th century to run dioceses in other parts of India. Goan intelligentsia was quick to resent the injustice, but could do nothing against the established order, where ignorant soldiers and dubious Eurasians were preferred to capable Goans.

That situation is best seen in the accounts of happenings in various convents and missions during this century. Frankly speaking, the exclusively European religious orders were in a sad state of disorder. Letters from viceroys and archbishops to the crown abound in complaints. The greed of the Dominican missionaries for ivory and gold in Africa or spices and sandalwood in Timor and Solor; the scandalous power-struggles of Augustinians in Bengal; extortionist and lax Franciscans in Bardez parishes; the business empire of the Jesuits.[56] The latter, however, were consistently praised for their work and dedication to duty, as were also the Goan Oratorians who did not have a fraction of the finances available to the Jesuits to support their self-sacrificing and pioneering work in Kanara and Ceylon.[57]

Then came Pombal's historic decrees of 1761 and 1763, commonplace to the modern mind but most enlightened for that age. And when he issued his Instructions in 1774 to the new viceroy and archbishop,[58] they were a charter of human rights to the Goans. Long pent-up resentment began to find immediate and vigorous utterance, and the crushed hopes of decades began to blossom again. Already in 1766 the *camara geral* of the Bardez *communidades* appealed against the innumerable outrages and injuries suffered by the people from the Franciscan Regulars who administered the 24 parishes of that province, and pointed out that the native clergy did the bulk of the the work of preaching, hearing of confessions and catechizing.[59] Though no friends of their, governor de Melo threw his weight in favour of the native clerics taking over the vicarships in question. The order was given by Pombal. A list of eligibles drawn in a petition of 1762 was instrumental in the appointment of the first native to the cathedral chapter, and a strongly-worded letter sent by the Goan clergy to the crown in 1771 was quoted in the famous 1774 Instructions.[60] Priests were henceforth to be selected for mission or parish posts on the sole criteria of learning and virtue, and without distinction of race.[61]

The local Theatines who had refused to admit natives into their ranks just as a few years before, in accordance with the accepted custom of other Orders, were the first to accept the Goan candidates. Soon they were reporting that "they are the most suitable for restoring the new missions and this has been amply proved in the kingdom of Kanara and the island of Ceylon... (where) they annually multiply the number of the faithful, because of the ease and skill with which they master the language of any place in this part of the East".[62] One by one, every religious Order in Goa began to receive Goan candidates. Parishes became theirs by right, not only where the Jesuits had been expelled and the Franciscans ousted, but all over the archdiocese and beyond. A matter-of-fact briefing of a new archbishop to Goa by the Lisbon Secretary of State in 1779 (following Pombal's downfall) pronounces the work of Goan priests as "fully and consistently satisfactory",[63] and several years later, a French historian comments on the "utter change for the better in the manners and morals" of Goan clergy,[64] both secular and regular, which, by the turn of the century, had become almost Indianised.

Padroado v/s Propaganda

A conflict of ecclesiastical jurisdictions plagued the Church of Goa all through the 18th century. Though not within the confines of the territory proper, it occasioned much bitterness and many unseemly disputes. Originally responsible for the problem was the limited geographical knowledge of the 15th and 16th centuries. When Portugal and Spain launched out on their epoch-making voyages, one eastwards and the other westwards, the Pope had blessed their missionary intentions by dividing the evangelical jurisdiction of the whole world between the two. Continents and oceans had yet to be charted. In 1534 the Portuguese king was given the right of royal patronage in the East, and successive papal briefs confirmed this right.[66] This meant that the crown could nominate all bishops, dignitaries and parish priests. In return it was bound to safeguard the Church interests and propagate the faith by supporting the clergy and religious institutions. Since all Catholics east of the Cape came under the dual control of Church and State, "mission and colonial expansion grew together", and defence of the "padroado" was almost a patriotic duty.[67]

Things worked well as long as the resources of the Portuguese crown in men and money sufficed. But dwindling resources and an increasingly greater number of Christians and Christian institutions brought the *padroado* up against practical difficulties. Within a century, Rome had realized that it was impossible for so small a nation to handle the colossal task of evangelizing the East. Therefore, it set about trying to rectify the initial error of judgement by setting up the *propaganda fide* in 1622.[68] The vicars apostolic of this Congregation were instructed "never to invade the rights and jurisdiction of the ordinary bishops, but only to supply when the prelates are impeded from exercising them, or have no means to supply for such a vast population in such vast areas.[69] Unhappily, no clear-cut agreement had first been worked out between Rome and Lisbon, since mutual consultations had ceased during the 60-year period of Spanish occupation of the Portuguese throne (1580-1640). The result was a conflict of jurisdictions, with the Portuguese king insisting on his "rights", and other colonial powers like the Dutch and the English making capital of the ensuing quarrels between bishops and priests appointed to the same posts.[70] Now, any priest leaving Goa for parish or mission work outside the territory was required to swear an oath that he would not accept "any usurpation of jurisdiction by the bishops of the *propaganda*, but rather the preservation of the privileges, exemptions and authority of the royal patronage... as confirmed and approved by the legally published and accepted Apostolic Ordinances".[71] One can easily imagine the difficult situations such as person could find himself in. Matters came to a head in the succeeding century, and were sensibly resolved only in our century.[72] In between the division of loyalties confused and dismayed all right-minded Catholics.

Education and Culture

As in other parts of the world, the Church of Goa was also in the vanguard of education, artistic and musical expression. We have described the little parish schools that made so many village lads literate from the 16th century onward. A Christian boy could also pursue secondary and higher education, if he could afford to live in the city of Goa or its suburbs. There were five colleges run by the religious Orders in the 18th century, namely the Dominican St. Aquinas College, the Franciscan St. Bonaventure College, the Augustinian Populo College, the Jesuit St. Rock's or New St. Paul's College, and the Oratorian college on *Boa Vista* hillock. There was also a grammar school attached to the Cathedral, meant mainly for the European and Eurasian students.[73]

Degrees in Arts and Humanities, Philosophy and Theology were dispensed by these "universities", as three of these colleges styled themselves. The undergraduate course in Portuguese, Latin, Greek grammar, Logic and Rhetoric was followed by a three-year course for a Master's degree and another three-year course for a Lecturer's qualification in Scholastic Philosophy. Doctorates were also awarded, but theses were usually referred to Lisbon or to Rome.[74] The syllabi of studies were thus moulded on those used by the great classical universities of medieval and contemporary Europe. The accent was religious, being primarily meant for the training of the candidates for priesthood. Both lay and secular interests took second place. Any layman aspiring to the teaching, medical or legal professions had first to take this University training at the colleges run by the religious.

After the expulsion of the Jesuits from Goa in 1759 the educational system lost its best teachers. But, though disastrous in many respects, their expulsion led to two major educational events in Goa: The foundation of the first diocesan seminary in ex-Jesuit Rachol,[75] and the introduction of Government-sponsored secular education in the form of primary, secondary and higher institutes of learning.[76]

In the "college for native boys and clerics which His Majesty orders to be re-established in the city of Goa", Minister Pombal hoped to introduce a modern system of education patterned on the English public school model, with the introduction of sciences and mathematics, subjects that had not figured on the curriculum before.[77] Things soon slipped back into the old mould since priests were still the only teachers available. Nevertheless the college grew into Goa's first diocesan seminary, fully controlled by the archbishop, and not by any single religious Order. It is still functioning as the major seminary of the archdiocese at Rachol.[78]

Similarly, in various secular primary and secondary schools that were set up together with different professional and scientific higher institutes, the monopoly passed out of the hands of the religious. But we can never forget the great debt we owe to these, and specially to the Jesuits. Had it not been for the latter's enlightened practice in studying grammatical and literary Konkani, for instance, the mother-tongue of the Goans may never have survived centuries of official neglect and discouragement. The Jesuits were responsible for the first literary works and grammars printed in the Konkani language. Even in the 18th century, a Czech Jesuit named Karel Prikryl (in Goa from 1748 to 1761) and a Spanish Jesuit named Hervas y Pandure (1735-1809) were working on the language and have left important works.[79]

Man has always given his artistic best to God who created his talents. The Church of Goa is rich in the cultural expressions of architecture, sculpture, painting, wood-carving and music. The West and the East have truly met in the cultural interplay and interaction of ideals as seen in the Christian churches of Goa. The classical lineage of Greece and Rome, the French Gothic, the Italian Renaissance and Mannerist styles came through Portugal to Goa. Much of the succeeding Baroque design and Roccoco decoration, however, are manifestly Indian, that is, Hindu and Islamic.

Building activity in the city of Goa had come to an end as the 17th century merged with the early 18th century.[80] But in the talukas of Bardez, Salcete and Tisvadi that activity was still alive, and continued right through the 18th century. In the churches of Calangute (1741), Socorro (1763) or Assagão (1775) we see obviously Indian faades. Little verandahs, false domes, octogonal towers, distinctive vaults, the tier-effect, horizontal bands and Indian motifs in wall and woodwork decoration show Indian expertise in handling the Baroque. Says an art critic: "It is an independent style and not a colonial variant of the Portuguese Baroque". In his opinion, two of the five masterpieces among Goa's churches are the "luminous" Our Lady of Piedade Church of Divar island (1700-24) and the "ornate" St. Stephen Church at Jua island (1759).[81]

Splendid crosses in this style of architecture adorn squares in front of major churches like Margão's Holy Spirit or St. Alexis at Curtorim, while many beautiful chapels like the one at Candolim belong to this century. The best existing examples of sculpture and painting of the time are also religious. The skill of the Indian craftsmen in sculpting, wood-carving and metal-work is evident in the altars, retables, and furniture of many a church in Goa, as for instance, the high Roccoco retable in Pomburpa's Madre de Deus church, and the many statutes of ivory or wood found everywhere.

Even in the field of painting, whose finest hour was in the previous century, we find notable examples in convents and churches of the old city of Goa. Goan craftsmen had certainly come of age by the 18th century.[82]

Meanwhile, religious music had profoundly influenced the Christian artist's ethos. A blend of eastern melody and western harmony, which had already been finding expression since the 16th century, resulted in compositions of heart-warming fervour. The 18th century church records contain innumerable examples of these hymns, masses, *motets* that are unique to Goa and worth a thorough study and classification. Most of the composers remain unknown and unsung. Related musical styles had also penetrated the secular sphere to evolve the different branches of folk music which are characteristic of the Christian Goans today.[83]

Summing Up

I have tried to examine the different facets of Church history in Goa during the 18th century in order to substantiate the claim that, although bereft of spectacular advances in Christianisation, it was a very important period from the point of view of modern principles and ideals in peaceful co-existence, self-government and true Christian evangelisation.

REFERENCES

Abbreviations used: HAG = Historical Archives of Goa,

MR = Monções do Reino
D.D. = Sumario Cronologico de Decretos Diocesanos do Arcebispado de Goa, ed. M. J. S. de Albuquerque.
DAG = Directory of the Archdiocese of Goa & Daman (1979)]

1. Hartmann, A., (ed.) *The Augustinians in Golden Goa*, Rome, 1968, p. 10.
2. Pereira, J., "Roccoco Goa", *In Praise of Christian Art*, ed. Mulk Raj Anand, Bombay: Marg Publications, 1980, p. 71.
3. Joppen, C., *Historical Atlas of India*, London, 1946, No. 16.
4. Silva Rego, A. da, *Portuguese Colonialism*, Johannesburg, 1959, p. 76.
5. Kloguen, D. L. C. de, *An Historical Sketch of Goa*, Madras, 1831. pp. 62-5.
6. DAG, p. 15.
7. HAG: *MR*, No. 127-B, fls. 261-2, 280, 291, 308-11, 315-19; No. 79, fls. 290-350.
8. Perera, S. G., *Life of the Venerable Fr. Joseph Vaz*, Colombo, 1953; *MR* No.

123-B, fls. 429-30, No. 127-B, fls. 319-25.
9. Priolkar, A. K., *The Goa Inquisition*, Bombay, 1961, p. 140.
10. *MR*, No. 68, fl. 239v.
11. *Ibid.*, No. 84-B, fls. 331-66.
12. *Ibid.*, No. 122-B, fls. 268-78.
13. Priolkar, *op. cit.*, pp. 98-105
14. *D. D.* , pp. 12-13, 27-28.
15. *Ibid.*, p. 13.
16. *Ibid.*, pp. 24-6, 19-20.
17. Bragança Pereira, A. B. da, *Etnografia da India Portuguesa*, II, Bastora, 1940, pp. 116-18.
18. *D. D.* , pp. 1, 3-4, 15-19.
19. *Ibid.*, pp. 3, 23.
20. *Ibid.*, pp. 19-20, 24-26.
21. *Ibid.*, pp. 28-35.
22. *Ibid.*, pp. 20-21.
23. *Ibid.*, pp. 1, 6-7, 17-19.
24. Menezes Bragança, L., "A Educação e o Ensino na India Portuguesa", *A India Portuguesa*, II, Nova Goa, 1923, pp. 18-22.
25. HAG: Ms. 7693, fls. 51v, 78v, 102v. ; D'Costa, A., *The Christianisation of the Goa Islands*, Bombay, 1965, pp. 151-3; Kamat, P., "Some legal aspects of the Socio-Economic Life of Women in Portuguese Goa", *Goan Soceity through the Ages*, Delhi, 1987, pp. 93-103.
26. Barbuda, C. L. M de (ed.), *Instruções com que El-Rei D. Jos mandou passar ao Estado da India*, Panjim, goa, 1841, App. VIII.
27. Xavier, F. N., *Bosquejo Historico das Communidades*, 2 vols., Bastora, 1903-7.
28. Martins, T., *Collecção de Decretos Diocesanos da Archidiocese de Goa*, Nova Goa, 1912, pp. 174-5.
29. HAG: Ms. 9529; *MR*, No. 83, fls. 250-65, 268-69.
30. HAG: Ms. 9529, fls. 147v-54.
31. Danvers, F. C., *The Portuguese in India*, London, 1894, I, xxviii ff. ; Boxer, C. R., "Portuguese and Dutch Colonial Rivalry", *Studia*, No. 2, Lisboa, 1958, pp. 7-42.
32. *MR*, No. 66, fl. 178; No. 68, fls. 102, 185-6, 238-48; No. 69, fls. 158-63; No. 77, fl. 88; No. 80, fls. 21-2.
33. *Ibid.*, No. 78, fls. 58-66.
34. *Ibid.*, No. 74-A, fls. 305-6; No. 81, fls. 178-201.
35. Priolkar, *op. cit.*, pp. 98-105.
36. Biker, J. F. J. (ed.), *Collecção de Tratados e concertos de pazes*, Lisboa, 1885, VII, pp. 15-20, 111.
37. *Ibid.*, VIII, pp. 1-4.
38. Xavier, F. N., *Collecção de Bandos*, Pangim, 1840, pp. 1-20.
39. *MR*, No. 129-B, fl. 552.
40. *Ibid.*, No. 150-B, fls. 430-9.
41. Gomes, F. L., *Le Marquis de Pombal*, Nova Goa, 1929; Soriano, *Historia do Reinado de ElRei D. Josée da administração do Marques de Pombal*, Lisboa. 1867, 2 vols. ; Smith, J., *Memoirs of the Marquis of Pombal*, London, 1843, 2 vols.
42. Chagas, P. (ed.), *Historia de Portugal nos seculos XVIII e XIX*, Lisboa, 1874. VI, pp. 123-6.
43. Gracias, J. A. I., *Catalogo dos Livros de Assentamento da Gente de Guerra que veio do reino desde 1731 at 1811*, Nova Goa, 1893, p. 18.

44. *MR*, No. 132-B, fls. 357-65; No. 118-A, fls. 64-9, 196-202; Ferroli, D., *The Jesuits in Malabar*, II, Bangalore, 1951, pp. 501-21; Nazareth, C., "Proscripção e Reclusão dos Religiosos em Goa", *O Oriente Portuguez*, Nova Goa, 1909, VI, pp. 201-8.
45. *MR*, No. 118-A, fls. 74v-85; No. 132-B, fls. 514-33; No. 137-A, fl. 221; No. 143, fls. 244-5.
46. *Ibid.*, No. 118-A, fls. 111-2.
47. Boxer, C. R., *Portuguese India in the mid-17th century*, Delhi, 1980, pp. 47-51.
48. Boxer, C. R., *Four centuries of Portuguese expansion*, Johannesburg, 1959, p. 84.
49. D'Costa, A., *op. cit.*, pp. 193-200.
50. Priolkar, *op. cit.*, pp. 53-63.
51. Saldanha, *op. cit.*, quoting the "History of the Principal Acts and Proceedings of the Inquisition in Portugal", Lisboa, 1845, p. 294.
52. *MR*, No. 192, fls. 290-5.
53. *Ibid.*, No. 152-A, fls. 149-68.
54. Boxer, C. R., *The Portuguese Seaborne Empire*, London, 1969, p. 270.
55. *DAG*, pp. 18-9.
56. *MR*, No. 81, fls. 1-5, 148-76, 204, 264; No. 132-A, fls. 1-8, 279; No. 143, fl. 243.
57. *Ibid.*, No. 80, fls. 122-5, 197; No. 81, fls. 210-12.
58. *HAG*, Mss. 1437 and 1438 (*Regimentos e Instrucções*)
59. *MR*, No. 139, fls. 406-9.
60. Cunha Rivara, J. H. da, *A Conjuração de 1787 em Goa*, Nova Goa, 1875, pp. 148-9.
61. Barbuda, *op. cit.*, Pt. II, pp. 14-31.
62. *MR*, No. 133-B, fl. 254.
63. *Ibid.*, No. 168, fl. 113.
64. Kloguen, *op. cit.*, pp. 92-3, 110-2.
65. Boxer, *op. cit.*, p. 256.
66. *HAG*, Ms. 1437, fls. 138v-141.
67. Saldanha, *op. cit.*, I, pp. 355-6; Ratus, L. (ed.), *Catholic India*, New Delhi, 1982, p. 4.
68. Boxer, *op. cit.*, pp. 230-5.
69. Gense, J. H., *The Church at the Gateway of India*, Bombay, 1960, p. 22.
70. Sa, M. de, *History of the Catholic Church in India*, Bombay, 1924, pp. 156-70.
71. *HAG*, Ms. 653, fls. 41-3, 46, 52.
72. Silva Rego, *Le Patronage Portugais de l'Orient*, Lisboa, 1957, pp. 264-8.
73. Menezes Bragança, *op. cit.*, , pp. 1-206.
74. *MR*, No. 118-A, fls. 91-3.
75. Melo, C. M. de, *The Recruitment and Formation of the Native Clergy in India*, Lisboa, 1955, p. 180.
76. Menezes Bragança, *loc. cit.*
77. *MR*, 118-A, fls. 178-9;No. 139, fls. 415-23.
78. Freitas, J., "Seminario Patriarcal de Rachol", *Memoria Historico-Eclesiastica da Arquidiocese de Goa*, Nova Goa, 1933, Ch. VIII.
79. Pereira, A., *The Makers of Konkani Literature*, Goa, 1982, Pts. I & II; Pereira, J., "Prikryl's Konkani Grammar", *Archiv Orientalni*, Prague, 1968; Gaspar de S. Miguel, "Sintaxis Copiossissima", ed. J. Pereira, *Journal of the University of Bombay*, September, 1967, New Series, No. 42.
80. Pereria, J., "Victims of Vandalism", *Sunday Navhind Times*, October 18, 1970, pp. 3-4.
81. Pereira, J., "Goan Architecture's Masterpiece in danger", *Sunday Navhind Times*, June 28, 1970, pp. 3-4.

82. Pereira, J., "Unnoticed Monuments: piazza crosses", *Sunday Nahind Times*, June 10, 1973, p. 5; and "The Goan Retable", *Sunday Navhind Times*, July 12, 1970, pp. 3-4; Azevedo, C., *Arte Cristã na India Portuguesa*, Lisboa, 1959, pp. 44-6, 53-5.
83. Mascarenhas, M., "The impact of the West on Goan Music", *Goa: Cultural Trends*, ed. P. P. Shirodkar, Panaji, Goa, 1988, pp. 189-204; "Social Life as reflected in Goan Christian Folksongs", *Goan Society through the Ages*, ed. B. S. Shastry, New Delhi, 1987, pp. 79-92.

10

SOME PROTESTING PRIESTS OF GOA

Pratima Kamat

Introduction

As the Indian History Congress chose to commemorate its Golden Jubilee in Goa in 1987, the Goans commemorated two centuries of the so-called "Conjuração dos Pintos" (=Conspiracy of Pintos). The generally-believed democratic nature and lofty ideals of this conspiracy made me think of piecing together the careers of a gallery of prominent protesting priests of Goa as a fitting salute to the spirit of the aborted revolt of 1787.

I shall try to analyse the causes and the nature of the rebellious careers of such priests in an attempt to discover the existence, if any, of a thread which binds together their anti-Portuguese activities. This will surely help to answer the specific question of whether these clerics can be called "freedom-fighters", and the more general question whether Goa had ever struggled for independence in the earlier centuries of the Portuguese rule.

Right from the 16th century when the Portuguese colonization of Goa started, till the 20th century which witnessed the flowering and the fructification of Goa's struggle for freedom, the Portuguese *Estado da India* (State of India) has been studded with revolts. It is interesting to note that quite a few of these revolts were engineered by Goan priests. "It is never lawful to rebel and should the rule be excessively tyrannical, than the appropriate remedy is to pray to God for help", so taught the Doctor of the Church, Thomas Aquinas.[1] Although 'priest' and 'rebellion' appear to be antithetical words, in Goa they have been coherent on different occasions. In 1654 Fr. Matheus de Castro attempted to free Goa from the Portuguese yoke with the assistance of the Adilshah of Bijapur. In 1787 a *coup d'état* was planned by some discontented clergymen who were inspired by the liberal writings of the French *philosophes*. In the political panorama of the 19th century, the foremost protesting *padres* were Frs. Pedro Antonio Ribeiro, Estevão Jeremias Mascarenhas and Antonio Francisco Xavier Alvares, while in the 20th century, it was Fr. Alberto Mendonça, who stoutly defended the case of Goa's merger with India. These clergymen believed that "the Church does not condemn those who wish to make their country independent of any foreign despotic power, nor does she blame those who wish to assign to their fatherland the power of self-government"[2], went ahead and raised their voices against the oppressive alien rule present in their homeland. What was it that prompted them to protest? It was more often than not the racist policy followed by the Portuguese in Goa. "Le Portugal n'a pas connu le prejuge de race", writes H. Bernard-Maitre, S. J. in *l'Histoire Universelle des Missions Catholiques*(Paris, 1957, tome iii, p. 50). There was no racial question anywhere in the Portuguese colonies according to another writer, namely S. R. Welch (*Portuguese and Dutch in South Africa, 1581-1640,* Joahennesburg, 1951, p. 137). Edgar Prestage stated in a lecture on "Portugal, Brazil and Great Britain", delivered at King's College of London on 8-10-1923 that "it is to the credit of Portugal that slaves and Jews apart, she made no distinction of race and colour and that all her subjects, once they had become Catholics, were eligible for official posts".[3] The truth, however, was that there did exist "a strong and tenacious colour-bar" in Portuguese Goa.[4] It was the racial discrimination practised by the Portuguese in filling up the higher posts in the Church hierarchy, and even in ordaining priests, that served as the chief cause for the clerical discontent in Goa.

Mid-Seventeenth Century

The first breach in the theory and practice of white superiority in the ecclesiastical hierarchy of Portuguese India was made when a Christian brahmin, Matheus de Castro, was consecrated Bishop of Chrysopolis in Rome in 1635 and was sent to India as vicar-apostolic of Bijapur three years later.[5] Matheus de Castro is indeed a typical example of a native priest suppressed by the *Padroado* and elevated to a high position by the *Propaganda Fide* (set up by the Vatican in 1622), which being in favour of indigenization of missionary work, enabled talented native clerics to climb in the ranks of Church hierarchy. Matheus de Castro Mahale was born at Diwar c. 1594 in a brahmin family.[6] Having probably been orphaned at a young age, young Matheus was brought up at the Reis Magos college of the Franciscan friars. It is said that he worked for them as a kitchen hand, devoting his spare time to academic pursuits. After doing this for five years, Matheus presented himself to the Archbishop of Goa for ordination, only to be rejected. As alleged by Matheus de Castro, the Archbishop, D. Christovão de Sa e Lisboa, had taken an oath not to ordain any native brahmin.[7] The Christian converts were led to believe that both the Pope and the Portuguese crown were against the induction of natives into the clergy.[8] Matheus de Castro was not to be deterred by this setback and proceeded to Rome in 1621. After journeying across Persia, Palestine, Syria, Armenia, he finally reached Rome in 1625. Here he won the patronage of the Secretary of the Congregation for the Propagation of Faith, Mons. Ingoli. Matheus de Castro pursued higher theological studies at the *Collegium Urbanum* from where he obtained a doctorate. Ordained in 1630, Matheus left for Goa in 1633 with the title of *Pronotario Apostolico*. In Goa the authenticity of his credentials was questioned by the Vicar Capitular, who found it hard to believe that a brown could be ordained by Rome, and that too with such extensive powers.[9] The Vatican had accepted him without any testimonials and had allowed his talents to bloom. He was rewarded with a deserving ecclesiastical post, but Goa under the Portuguese refused to accept the evidence of his consecration and appointment. Dejected by this extremely narrow-minded display of racial prejudice and convinced that no Goan could ever hope to hold a position of responsibility and respect under the Portuguese Matheus de Castro returned to Rome. In Rome Matheus de Castro vehemently denounced the working of the *Padroado* in India and launched a determined campaign to rid the ecclesiastical set-up of Goa of the abuses which were so prominently present in it. In frequent memorials to the *Propaganda Fide* he lamented about how Goan Christians were being treated as slaves, with the doors of Religious Orders, priestly colleges, and high offices closed to them. They could only function as servants. Though exaggerated, these reports were heeded by the *Propaganda* authorities as they were complemented and supplemented by complaints received from the native Christians of Goa and by the accounts of European priests returning from Goa to Rome. The establishment of *Propaganda Fide* had raised the hopes of many a Goan Christian. In those days priesthood was the only avenue open to the common man (or rather to a converted brahmin, because for a long time the other castes were denied this privilege) for commanding some respect in society. Almost as soon as the Congregation was founded, it started receiving complaints from the native Christians of Goa to the effect that they were being denied admission to institutions of higher education and to priesthood. Intellectual deficiency, inconsistency of character, general softness of disposition, want of firmness in faith, and inability to maintain celibacy were some of the reasons generally quoted to keep the Goans out of the Church offices.[10] Matheus de Castro proved the fallacy of such arguments both in words and by his actions. The real reason for keeping the Goans out of priesthood were because they were brown-skinned, and because if they were recruited in large number and promoted according to merit, they would replace the Portuguese as leaders of the people.[11] This policy of the *Padroado* frustrated the ambitions of the brahmin Christians of Goa who yearned to again occupy the high social standing that had once been theirs. Although some Goans were reluctantly ordained as secular priests, they were treated with contempt by their white correligionaries. The contemporary accounts tell us that the Portuguese would not "deign to offer a seat to the native priests when these pay them a visit"[12], and that they would not "make their confessions to a native or a mestio priest".[13]

As vicar-apostolic in Bijapur Matheus de Castro soon fell out with the Archbishop of Goa for ordaining Goan natives at Bicholim without his permission. The Portuguese authorities were eager to lay their hands on this bellicose Bishop, and he was accused of "many connivances with the vassals of the Adilshah and particular friendship with the Dutch".[14] This brings us to the political exploits of the Bishop of Chrysopolis. He believed that Christianity would not be able to take firm roots in Goa as long as the Portuguese dominated the political scenario there, and that no matter how intelligent and capable a brahmin was, the *Padroado* would never allow him to occupy the upper echelons of the Church organization. The panacea for these ills, as suggested by the Bishop, was the removal of the Portuguese from the Goan soil. In 1653, when he returned to Bicholim after his third visit to Rome, Matheus de Castro was more determined than ever to liberate his people from the shackles of the Portuguese colonialism. He evolved a three-pronged strategy to achieve his goal, namely to attack the Portuguese from within, and by land and sea from without.

In order to win the support of the local people Castro wrote a letter to the brahmins of Goa entitled *O Espelho dos Brahmanes* (=The mirror of the brahmins). It was worded in a highly provocative language, inciting his fellow caste-men to rise up in arms. Declaring that "sou pronto pera dar mil vidas pera defesa da patria" (=I am ready to die a thousand times for the defence of my country), he tried to whip up similar patriotic feelings in his countrymen. He contemptuously asked the brahmins whether they as traditional leaders of the Indian society were not ashamed of being led like sheep by the alien rulers.[15] Citing the example of Sicilians who had revolted against the French with the help of Spain, Matheus de Castro exhorted the brahmins to take up the lead in expelling the Portuguese from Goa, if necessary with the help of Bijapur.[16]

Realizing fully well that the local population could not be relied upon for the requisite determination, unity and strength to fulfill this task, Matheus de Castro decided to exploit the existing political situation in India to win allies for his cause. Believing firmly that the enemy of one's enemy is one's friend, Castro selected a local potentate, the Adilshah of Bijapur, and an European trading company, the Dutch East India Company, to put his plan into action. Bijapur had not yet reconciled itself to the loss of the islands of Goa in 1510, and of the outlying provinces of Bardez and Salcete later on. The Adilshah was convinced by the Bishop that the moment was ripe for the recapture of Goa, Bardez and Salcete. He was also urged to take advantage of the escalation in the hostilities between the Portuguese and the Dutch to attack Goa. He was also informed that the local people were eagerly awaiting their deliverance from colonial suppression. His intense dislike for his Portuguese co-religionaries prompted Castro to join forces with the Dutch Calvinists, who at this stage were engaged in a determined effort to divest the Portuguese of their colonial possessions in Asia. In order to divert the Portuguese attention from the defence of Ceylon, which they coveted, the Dutch cajoled the Adilshah to invade Goa. The Sultan requested the Dutch to simultaneously venture their offensive at Goa.[17]

The political situation seemed ideal to Matheus de Castro for the realisation of his dream of liberating Goa from the Portuguese yoke. He visualised the brahmins leading the Goans against the Portuguese from within, and the Adilshahi army invading the frontiers and the Dutch blockading the coast. The division of spoils was also pre-arranged: Adilshahi would recover the territorial jurisdiction, the Dutch would benefit commercially, and Castro would have the control over the Archdiocese.[18] It is not known whether the last named had a more temporal ambition in mind, that is, of becoming Adilshah's Governor in Goa. However, things did not turn out as Matheus de Castro had expected. The Portuguese, upon receiving the intelligence reports of an imminent attack from across the border, strengthened immediately their land and riverine defences.[19] On the other hand, the Adilshah, over-confident of a victory, sent a meagre force to attack Goa. The invasion commenced on 12-8-1654, but met with a total failure. Totally frustrated, bereft of Adilshah's favour and hounded by the Portuguese, the Bishop of Chrysopolis left for Rome in 1658 and died there in 1677, and exile from the motherland which he had tried to liberate.

The Eighteenth Century

Although Matheus de Castro had been unsuccessful in his political aims, the frequent representations that he had made to Rome against the abuses of the Padroado yielded good response from the Vatican in the form of *Sacrosancto Apostolatus Officii*, issued by Pope Alexander VII to the Vicar-Capitular of Goa.[20] However, the enthusiasm of the Holy See in favour of the native clergy was not shared by the Padroado. In 1718 Lisbon outrightly denied to the Goans equality with the Portuguese in the distribution of official posts.[21] Hand in hand with such arrogant displays of colour-bar there was administrative corruption, both ecclesiastical and lay. Marquis of

Pombal tried to bring in some liberal air into the stifling and prejudice-filled atmosphere of Goa. As a follow-up to a decree ordering that "His Majesty does not distinguish between his vassals by their colour but by their merit",[22] a new Governor and a new Archbishop were sent to Goa with "Instructions" to not merely throw open the doors of the civil, military and ecclesiastical services to qualified natives, but to give a preferential treatment to them.

The Pombaline "Instructions" had raised the hopes of the people, but the utterly arrogant refusal of the whites to do full justice to them soon dashed these hopes to the ground. After the fall of the Marquis of Pombal from power, the few liberal changes that had been introduced were promptly withdrawn. Having tasted equality, albeit in paper, the Goans were reluctant to let matters rest.

Determined to get episcopal postings for themselves, two Goan priests, Fr. Caetano Francisco do Couto and Fr. Jose Antonio Gonsalves, set sail for Lisbon where they hoped to appeal to the Crown for a redressal of their grievances.[23] In Lisbon the two priests came in contact with Fr. Caetano Vitorino de Faria, the father of the renowned Abbé Faria, who too had come to the Portuguese capital in search of better prospects. Fr. Faria tried to persuade the authorities to fill up the vacant benefices of the *Padroado* with Indian appointees, proposing the name of Fr. Couto for Cochin, of Fr. Gonçalves for Mylapore, and his own for the Metropolitan See of Goa.[24] The Crown, however, went ahead with its own European appointments. This was all the more frustrating because both Fr. Faria and Fr. Gonçalves had obtained their doctorates in Rome, and Fr. Couto had already held the post of the Governor of the Cochin diocese. Thus disillusioned the three priests started conspiring with a section of the Goan clergy and laity present in Lisbon, to overthrow the Portuguese regime in Goa. On their return journey Frs. Couto and Gonçalves travelled with Fr. Joseph Kariatil of the Syro-Chaldean rite, who had been favourably heard and granted the position of Archbishop of Cranganore.[25]Kariatil's appointment further strengthened the resolve of Frs. Couto and Gonçalves to ring the curtain on the racist regime of the Portuguese in Goa. The Portuguese appeared to prefer even Malayalees to their own tax-payers, the Goans.

Upon returning to Goa the two clerics set themselves to the task of winning over Goan priests, military officials and civilians to their cause and planning a *coup d'etat*. It was alleged that Fr. Gonçalves, in an attempt to rally the common folk round him, claimed to have received special powers from the Pope to liberate Goa.[26] The conspirators were aided by the Pintos of Candolim village, and it was in their palatial house that the uprising was being planned. It is for this reason that the whole episode came to be called "Conspiracy of the Pintos". The regiments of Bardez and Salcete, consisting chiefly of natives, were to serve as a means to implement the plans. The *coup* was scheduled for 10-8-1787[27], but it was denounced to the authorities five days earlier and was aborted as a result with a heavy hand.

Although it was nipped in the bud, the conspiracy excited much debate. Due to absence of sufficient written evidence in possession of the arrested conspirators, the details are sought to be revealed on the basis of confessions that were rung out from them. Was the conspiracy to be carried out entirely from within with the military assistance or "poisoned bread"?[28] Or did they seek external aid? To answer these questions it is necessary to keep in mind the political situation prevailing in the neighbouring territories around that time. The Indian subcontinent was a bone of contention between the European arch-rivals, England and France. Most of the native rulers were drawn in this struggle. Goa was the cynosure of European imperialists as well as of Indian chieftains like the Sawant of Wadi and the Sultan of Mysore. With the attention of the Portuguese government diverted on so many fronts, conditions were propitious for an outbreak of armed rebellion from within. The conspirators were surely intelligent enough to exploit this volatile situation to their advantage. To which of the external powers did the conspirators turn for support? At this time the Sawant was maintaining a low profile as a result of a recent defeat. The king of Sunda had lost his kingdom and was living in Goa as a Portuguese vassal. The Marathas were on friendly terms with the Portuguese. But Tipu Sultan definitely posed a threat. He had been on a victory spree and just conquered Piro, south of Goa. The collusion of the disaffected Goan elements with Tipu has been generally accepted by the chroniclers of the "Conspiracy", although this remains to be proven more conclusively. It has been suggested that the idea behind Fr. Gonçalves' disembarking at Ceylon on his return journey from Lisbon, and then travelling northwards along the coast was meant to feel the mood of the people and the chieftains of peninsular India, and particularly of Tipu. Besides, Narain Sinay Dhume, the Portuguese emissary at the court of the Peshwas, wrote to his superiors in Goa on 15-10-1787 about having learnt from Nana Phadnis that Tipu had crossed Tungabhadra with 15, 000 men in a bid to capture Goa.[29] However, since this letter was written in October, Tipu's alleged plans could not have meant to coincide with the local uprising in the early August. The lack of any concrete evidence in this connection makes one wonder whether the news of Tipu's intended intervention was not just a ploy to secure the whole-hearted backing of the local populace. In case there really was a connection with Tipu, what would he gain by invading Goa? This requires a look at the French connection. Tipu had joined hands with the French in his struggle with the British efforts to control and destroy him. It is possible that Tipu was agreeable to conquering Goa and delivering it to the French in exchange for substantial French assistance against the British.[30] The French and Tipu might have had an agreement to capture Goa, but the link of such a pact with the Goan conspirators is yet to be firmly established. It is to be noted here that there is a tendency among the present-day historians to read the later Napoleon-Tipu alliance into the Goan situation of 1787. In most of the pre-Liberation (1961) writings, the conspiracy of 1787 has been portrayed as nothing but a disorganized attempt on the part of some disgruntled local elements to avenge their frustrated ambitions. Some of these interpretations even suggest that the conspiracy existed only in the minds of a few discontented clergymen. On the other hand, more recent writers tend to over-glorify the episode and even hail it as "the second anti-colonial revolt in modern history"[31], organized by priests and military officials to establish in Goa a sovereign republic along with a new social order erected on the enlightened foundations of liberty, equality and fraternity. The truth seems to lie in between these two extremes. The first point of debate that arises in the unveiling of this truth is the nature of the spirit which spurred the conspirators: Was it a spiteful one of revenge or an altruistic one of liberating one's motherland from the grip of colonialism and giving the people a better deal? It is true that the immediate motivation was the thwarted ambition of two priests. But they had also imbued the egalitarian and republican philosophy of the French Enlightenment. They had also witnessed the reactionary regime of the Portuguese Queen D. Maria I. Yet one still wonders if these priests would have revolted if their demands for certain posts had been satisfied. It must also be kept in mind that these priests could have left the *Padroado* and joined *Propaganda Fide*. But they did not take this easy way out, but opted to plot a revolt. The second debatable issue is about the system of government which the conspirators wished to set up in Goa after driving the Portuguese out. It has been generally stated that they aimed at creating " a new republic in which the natives, through a Council, would govern and would exercise sovereignty".[32] Had they succeeded in this undertaking they would surely have been the forerunners of the French Revolution in Asia. However, another theory has it that the conspirators had intended to fight the Portuguese under the flag of the local king of Sunda.[33] Having witnessed the rise of Christians in the armies at the courts of Indian rulers like the Peshwa, the conspirators preferred a native ruler, irrespective of his religion, to the Catholic monarch of Portugal. If the setting up of a republic was indeed the goal of the rebels, it is not known whether it was to have been a secular one. Except for the case of a lone *Desai*, Narba Naik, who was arrested as a conspirator, not much is known about the involvement of the Hindu population of Goa in this plot. Another question is whether a republic would have been feasible in the prevailing political situation. If the conspiracy did have a Tipu-French backing, would it have been an anti-colonial or just replaced one colonial master with another? Would the Portuguese remain idle without making efforts to recover their "Pearl of the Orient"? And would the ambitions of the other European rivals or native chieftains left a little republic to survive? The conspirators could have never hoped to secure and maintain the sovereignty of Goa in the face of aggressive posturings around. As Cottineau de Kloguen has observed, the Europeans occupied the topmost positions in the class hierarchy of Goa[34], and their removal would have elevated the brahmins to the top. If the conspiracy was aimed at this, would the lower castes willingly accept such a transfer of power? It is said, however, that the conspirators aimed at creating an egalitarian social order. But would this be a practical proposition in a land of deep-seated caste prejudices even among the Christians themselves? Would the brahmins be willing to share the privileges of priesthood with the socially inferior brethren? One needs to churn much more the official and private archives in Europe and in India to fill in the answers to the various questions and to solve the historical puzzle.

The Nineteenth Century

The second decade of the 19th century witnessed the stormy birth of constitutionalism in Portugal and in Goa. Goans were given representation in the Portuguese *Cortes* (Parliament), albeit through the exercise of a limited franchise. A native member of the ruling Junta that had replaced the viceroy of the absolute regime, namely Antonio Jose de Lima Leitão, was amongst the first three representatives of Goa. The seat vacated by him in the Junta was filled up by coopting Joaquim Mourão Garces through the medium of a carefully chosen electoral constituency. This mock election did not enjoy the sanction of the people of Bardez which was represented by Lima Leitão.[35] It was against this usurpation of their rights that the people of Bardez vehemently protested under the leadership of Fr. Pedro Antonio Ribeiro of Pilerne. The reaction of the government was to silence the protest by disarming the native officers and soldiers, by stationing a strong unit at Guirim, by asking the Archbishop to instruct his priests not to "incite" the people and by ordering the arrest of the leader of the people, Fr. Ribeiro, who marched at the head of 250 badly-armed men against the fort of Colvale on 9-5-1822.[36] The plan was to capture the ammunition housed there and use it to overthrow the Junta. The plan failed and Fr. Ribeiro had to flee to Malvan. It is interesting to note that out of 49 persons arrested in this connection, eight were clerics. In the 1850s two priests, Fr. Sebastião Salvador Baptista Cana and Mons. Estevão Jeremias Mascarenhas displayed their patriotic fervour on the floor of the *Cortes* by making stirring speeches in the defence of the rights of their motherland. Fr. Mascarenhas was elected to the *Cortes* in 1848 and re-elected in 1855 and in 1856. On 24-5-1853, in a speech made in the Parliament, he extolled the virtues of independence and censured those who "having the necessary strength and intelligence to live independently would not desire it, would not employ all the means to achieve it".[37] However, this does not mean that he was demanding immediate independence for Goa. On the contrary, he acknowledged the emancipatory role of Portugal as a mother country and declared that circumstances were not right for the independence of his land. He believed that if Goa got out of Portuguese dependence it would fall prey to some other nation. He had England in mind. Fr. Mascarenhas was such a dedicated *deputado* that at the time of his death, Antonio Rodrigues Sampaio, a minister of the Portuguese government, stated that "never did a deputy show himself to be more zealous about the interests of his province, never was one more constant and more pertinacious in advocating the cause of his country"[38] than Fr. Mascarenhas. Earlier this priest had, through his writings and speeches, boldly championed the cause of Bernardo Peres da Silva, a Goan who had been appointed Prefect of Goa, but had been deposed by the mestiço elements of Goa.

In the last quarter of the 19th century it was Fr. Antonio Francisco Xavier Alvares, who protested against the Church and the Government in Goa. Fr. Alvares was an editor, a writer, a founder of educational and social institutions, and a dedicated social worker. Unable to see eye to eye with the Archbishop, Fr. Alvares left the Church in which he had been ordained to join the Syrian Church which consecrated him Bishop of Goa, India and Ceylon with the title of Mar Julius I. In his book entitled *A Supremacia Universal na Igreja de Cristo*, Fr. Alvares has a tirade against the abuses of the *Padroado* and the Papacy. He denounced the universal claim of the Pope in favour of the Syrian Patriarch of Antioch, who being an Asian, was considered by Fr. Alvares to be the rightful head of the Christian Church in Asia. It was in Asia that God's revelation had taken place first. His pride in Asia assumes on several occasions a more *swadeshi* colouring as is apparent from his strong advocacy of the use of Goan commodities in the place of the foreign substitutes. He urged the young to renounce wasteful merry-making, and instead to take up the lucrative cultivation of mandioca, which would improve the finances and the food stock of their motherland. Through his newspaper entitled *O Brado Indiano* (=The Indian Cry), Fr. Alvares conducted a determined campaign against the corrupt and negligent officials of the Portuguese administration of Goa. For his clerical protests, Fr. Alvares was excommunicated by the Roman Catholic Church and for his political protests he was charged with sedition.

The Twentieth Century

In the 20th century, when Salazar was using the Church to perpetuate Portugal's hold over Goa, Fr. Alberto Mendonça staunchly championed the cause of Goa's merger with India. As a student in Portugal at the Coimbra University he spoke against the Portuguese imperialism. He was so much impressed by Gandhi that upon return to India, he went to spend a few days at the Sabarmati Ashram. Proud of his rich Indian heritage, he taught Indian philosophy, especially the Buddhist philosophy, with all the respect due to it.

He also criticised the anti-Indian activities of the Jesuits and their fanatical idea of creating a Catholic State of Goa. For this he had to face the conflict with his Spanish Jesuit superiors in Bombay and was relieved from his teaching post at St. Xavier's College. Fr. Mendonça decided to leave the Jesuit membership as a result of this conflict, but continued to be a priest and to hold his views.

CONCLUSION

I have tried to pose some probing questions about the nature of the protests launched by some protesting priests of Goa in order to determine whether these clerics are entitled to a place in the wide spectrum of Goa's freedom fighters. Matheus de Castro fought, but not for Goa's independence. He was helping Bijapur to recover it. Even if the Pinto Conspiracy of 1787 had a republican flavour, its lack of realism in the context of the prevailing political-military scenario around did not make it a viable struggle. In both these cases the question of attaining an independent status for Goa was either never on the cards, or it was impossible. The absence of an adequate defence system made it virtually impossible for the Goans to preserve their sovereignty. Besides, the caste-ridden society of Goa prevented any real popular uprising as a nation against the colonial subjugation. Castro's appeal was not only communal, but also casteist. And when his plot in 1654 was discovered and many of his disciples were arrested in Goa, he seems to have made a volte-face by claiming that he had dissuaded the Adilshah from invading Goa and by stating that once the abuses in the civil and ecclesiastical administration of Goa were weeded out the Goans "will continue to be your (Portuguese crown) subjects and servants as we have always been".[39]

The 1822 protest of Fr. Ribeiro was directed not so much against the presence of the Portuguese regime in Goa as against the reaction that had set into the nascent constitutional Junta. Fr. Mascarenhas was of the opinion that Goa was not mature enough to break away from the "maternal" influence of Portugal. According to him the parting had to be achieved through a friendly way and not by a violent upheaval. Fr. Alvares was more of a social reformer, and rather than attacking the concept of the Portuguese rule, his fire was focused on the malpractices in the administration.[40] His swadeshi spirit was more economic than political in character. The last of the protesting priests discussed in this paper, Fr. Mendonça advocated the integration of Goa with independent India through his writings. However, it must be remembered that the main target of his vocal and verbal attacks were the foreign Jesuits at St. Xavier's College, Bombay.

Thus, the protests of these priests were by and large manifestations of their immediate personal grievances arising out of racial discrimination and administrative abuses and did not form part of Goa's struggle for freedom a such.

REFERENCES

1. Nicolau Menezes, "Revolutionay Priests of Goa", *Goan Tribune*, Bombay, IV, n. 4, p. 8.
2. *Loc. cit.*
3. Quoted by Boxer, C. R., "The Colour Question in the Portuguese Empire", *Proceedings of the British Academy*, Oxford University Press, London, 1961 XLVII, p. 123.
4. *Ibid.*, p. 113.
5. Boxer, C. R., *Race Relations in the Portuguese Colonial Empire*, Clarendon Press, Oxford, 1963, p. 67.
6. For biographical data cf. Pereira, B., "O 1o. Bispo goes, D. Mateus de Castro", *Heraldo*, Nova Goa, 2-1-1942, p. 1; De Souza, T. R., "An Unsung Hero: Matheus de Castro Mahale", *Goa Today*, Panjim, January, 1975, pp. 18, 28; Fernandes, A. P., "Matheus de Castro Mahale -- His Role", *Goa Wins Freedom*, ed. K. M. Mathew, Goa University Publication, 1986, pp. 45-59.
7. Cronin, V., *A Pearl to India: The Life of Roberto de Nobili*, London, 1959, p. 205.
8. Melo, C. M. de, *The Recruitment and Formation of the Native Clergy in India (16th-19th century)*, Lisboa, 1955, p. 126.
9. *Op. cit.*, p. 155.
10. Thekkedath, J., *History of Christianity in India*, Bangalore, 1982, p. 401.
11. Melo, *op. cit.*, pp. 155-156.
12. *Op. cit.*, p. 250.
13. Silva Rego, A. de, *Documentação para a Historia das Missões do Padroado*

Portugues no Oriente, Lisboa, 1950, vol. IV, p. 183.

14. Pissurlencar, P. S. S., *Assentos do Conselho do Estado (=ACE)*, III, Bastora, p. 474.
15. Fernandes, A. P., *op. cit.*, pp. 50-52.
16. He believed that Christians could thrive under a Muslim rule as he had witnessed in Turkey and Persia, and intended to unify the Christians of India with those of the Middle East. Cf. *ACE*, III, pp. 296-297.
17. Sequeira, A. J. L., *Relations between the Portuguese and the Sultan of Bijapur* (Unpublished Thesis), University of Bombay, 1932, pp. 551-554.
18. *Ibid.*, pp. 553-554. Cf. "Monumenta Historiae Indiae", *Journal of Bombay Historical Society*, I, n. 2, Bombay, 1928, pp. 199-202.
19. *ACE*, III, pp. 337-39, 347-49.
20. Melo, *op. cit.*, p. 150 ff.
21. Boxer, C. R. "The Colour Question in the Portuguese Empire", p. 129.
22. Boxer, C. R., *The Portuguese seaborne empire 1415-1825*, London, 1969, p. 256.
23. Fr. Couto had been named governor of the diocese of Cochin by the liberal Archbishop, D. Fr. Francisco da Assuncao e Brito. However, he was later removed by D. Fr. Manuel de Santa Catarina, a thorough racist. Cf. Cunha Rivara, *A Conjuração de 1787 em Goa e varias cousas desse tempo: Memoria historica*(Henceforth *Conjuração*), Nova Goa, 1875, p. 13.
24. Moraes, G. M., "Padre Caetano Vitorino de Faria -- a would-be Archbishop of Goa", *Boletim do Instituto Menezes Braganza*, Bastora, 1971, n. 96, p. 315.
25. *Loc. cit.*
26. Ayalla, F. D., *Goa Antiga e Moderna*, Nova Goa, 1927, p. 173.
27. *Conjuração*, p. 23.
28. Ayalla, *op. cit.*, p. 171.
29. *Conjuração*, p. 100.
30. *Loc. cit.*
31. Azevedo, C., "Pinto's Revolt of 1787", *Armed Coups against Portuguese Regime*, ed. Vikas V. Desai, Canacona, 1986, p. 14.
32. *Conjuração*, p. 22.
33. *Ibid.*, p. 95.
34. Kloguen, C. de, *Bosquejo Historico de Goa*, Nova Goa, pp. 145-46.
35. Bruto da Costa, A. A., *As Revoluções Politicas da India Portuguesa de seculo XX*, Margão, 1896, p. 32.
36. Abreu, M. V. de, *Relação de Alterações Politicas de Goa desde 16 de Setembro de 1821 ate 18 de Outubro de 1822*, Nova Goa, 1862, pp. 115-116.
37. De Souza, R., "Political Consciousness among the Goans - II", *The Navhind Times*, Panjim, 9-4-1967, p. 3.
38. Abreu, M. V. de, *Noção de alguns filhos distintos da India Portuguesa, que se illustraram fora da patria*, Nova Goa, 1874, p. 41.
39. Jesuit Archives (Rome), *Ms Goa 40*, fls. 384-386v.
40. Alvares, A. F. X., *Prelecção sobre a situação actual no interior e exterior do paiz*, Nova Goa, 1886, *passim*.

11

FRENCH SLAVE-TRADING IN PORTUGUESE GOA (1773-1791)

Teotonio R. de Souza

Introduction

The Portuguese were not inventors of the institution of slavery, but they certainly contributed to its massive expansion on a global scale from the beginning of their colonial expansion. This did not give rise to any serious problem of national conscience. Even men like the Jesuit Antonio Vieira in the late 17th century could denounce from the pulpits of Brazil that black colour did not make the slaves less of men, but all he had to offer the slaves was only moral consolation and God's reward in after-life. He preached that through Baptism their souls were cleansed snow-white, but this did not prevent him from justifying slavery for sustaining colonial economy.[1]

Slavery was not unknown to the Indian society since the early times. There are references to *dasas* and *dasyus* in the Vedic literature and in *Artashastra*. The arrival of Islamic power in India seems to have given slavery a greater impetus, and the African slaves (*Habshis*)became ubiquitous in India. The arrival of the Portuguese in India gave a new boost to slavery, and Goa's slave market has been described in the 16th century as providing abundant and wide variety of slaves from West African Guinea to Macau and Japan in the Far East.[2]

I do not intend to delve in the aspects of slavery in Portuguese India that have been quite well studied in various recent studies, both published and unpublished. To mention some of their authors, C. R. Boxer, W. F. Rea, Ann M. Pescatello, P. P. Shirodkar, G. Clarence-Smith, Jeanette Pinto, have studied the subject to different extent and in different contexts.[3] I am keeping the scope of this paper restricted to information available in the private papers of Mhamai Kamat family, a Goa-based agency house that from 1760's was associated with the French in India.

Very surprisingly this association has received only passing references in the studies on the French presence and activities in India, and even a comparatively recent work of the late S. P. Sen has failed to identify the Goa connection of Montigny and other Frenchmen in India. The Camotins of Goa figure in the catalogues of the old manuscripts of French India edited and published by G. Gaudart, but these references are very official in nature and one has to depend upon the inward-outward correspondence of the Mhamai Kamat family with many prominent and less prominent names of Frenchmen in India till 1791 to imagine that much more was transacted than met the eye. And that is where I thought I was in a position to throw some light on what Toussaint and Filliot regard as prevailing vagueness about the Indian side of the slave supply during 1773-1810 compared with the supplies arriving from the African coast or from Madagascar. It was the period when the commerce in the Indian Ocean was no longer a monopoly of the French Company, and Goa had become a much frequented "comptoir".[4] The British occupation of Goa during the Napoleonic period may explain why the French connection with Goa suddenly thins out and disappears after 1791.

Mhamay Camotim: Background History and Legends

Camotim was the Portuguese corruption of native *Kamat*, a family name designating a hereditary function in the agrarian village-community set-up. A *kamat* headed a hereditary association or *bhaus*(literally *fraternity*) of peasants whocultivated reclaimed lands (*khazans*) which needed cooperative labour to reclaim and maintain against inundations. Hence, one could find Kamat families wherever there were large areas reclaimed for rice cultivation. Caste-wise they happen to be always Brahmins, which goes to suggest the important role played by this caste not only in the socio-political organization of the country, but also in planning and directing the agricultural development in the difficult times of initial settlement.

In the wake of the conversion drive initiated by the Portuguese in Goa in the mid-sixteenth century several Brahmin families opted for loss of their landed rights and privileges instead of betraying their ancestral faith. However, they proved their resourcefulness in the midst of such a trying situation: The development of Goa into an important commercial entrepot, as well as the needs of colonial administration provided ample opportunities to make good their economic losses in spite of the official discriminating legislation on religious grounds.[5] One such piece of legislation denied the non-Christians the right to own immovable property within the Portuguese jurisdiction. This ban seems to have freed the non-Christians for entrepreneurship with borrowed capital, or with capital accumulated through revenue farming.[6]

Farming of revenue-collection in the Portuguese administration had become almost an exclusive business of the Saraswat Brahmins, predominantly Sinays. The Portuguese administration could not help depending on their knowledge of local usages, and these natives exploited this fiscal need to the utmost to accumulate capital that they slowly invested and reinvested in business. I have not come across Camotins in the registers of the revenue administration of Portuguese India until mid-seventeenth century[6], but before mid-eighteenth century some Camotins had already risen to remarkable financial power. In the wake of the anti-Hindu feelings whipped up in Goa during the Maratha invasion of the territory in 1739, the city rabble was provoked by some clerical leaders to mob the house of Phondu Kamat who is described as the wealthiest merchant of Goa, under the pretext of having sheltered some enemies. In addition to much that he lost in this mob-attack, the State demanded from him alone 130, 000 xerafins to pay for the retreat of the invading Maratha forces.[7] Probably it is the same house that in 1770's is administered by the widow of Raulu Camotim, Bhagwatiny Camotiny. In a representation addressed to the crown on behalf of her house, which she describes as "the most important business house of the city of Goa and greatly involved in the seaborne trade of the empire", she refers to her loss of a consignment worth 96, 000 xerafins on the occasion of the Lisbon earthquake. With the suppression of the Society of Jesus the house had been left unpaid 203, 370 xerafins which the Jesuits of China owed to it.[8]

It is difficult to identify the links of the various Kamat families merely on the basis of the documentary references to the name. I could not find any reference to the additional distinguishing surname - *mhamay* - adopted by our Camotins until 1781.[9] This new distinguishing name was assumed by the Camotim family from its family deity *Mhamaya*(= the great love), an important deity of their original village of Guirdolim in the Salcete taluka of South Goa. According to the oral tradition maintained by the family, they had to leave their ancestral village to escape conversion drive and sought shelter in the neighbouring territory of the Sunda rulers. That is how they seem to have reached Ponda in the neighbourhood of the capital city of Old Goa. It is very likely that Mhamai Kamat were engaged in business in Old Goa before they shifted to Panjim at the time of the transfer of the capital to this town in 1759, because already in 1757 Suba Camotim, who founded the business house in partnership with his four sons, was appointed as one of the four official brokers of the Goa customs.[10]

Suba died before November 1765. One son Madhav died very early, and Yeshwant (alias Exa) who looked after the business of the house in Bombay died in 1815. Narayana and Venkatesha, the two older sons continued to run the business jointly from Goa and the voluminous business correspondence that has survived was addressed to them or drafted by them. Besides documentation in Modi (Marathi) and Old Kannada scripts, the bulk of the documentation is in Portuguese. The collection includes nearly 800 letters in French of the Frenchmen dealing with the Mhamais. They date from 1777 to 1819. The drafts (*borradores*) of the letters written to them by the Mhamais are in Portuguese, with occasional copies in French.

Business Involvement of the Mhamays

As mentioned earlier the Mhamays laid the foundations of their business by joining the club of the revenue-farmers. In addition to some other branches of revenue, it was the tobacco revenue-farming that seems to have brought them much gain. But in the course of time they ended where they had begun. The administration under the viceroy Count of Rio Pardo sought to clean the corruption and fiscal abuses with singular tenacity, and that is when the Mhamays were caught on the wrong foot. They were declared debtors to the State to the tune of 180, 000 and plus xerafins in 1818.[11] With their properties confiscated, goods and credits mortgaged and frozen to pay the debt, the Mhamays entered into decline and never again recovered their prosperity of the first decade of the 19th century. Their decline was also linked with the general phenomenon of high mortality among small agency houses in Bombay following changed commercial-fiscal policies of the English East India Company. Mhamays depended very much on the Bombay network for feeding their commission agency and to act as their retailers. Their other major clients seem to have been the French, and with the French withdrawal from the scene, one important client was lost to the Mhamays. These factors cannot be taken lightly in assessing the declining fortunes of the Mhamays at the close of the 2nd decade of the 19th century.

There were many sides to the business involvement of the Mhamays, and some of these made their agency house particularly attractive to their clients, including the French. The Mhamays were attending to the furnishing and provisioning of Viceroy's palace in Panjim. They also supplied the needs of the State shipyard by taking care of State and private vessels that came into Goa harbour for wintering or needed refittingand provisioning. This gave the Mhamays an execellent opportunity to further their interests in many ways: They could satisfy the requests of their clients for the Portuguese safe-conducts (*cartazes*), for ordnance pieces from the State shipyard, for political information, or for pursuing any cases with the local judiciary.

The French-Mhamay Connection

Although the Mhamays seem to have functioned from 1764 as

the "courtiers" or brokers of the French in Goa, the correspondence of the Mhamays with the French begins picking up from 1777. That was the beginning of a new active period of French political intrigues in India, coinciding with the French active interest in the War of American Independence. In India the new phase was marked by the arrival of M. de St. Lubin and Montigny to the Maratha and Mughul courts. The Mhamays were actively involved as bankers issuing Bills of Exchange on Poona, Bombay or Surat to meet the expenses of these French envoys,[12] as well as friends of the Poona *savkars* to obtain political information or to mediate with the Poona court when J. Warnet was arrested over his sale of the cargo of *Le Sartine* in 1778 or when the Marathas seized the vessel *l'Adelaide* of Nicholas Comarmon, a merchant of Port Louis in Mauritius in 1788.[13] As it should be sufficiently known to the students of the history of the French in India, the Mhamays had also to put up with the characteristic French ways of political evasion and adventurism. The Mhamays were forced at times to hesitate and delay payments. Complaints of Montigny in this regards, accusing the Camotins of dishonesty or lack of cooperation, need to be understood in the proper context of the French diplomacy and near chronic paucity of funds for repaying their borrowings.[14]

Presently I shall not go into every aspect of the French-Mhamay connection that could be studied with the help of the records in hands. The Mhamay papers reveal a high degree of dependance of French merchants, agency houses and Mauritian country traders on them. It was on the resourcefulness, contacts and business acumen of "courtiers" like Nasserwangy Manockjee of Bombay and the Camotins of Goa that the bulk of the private trade of the French colonial administration rested. I shall proceed to present only the information relating to the slave-traffic between Goa and Mauritius. Although the correspondence in French continues till 1819, our last document dealing with slaves for Mauritius is dated 1791. The French correspondence after that is almost exclusively with the Mahé-based house of Brown and Dineur.

Couronat and Warnet, who came with St. Lubin in *Le Sartine* to Chaul and Poona in the Maratha territory are the first recorded dealers in slaves in the Mhamay correspondence. Couronat wrote to Mhamays from Pune on 15 October 1777 asking to arrange young and strong negro-slaves. He wanted 400 of them and would invest 20,000 rupees. He gave clear specifications: They ought to be young and strong, half of them adult males, one-fourth females, and the rest young males. All should be healthy and without any deffects. Whatever be the cost, he wants two male slaves who can sound horn, and two young and graceful females. He wants strict secrecy to be maintained, and complaints that a Brahmin friend of the Camotins in the Poona court talks things too easily with the ambassador. The Mhamays replied to his letter on the 1st of November 1777 with the promise of full assistance and confidentiality. They inform that Mr. Galinem had come with his *chalupa* from Mauritius and had taken 160 slaves, and that Mr. Larochet was presently in Goa with his vessel to take 140 slaves. The ship from Mossambique had arrived with nearly 700 slaves.

Mr. Moracin, a seasoned French official and holding important position in the administration and company affairs in Pondicherry for many years since 1765 seems to have been carrying on private trade and is known to have amassed a considerable fortune. He had his establishment in Mauritius, and a certain Goa-based French businessman named Mr. Frederic Breauchaud had acquired 100 slaves on his account. Mr. Martin from Pondicherry had come to Goa to collect them on behalf of Mr. Moracin, but for some unknown reason only 30 were handed over to him. One day later the businessman fell ill and died, and the government took charge of all his possessions including the remaining slaves. Mhamays made arrangements for the transport of the 30 slaves from Goa, but two slaves had run away and one was sick. Mhamays were sending the remaining 27 to Mahe in a ship belonging to Mr. Lorecet to be handed over to Mr. Picot de la Motte, who would then arrange to convey them to Mr. Moracin. It is clear from the correspondence that these slaves were to be sent to Mauritius for sale. Mhamays would continue to look after the interests of Mr. Moracin, and particularly about recovering the remaining slaves in Government custody in Goa. In the correspondence Mhamays refer to the good correspondence his uncle Moracin had with their deceased father Suba.

On 19 February 1778 the Mhamays obtained customs clearence for three Frenchmen named Chapam, Lefebre and Rostum to sail from Goa to Mahe carrying with them their four "servidores". It is likely that slaves passed as servants for clearence convenience.

On 1 November 1779 Mhamays wrote to J. Warnet in Poona reminding him about payment of Rs. 200 for a black slave sent to him to look after horses. Apparently, as reported in a letter of 24th of the same month the slave had run away while being taken to Poona and was caught near Colvale river-crossing well within Goa territory. The Mhamays had taken charge of him on behalf of Warnet.

On 11 April 1782 Mhamays obtained State permit for Mr. de Beaubrin, the French agent in Goa, to take out of the Powder House (which served as jail and a place for safe-keeping of slaves) the slaves that had escaped from the *corsarios* of Mr. Dechien. It is said in the application for the permit that these slaves are to be sent to Mauritius. Dechien had come with ships *Philipina* and *Philipa*, and two other vessels captured from the China merchants. Apparently Dechien worked for Pitot & Freres, businessmen of Mauritius. The Mhamays wrote to them on 4 April 1782 giving news of the 14 slaves they had acquired for them and that seven were being embarked to Mauritius in a ship (*La Perle de Goa*?) belonging to Camille, an Armenian merchant. Four of the remaining were sent a month later in a *curveta* sent by J. Ribeiro under captainship of Mr. Portello. Two slaves seem to have run away while being embarked.

In December 1783 two ships belonging to Barbier & Co. of Mauritius arrived in Goa. They were looking for slaves in Goa before proceeding to Malabar for pepper. Mhamays sent this information to Mr. Amiot in Poona for whom they had purchased two black slaves for Rs. 210.

Mhamays were corresponding with three Monnerons, one in Mauritius, one in Pondicherry and one in Colombo. Their first names appear as Janvier, Pierre and Antoine respectively. Among other items, small number of slaves figure in the consignments sent to Monneron in Mauritius between 1785-1787.

In December 1786 Mhamays sent five black slaves to De Court, the Director of the French Co. in Mahe for 822 Bombay rupees. The names of the slaves are given as Januario, Alberto, João, Ignacio and

Joaquim. Mhamays say that they got them relatively cheap because the Governor D. Frederico de Souza disposed of them while returning to Europe.

There is a letter of Mr. de Canaple, who was earlier posted as Agent at Haider Ali's court and later administered Mahé for three years till he left for Mauritius in April 1790 aboard *Thetis*. He died on arrival in Port Louis caught in a popular upsurge. This letter he wrote two years before his departure from India, asking the Mhamays to buy a black slave 19-20 years old, of good strain, able to cook and speak Portuguese, intelligent and with agreeable looks, and not foul-smelling. He was willing to invest up to Rs. 190. He wanted two other slaves aged 15-20, who should be healthy, honest and not given to drinking. They should also have had small-pox already. He seems to have been told that blacks were being sold for cheap prices by their masters in Goa.

In a letter dated 17 April 1787 Mhamays informed P. Monneron on the Malabar Coast that Mr. Bonhomme had caused the prices of slaves to go up to Rs. 200 per piece, and that Mr. Carosin did not want to take five slaves for Monneron even with freight paid in his ship *Alexandre*.

Messers Amalric Michel & Cie. in Pondicherry are informed that young blacks (*cafrinhos*) from Mossambique ordered by them cost twice as much as calculated by them.

Writing to Mr. Canaple on May 1, 1788, Mhamays say that they have not forgotten about his request for slaves, but that they had to wait because of the difficulty of obtaining good quality slaves. Two French ships had taken slaves and raised the prices very high, and the cost of a palanquin slave had gone up to Rs. 200. Presently the Macau vessels were in the port and were also looking for slaves. He suggests that it will be advisable to wait for the arrival of the Mozambique ship in September for better bargain. However, in a post-script to the same letter Mr. Canaple is told that they have at last been able to secure a black slave for him. He is named Domingos and is entrusted to a *tandel* called Duma to be taken to Bombay. They hope that the purchase will satisfy him. The price is stated to be 165 rupees of Goa, including all expenses.

Mhamays wrote to Mr. Dayot in Bombay on 28 September 1788 that the ship *Le Peron* will soon arrive in Goa to take slaves for Mauritius.

Mr. Chalamont in Mahe is informed by Mhamays on 9 September 1788 that the Mozambique ship with slaves has not arrived.

Mr. Boyes, also at Mahe, is informed that they are trying to find one black slave for Mr. Rossily as requested.

On 9th October 1789 Mhamays secured permit for the captain of a French "curveta" that had arrived in the Goa port to purchase 250 fardles of rice and was going away with slaves (*escravatura*). No more details are available.

One Mr. Rondeau, surgeon in Mauritius is informed on 18 April 1790 that in respect of the powers of attorney left by him with Mr. Mutel they have helped to recover his slave that had run away a second time. It cost them Rs. 40 to do that. They have then sold the slave to Mr. Avier and are sending the balance to Mr. Rondeau after deducting the costs through the captain of brig Landis.

A bill of lading signed by Michel Pierre, the supercargo of *l'Alexandre* at Goa on May 11, 1791 states having taken for safe delivery to Messrs. Villeaulet (?)and Neucent in Mauritius two consignments, one of 111 heads (including 104 blacks and seven Malabaris), and another with six slaves.

Conclusion

The papers of the Mhamays are yet to be fully ordered and classified, particularly those in the vernacular languages, and it is possible that more papers on this subject may come to light. However, as suggested earlier it is not surprising that the information about their dealings with the French and with slaves for Mauritius thins out and disappears after 1791. That was the disturbed period of the Revolution that created local disturbances in the French settlements in the East. The Mascareignes islands had their own problems with the revolutionary government in France and had to face its wrath for a while, chiefly because of its refusal to adopt the anti-slavery legislation. With the eruption of the war France lost its Indian possessions in 1793. Though Mauritius continued to be an active base for French privateering till its capture by the British in December 1810, its normal trade network with India was disrupted. And in Goa the pressure of the British was mounting from 1783 to accept British occupation forces to defend it against any French attack. And the British did base their forces in Goa from 1798 till the Napoleonic threat was over and they were guarding the entry to the harbour.

Apparently the disturbed situation had its effect upon the slave market. A Mozambique-based businessman named João da Silva Guedes was writing to the Mhamays in Goa on 22nd August 1800 describing the slump in the slave market there. And he believes that only when the wars with France cease and the Frenchmen return to that port as before the slave trade might pick up and the colony might breathe again!

The correspondence of the Mhamays in the later years contains stray references to slaves that they sent for sale to Macau at the request of their Bombay-based friend and opium-dealer, Sir Roger Faria.[15] On recommendation from Faria they also helped Charles Forbes of Bruce Fawcett & Co. of Bombay to purchase a large number of slaves in Goa for the Government of Ceylon in 1813.

N. B. I wish to express my gratitude to Dr. Robert Newman of La Trobe University (Australia) and to Dr. Richard B. Allen (Illinois, U. S. A.) for their generous cooperation in the form of reference material and useful comments they sent to me on the subject of this paper.

REFERENCES

1. C. R. Boxer, *Race Relations in the Portuguese Colonial Empire, 1415-1825*, Oxford:Clarendon Press, 1963, pp. 102 ff; T. R. de Souza, "Afro-Asian Church in the Portuguese *Estado da India*"(Paper presented at a Consultation of Church Historians of Africa, Nairobi, August 1986).
2. P. P. Shirodkar, "Slavery in Coastal India", *Purabilekha-Puratatva*, III, n. 1, Panjim (January-June 1985), pp. 27-43; *The Cambridge Economic History of India*, I, ed. T. Raychaudhuri & Irfan Habib, Delhi: Orient Longmans, 1984, pp. 90-93; A. L. Basham, *The Wonder that was India*, Bombay: Rupa & Co, 1967, pp. 153-54; T. R. de Souza, *Medieval Goa*, New Delhi:Concept Publ. Co., 1979, pp. 115, 125-26, 265-267, 277-78.
3. C. R. Boxer, *The Portuguese Seaborne Empire*, London:Hutchinson & Co., 1969; *The Church Militant and Iberian Expansion*, Baltimore:The Johns

Hopkins Univ. Press, 1978; W. F. Rea, *The Economics of the Zambezi Missions, 1580-1759*, Roma:Institutum Historicum S. I., 1976; Ann Pescatello, "The African Presence in Portuguese India", *Journal of Asian History*, XI, n. 1 (1977), pp. 26-48; P. P. Shirodkar, *op. cit.* ; G. Clarence-Smith, *The third Portuguese empire, 1825-1975*, Manchester, 1985; Jeanette Pinto, *Slavery in Portuguese India, 1510-1842* (Unpublished Ph. D. dissertation submitted to the University of Bombay, 1985).

4. A. Toussaint, *Histoire de l'Ile Maurice*, Paris, 1974; *La route des iles. Contribution a l'histoire maritime des Mascareignes*, Paris, 1967; J. -M. Filliot, *La traite des esclaves vers les Mascareignes au XVIIIe siecle*, Paris, 1974.
5. Teotonio R. de Souza, "Mhamai House Records: Indigenous Sources for Indo-Portuguese Historiography", *II Seminario Internacional de Historia Indo-Portuguesa*, Lisboa, 1985, pp. 933-947.
6. Goa Historical Archives, Ms. 1371, *Fianas*, n. 3, fls. 33v, 94, 99, 132, 190; M. N. Pearson, "Indigenous Dominance in a Colonial Economy:The Goa Rendas, 1600-70", *Mare Luso-Indicum*, II, Paris, 1973, pp. 61-73. T. R. de Souza, "Glimpses of Hindu Dominance of Goan Economy in the Early Seventeenth Century", *Indica*, XII, Bombay, 1975.
7. P. S. S. Pissurlencar, *The Portuguese and the Marathas*, ed. P. R. Kakodkar, Bombay, 1975, pp. 276-81, 302.
8. Arquivo Historico Ultramarino (Lisboa), *Mao* I (India), doc. 46.
9. Goa Historical Archives: Loose and unclassified doc. dt. 24. 3. 1781: It is a petition of the Hindu businessmen of Goa to the crown to lift the ban on the public celebration of their weddings with customary ceremonies. They quote the precedent of some prominent businessmen, such as Suba Camotim Mhamay who had been granted such a permission during the viceroyalty of the count of Ega (1756-65).
10. Goa Historical Archives: Ms. 1378, *Portarias do Governo*, n. 3, fl. 105.
11. M. V. Abreu, *O Governo do Vice-Rei Conde do Rio Pardo*, Nova Goa, 1869, p. 120, doc. 46.
12. The information in Mhamai Papers finds corroboration in *The French Records Relating to the History of the Marathas*, I& II, ed. V. G. Hatalkar, Bombay, 1978, pp. 146-148; Cf. also *Catalogue des Manuscrits des Anciennes Archives de l'Inde Française, 1739-1808*, Tome II, ed. E. Gaudart, Pondicherry, 1934, pp. 187-88.
13. Ruchira Bannerjee, "A French Document from Mhamai House Records", *Rojnishi* (Research Bulletin of History Academy, University of Poona), I, n. 2 (July 1983), pp. 33-36: The case of seized vessel has been studied on the basis of this document. The documents regarding the Warnet's case are yet to be studied, and they include originals in Marathi with seals of Mahadji Sindhia.
14. One of the longest letters addressed by Mhamays to Montigny and dated 30 september 1785 deals precisely with the unhappiness of the Mhamays over Montigny's complaints to his superiors about Mhamays. Mhamys state that they have lost more than gained by serving the French as their "courtiers". They record a loss of about Rs. 51, 000 in the course of years. This includes Rs. 30, 000 that they had lent to or through Warnet, and Rs. 15, 000 that Gattereau Co. of Mauritius refused to pay them by declaring insolvency. Mhamays have serious grudge against the French agent in Goa, namely Beaubrun and his successor Dhoudon. And says of the latter that he is more busy and understands more of his Catholic devotional practices than matters of business and politics! The letter ends by asking Montigny to relieve them from their "courtier"-ship if he has the authorization to do so. *Cf.* also

E. Gaudart (ed.), *op. cit.* , p. 188.

15. T. R. de Souza, "Capital Input in Goa's Freedom Struggle: The Bombay Connection', *Indo-Portuguese History: Old Issues, New Questions*, ed. Teotonio R. de Souza, New Delhi, 1985, pp. 102-113. This Bombay-based Goan businessman who had made his moneys by trading in opium and did not mind requesting the Mhamays to send slaves for his friends in Macau, was writing to the Mhamays on 11 October 1812 that "the gain and profits made on trading in rice and slaves has led to ruin and caused the downfall of many".

12

FRANCISCO LUIS GOMES: THE HISTORIAN

Joseph Barros

Among the great intellectuals that have adorned this land with their fine achievements in several fields of human endeavours, the name of Francisco Luis Gomes stands head and shoulders above many others. Some are born great by birth, some achieve greatness and immortality by the sweat of their brow, and still others have greatness thrust upon them and it is nothing but a passing show of human vanity. Francisco Luis Gomes achieved greatness, immortality and international fame in the intellectual circles of Europe by his self-erudition, self-enlightenment and his steadfast devotion to intellectual pursuits. Such is the superman whose life and work I propose to assess in this essay.

Francisco Luis Gomes had an extraordinary intellectual organization. Elements usually the most incompatible were mixed in the most natural harmony.[1] Science and literature, history, politics, sociology and economics. Criticism, realism and idealism were all woven together creating so excellent a blend that one could say in a Shakespearean way: This was a Man. And indeed he was gigantic man of whom it is recorded that

"He trailed the splendours of the Rising Sun
To the far heavens of the purple West;
And that land confest
Of all the Eastern glories this was one...
Then, seeking back his nest
-- The home of Kalidas and Valmiki.
"Of chess and epopee"--,
Sore-stricken, from the strife
Of Life,
He felt his mortal race was run,
Burst his noble breast,
And laid him, in the vast deep
Asleep,
Under the sea
Of Immortality. "[2]

He was born in the picturesque village of Navelim (Salcete, Goa) on 31 May 1829 where he spent his early youth among the slender green palm trees full of coconuts and among the smiling rice-fields.[3] It appears that he was a very precocious child for even at the tender age of eight he was wielding the Portuguese language quite comfortably and by the age of twenty-one he had completed his medical course in the *Esçola Medica* of Nova Goa, the first institution of this kind in the East. He was appointed professor of the same in view of his academic merits and was even granted a commission in the colonial army (*exército colonial*). He was honoured by the Portuguese government with the knighthood of the *Ordem Militar de Nosso Senhor Jesus Cristo*,[4] a very high condecoration of the Portuguese government in those days. It was granted to him probably because of his great faithfulness to Portugal and his love and enthusiasm for the Portuguese language and culture. He was well accepted in the Portuguese court and by the Portuguese king. The Portuguese nobility greatly admired him and hailed him as their own, but at heart he remained an Indian, till the end.

In spite of its geographic smallness, Goa has been throughout her history a cradle of quite a few literary figures, political stalwarts and erudite scientists and scholars. Gomes was a literary giant and an extraordinary orator in several languages. He could command very fluently several western languages as well as Indian ones. He was very much at home and conversant in English, French, Spanish, Italian, Latin, Portuguese, Konkani and Marathi. Thus, he was rightly called "um linguista por excellencia".[5] The knowledge of these languages enabled him to collect source material for his historical works from various authors writing in various languages. He is perhaps the only Goan historian having so extensive a knowledge of foreign and Indian languages.

The exact place of his birth, namely the *vaddo*[6] where he was born is clearly indicated in the Register of Births of Our Lady of Rosary parish church of Navelim village. Thus English rendering of the birth registration runs as follows:

"Francisco Luis, son of Francisco Salvador Gomes of Collomoroddo. On 9th June of the year 1829 in the church of his parents I have baptised Francisco Luis, son of Francisco Salvador Gomes and of his wife Deodata Furtado. He is an infant of 9 days. I have anointed him. He is grandson of Minguel Gomes and of Rita da Silva, both residents of Chinchinim. His god-parents were Manuel Francisco Correia de Sa e Gama and Dona Luiza Pereira Garcez, residents of Ribandar. Joaquim João de S. Anna.[7]

But just because he could express well in Portuguese language some authors affirmed that he was a Portuguese writer. For example, the author Jayme de Seguier records that Francisco Luis Gomes was a Portuguese writer.[8] F. L. Gomes was very much a Goan, and brought up and educated in Goa. It may be noted that Goans, Mangalorians, East Indians and Sinhalese have Portuguese names and surnames, but they are not Portuguese *firanghis*. This is one of the paradoxes of the Indo-Portuguese history.

Although his life was short-lived, he produced several works in the field of literature, history and politics, such as *Os Brahmanes*, *Le Marquis de Pombal*, *A Liberdade da Terra e a Economia Rural*, *Notas a Gramatica de Lingua Concanim*, *Essai sur la Theorie de l'Economie Politique*, and *Os Brigadeiros Henriques: Carlos Henriques e Joaquim J. X. Henriques*. Besides these he wrote several articles to the Press in Goa and in Lisbon, and also pronounced many important speeches in the Portuguese parliament. Such was his intellectual output within a short spell of time that Julio Dantas, a reputed Portuguese writer, could say:" *Os pensadores, ou sabios vivem para alem da morte, perpetua juventude, como arvores eternamente em flor. Eu presto a minha homenagem nao apenas ao pensador que ele foi, mas ao que ha de luminoso e de imortal na perpetua juventude da sciencia.*"[9] (*Transl.* The thinkers or the wise live beyond their death. Theirs is an eternal youth, like trees forever blooming. I wish to pay my respects to the thinker in him, as well as to the brilliance and immortality in the eternal youth of knowledge. *Ed.*)

As an historian he was a critic and a philosopher of history, not a mere compiler of facts. Commenting on his merits, Prof. G. M. Moraes wrote: "Goan contemporaries of Francisco Luis Gomes, like the late Dr. Panduranga S. S. Pissurlencar of our own days were archivists of documents and had little critical work to their credit. Francisco Luis Gomes towered far above these scholars, displaying in his *Marquis of Pombal* in a sufficiently high degree all the qualities that are demanded of a competent historians -- zest for truth, objectivity, critical acumen, accuracy and thoroughness.[10]

His other historical work on the life, personality and achievements of the two brigadiers displays his psychological acumen and insight into the motivations of their actions. His medical knowledge enabled him to diagnose the propensities of their minds and assess their motives and actions. This biographical work also reveals his impartial historical bent of mind and his careful and elaborate search and research into historical facts.

In another of his short works written originally in Portuguese and entitled *A Liberdade da Terra e a Economia Rural da India Portuguesa*, he reveals a profound grasp of the agrarian economy of Goa. In this economic history of Goa he dwells on the various handicaps of the native agriculturist and wishes to liberate the land and share it among the local people to whom it rightly belongs. That was his socialism of "land to the tiller". He puts forward his doctrine in the introduction to the book:"*Não temos monarchias por direito divino; não carecemos d'um clero influente pela riqueza; não queremos familias poderosas entre o rei e o povo. Procuramos a egualdade do direito quanto as pessoas, a uniformidade da legislação quanto aos bens.... E' tempo ja de democratisar a propriedade.* "(*Transl.* We do not have monarchies by divine right, we do not lack influential and wealthy clergy, we do not want rich families between the crown and the people. What we are looking for is equal rights for people, and uniform distribution of goods.... It is time for democratising the right to property. *Ed.)* [11]

In this same work he gives us a brief historical survey of Portuguese India of his days. He analyses in several chapters the social, political and economic problems of the land and offers his own solutions and suggestions to the Portuguese government. This historical-cum-economic treatise was quite good for his times, but may be regarded today as outdated. It gives us a good insight into the economic history of Goa and no serious economic historian of Goa will easily ignore reading it.

Even in his *Brahmanes* there are many historical references. The sepoy mutiny of 1857 and some other developments in India of those times are carefully considered and evaluated. As history is the root and politics its fruit, the author minutely assesses the historical weightage on several of the socio-political events of his days. One is tempted to consider *Os Brahmanes* as an historical novel.

Regarding *Os Brahmanes* he himself wrote in the first Lisbon edition of 1866. He confesses his inadequacy as a novelist, but states using the novel form with the sole purpose of conveying better his ideal:" It is necessary that the principles of liberty, equality and fraternity, eternal in their duration, be universal in their application, that being realised in institutions, law and customs they spread over the surface of the globe and filter down to its lowest strata. Only then shall the regeneration of man be accomplished."[12]

In this work Francisco Luis Gomes has built his scenario around the life of the Anglo-Indian community in the district of Fyzabad and its social relationships with the native neighbours. He reviews the traditional festivities in Kanpur and finally dwells in detail on the causes and effects of the Indian mutiny of 1857.

REFERENCES

1. *Selected Works: F. L. Gomes Memorial Volume*, Bombay, The Centenary Committee, 1931, p. xxxiii.

2. *Ibid.*, p. 392.
3. Pereira, F. Gonsalves, *Apontamentos para a biographia de Francisco Luis Gomes*, Bombay, 1809, p. 7.
4. Cruz A. da, *Goa: Men and Matters*, Vasco da Gama, 1974, p. 2.
5. *Ibid.*, pp. 4-6.
6. Konkani expression for a village ward.
7. Extracted from the Navelim parish archives, Salcete, Goa.
8. Jayme de Seguier, *Dicionario Pratico Illustrado*, 2nd ed., Porto, 1928, p. 1641.
9. *Souvenir de Comemoraçao do Primeiro Centenario do Falecimento de Francisco Luis Gomes*, ed. Alvaro da Costa, Margão, Gomant Printing Press, 1974, p. 3
10. *Ibid.*, p. 12.
11. F. L. Gomes, *A Liberdade da Terra*, Lisboa, Typographia Universal, 1862, p. 17.
12. F. L. Gomes, *Os Brahmanes*, p. 6.

N. B. I suggest that readers of this essay should refer to a good critical essay on the writings of F. L Gomes by H. Scholberg in *Indo-Portuguese History: Old Issues, New Questions*, ed. Teotonio R. de Souza, New Delhi, Concept Publ. Co., 1985, pp. 203-215.

13

FR. CAETANO VITORINO DE FARIA

Mariano Dias

Re-writing of Goan History is required for several reasons. One of these is to remove distortions arising from the colonial view of historical facts and personalities. In this process we can expect many a "villain" to be re-habilitated and restored to his rightful place. One such *bête-noire* in need of re-habilitation is Fr. Caetano Vitorino de Faria.

Rivara's Disinformation

More than a century has elapsed since J. H. da Cunha Rivara's *A Conjuração de 1787 em Goa* was published[1], and it has remained the only source book, all its deficiencies notwithstanding. Even a senior historian, who published recently an assessment of Rivara's work, has blindly followed Rivara's opinion regarding the attempted revolt in 1787. He writes: "There were confusing traditions circulating in Goa of a conspiracy which is commonly known as *sublevação dos Pintos*. Cunha Rivara wanted to know the truth of the matter. He examined the documents, and in his *A Conjuração de 1787 em Goa e varias cousas desse tempo*: *Memória Histórica* he sets forth the results of his investigations bringing out the truth of the matter as revealed by the historical sources. Viewing the incidents, as he does, in the political situation of the times, the treatment is masterly".[2]

The above quotation manifests uncriticality that prevails in the appreciation of the "authorities". The burden of this essay will be to show that it is preposterous to propound in 1980 the idea that Cunha Rivara's treatment of the revolt of 1787 is "masterly" and that it brought out the truth.

Rivara was in Goa most of the time as Chief Secretary of the government from 1855 to 1877, the period when the British saw their colonial aspirations seriously threatened in India by the valiant but abortive revolt of 1857. The Portuguese authorities in Goa were profusely thanked by Lords Canning and Elphinstone for the assistance rendered in quelling the disturbance.[3] In such an environment Rivara could not but show his deep-seated hostility to anything smacking of nationalist pride in Goans, and this pride had reached its climax among others in Fr. Caetano Vitorino de Faria. And this is precisely what he achieved with success in his research on *Conjuração*. He successfully tarnished the image of the Goan patriots who laid down their lives in the gallows and languished in the prisons of Lisbon for long years without trial. Rivara's claim that he deals with the revolt without bias (*limpa da macula da paixão*) and of doing it with historical sincerity does not withstand the test of criticism.

Rivara deemed convenient to devote a chapter to what was then written about the revolt. This chapter had to be an exhaustive exposition of the representative views expressed till then in order to enable him to vindicate his own. What we actually have is a feeble and cursory treatment restricted to what was mentioned in the *Refutação Analytica do Governo Provisional*(Bombay, 1835), the only source where the badly mutilated text of the infamous judicial sentence of December 9, 1788 was available to him. He could not have been unaware of what Bernardo Francisco da Costa of the Margao *ULTRAMAR* fame had written in 1865 in the context of the Tiracoi patriot Mariano Jose Conceião da Rocha in the *Illustração Goana* about the foul intrigues that had landed the "conspirators" to the gallows and about their rehabilitation that had started with the advent of liberalism in Goa.[4] Rivara's attempt in his *Conjuração* was to put the clock back on this rehabilitation process. Intellectual honesty demanded that he stopped short of an unimaginable suppression. It defies comprehension how in the chapter that we have mentioned he could remain silent on what is suggested in this essay as a prime provocation for the *Conjuração*: The writings of the youthful and courageous Goan writer Jacinto Caetano Barreto Miranda (1842-1879), particularly those designed to shed light on Fr. Caetano Vitorino de Faria and on the Revolt of 1787 during Rivara's presence in Goa.[5]

The publication by Barreto Miranda in the *ULTRAMAR* of May/June 1867 of the "Glosas" attributed to Fr. Faria proved to be a red rag for Rivara. His incisive allusion to the iniquitous sentence of December 9, 1788 as a juridical murder of the martyrs of Bardez[5] was too strong stuff for Rivara to stomach. This was all the more difficult for Rivara to take lying, because it touched the sensitive elections of 1861 in Nagoa (Bardez) in which Rivara was emotionally involved on behalf of the white interests. Barreto Miranda had quoted an expression used by Rivara in the *Boletim do Governo* in the context of the above mentioned elections describing the natives as having a character marked by meanness and duplicity *mesquinho e dobre*).

While ignoring the blunt analysis of Barreto Miranda mentioned above Rivara did not find it irrelevant and unfounded to quote Barreto Miranda's introduction to the "Noticia" in *ULTRAMAR* of May 18, 1865.

As a result of Rivara's disinformation campaign Fr. Faria emerged badly disfigured as notorious and mediocre. No new documentary evidence was produced, besides private correspondence obtained through Julio Gonçalves (1848-1896) from the Pinto family archives. The major part of the 25-page vicious biographical note is a prolix and ineffective refutation of the "Glosas" published earlier by Barreto Miranda. It is this difficult to accept as tenable Rivara's claim that he sought accurate information from authentic documents.

A re-appraisal

It is inconceivable that while quoting the correspondence of the

Minister Martinho de Melo e Castro (1716-1795) of March 1779 regarding Fr. Faria, Rivara could just "miss" two extremely pertinent documents in the book of *Monções* of the same year. One of these documents is a letter of March 22, 1779 addressed by the Minister to the Governor D. Frederico Guilherme de Sousa (1779-1786). The other document is a letter of March 20, 1779 addressed by Fr. Faria from Lisbon to the Camara Geral. Both these documents can be found in the Historical Archives of Goa, Ms. *Monções 159 B, fls. 499-500* and *502-503v*. The details contained in these documents seem to have been inconvenient for Rivara in his bid to denigrate the memory of Fr. Faria. Had he utilised these documents, the reference made to Fr. Faria as "celebrated" by Martinho de Melo e Castro would not have been put into a wrong context as it has been done in the *Conjuração* at page 84. It was only Rivara's prejudiced mind that could warrant his finding the epithet "celebrated" as pejorative and contemptuous. Rivara knew well that the inclusion of Minister's letter would remove the sting from his uncharitable assessment.

The Portuguese Nobel prize winning neurologist and biographer of Abbe Faria, Dr. Egas Moniz deserves our gratitude for having shown exemplary honesty by bringing to light these two letters that were supplied to him by the late Dr. Germano da Silva Correia and by endorsing courageously the nationalist aspirations of Fr. Faria against the background of the oppressive rule of the Portuguese.[6].

We learn from the letter of the Minister that Fr. Faria was quite vociferously critical of the Portuguese in India (*clama igualmente contra os Ministros e enfim contra tudo o que he Portugues na India*) because of the ill-treatment and extortions to which the Goans were subjected (*por causa das vexações e abatimento com que tratam os naturaes, maltratando-os com dispendios e violencias e extorquindo-lhes tudo quanto tem*). He castigated unsparingly the bribery prevailing in the selection of the army recruits from 1775 onwards. He submitted various plans of reforms in Goa to the Ministry in Lisbon, mostly designed to favour the Goan Congregation of the Oratory, in contrast with the fulminations against the other European-dominated religious orders in Goa.

Minister's appraisal concludes stating that Fr. Faria did not belong to the tribe of self-seekers and that his reputation in the highest circles in Lisbon was that of a well-behaved and selfless priest as far as he himself was concerned, but at the same time whimsical, machiavellian and very much lacking in sincerity, with a marked propensity to use subterfuge to achieve his aims.

The picture that emerges from the above report is that of a respected personality whose only aim was to make the best of his position in Lisbon to serve his country fearlessly. In this regard Rivara's comment that Fr. Faria was the patriarch and patron of the Indian community is realistic and true to facts.[7] His reforming zeal must not have escaped the observation of Fr. Luis Antonio Verney (1713-1792), the pioneering and controversial author of the *Verdadeiro Methodo de Estudar*, to whose ideological thrust are attributed many reforms in Portugal during Pombal's regime and that of Queen Maria I.[8] Incidentally, Verney was educated by the Portuguese Congregation of the Oratory and was very close to the Goan Congregation of St. Phillip Neri and he maintained correspondence with it from Pisa, Venice, and Rome. He also procured favours for it from the Roman Papal curia. Some of these letters were first published by Cunha Rivara in Goa in 1858[9] and were reprinted in Lisbon by L. Cabral Moncada as appendix to his book.[10] Since Verney lived in Italy until his death, it is not improbable that Fr. Faria may have known him during his stay in Rome.

The most impressive, dignified and distinguished trait of Fr. Faria as reported by Martinho de Melo de Castro was his utter selflessness, even in times of penury, unlike the normal breed of powerbrokers and sycophants. Undoubtedly, he could not afford to display seraphic simplicity while dealing with the difficult and sensitive situations he had to face and the uphill tasks he had undertaken. He could not help revealing his innate Indian subtlety which was construed as machiavellian. He was cunning, shrewed and result-oriented, and all for the cause he had vowed to serve in Lisbon, namely the advancement of Goa.

It is important to note that Fr. Faria's forceful and passionate advocacy of Goan interests was not an exercise in futility. He would normally not waste his talents in trivialities and inconsequential matters. Response did come and was seen to have in Goa, as we shall see soon. The end of the odious colour discrimination in the

Religious Orders in Goa could not be deferred any longer as it was an affront to the dignity of Goans that had lasted for too long.

Under cover of his letter of March 21, 1779 to the Goa government, Martinho de Melo e Castro sent a copy of his letter of the same date addressed to the then Bishop of Cochin and Administrator-Apostolic designate of Goa. In this letter he instructed that all religious superiors established in Goa ought to be made to admit Indian novices and do away with the prevailing discrimination despite orders issued in 1774.[11] Similarly the long overdue abolition of the distinct colours of veils for Santa 'Monica nuns, namely black veils for those of Portuguese lineage and white veils for the Indians.[12] Significantly Rivara records in the *Conjuração* (p. 69) that before his departure to Rome in 1772, Fr. Faria had addressed a petition to the Crown on behalf of Inacio Pinto of Candolim (1723-1797)[13] seeking measures to do away with the "veiled" discrimination! This is confirmed in the above mentioned letter of Fr. Faria addressed to the Camara Geral.

The question of limited access of Goans to civil and military posts in their own country had for long been a cause for bitter resentment. By another letter of March 21, 1779 Martinho de Melo e Castro reiterated the earlier orders to allow Goans free access to all civil and military posts. Specific reference was made to the selection of army recruits.[14]

The reform of the Religious Orders in Goa was felt for long, but no positive action was forthcoming. The same Minister ordered by his letter of January 25, 1783 addressed to the Bishop of Cochin that he should use the canonical powers vested on him by the Council of Trent to undertake reform of the two Franciscan provinces in India, threatening to suppress them if they did not show willingness to accept the orders.[15]

By his letter of April 9, 1778 the Minister had forwarded to Goa government some applications submitted to him by Fr. Faria on behalf of the petitioners and recommended earnestly that the requests be looked into with the same good-will that is shown to Fr. Faria in the court of Lisbon. This was designed, it is stated, to do away with the horror that Goans had for the military service, not seldom for valid reasons arising from rank discrimination against them.[16]

Against this outline background it could be safely stated that Fr. Faria stands out as one of the little known Goan patriots, who enjoyed a unique position and wielded power owing to his personal prestige and rapport with the highest authorities in the royal court in Lisbon during the last quarter of the 18th century. So far he has been known only as the father of Fr. Jose Custódio Faria (1756-1819), better known as "Abbé Faria" or "Abade Faria". Details regarding the life of this uncommon instance of a Catholic priest being the legitimate son of another Catholic priest have been published by the late Msgr. Gomes Catão and some more inaccuracies of Rivara have been rectified.[17]

It is widely stated that Fr. Faria took a doctorate during his stay in Rome from 1772 to 1777. In fact he is referred to in some documents as *Doutor* and in one notarial deed as *Doutor em Theologia*. My investigations at the Urban University (Rome) tend to indicate that he was not awarded any doctorate. I could not however elicit any information from the Sapienza University (Rome) where Fr. Faria's contemporary and colleague Fr. Jose Antonio Gonçalves obtained his doctorate and was directed there by Fr. Faria himself. Rivara does not substantiate his statement that Fr. Faria took a doctorate in Rome. Had Fr. Faria done so, Fr. Thommam Paremmakkal would not have failed to mention it while specifically referring to his 5-year long sojourn in Rome.

Even before his ordination in 1767 Fr. Faria is known to have been living with Inacio Pinto at Candolim along with his son for over seven years. In February 1771 the father and the son left Goa for Lisbon, where they arrived on November 23, 1771. It is known that their ultimate destination was Rome.[18]It is significant what Inacio Pinto asserts about his having relented in his opposition to Fr. Faria's departure, because the purpose underlying it was "pious and meritorious". Hence, he must have left with the blessings of the distinguished members of the Pinto family, such as Antonio João Pinto (1714-1783) and Fr. Pascoal Pinto (1718-1788). This meant automatic access to high contacts among the nobility in Lisbon. This brings to the fore the ecclesiastical significance of Fr. Faria's initiative in Rome, particularly strengthened with the support of the

Apostolic Nuncio in Lisbon.

Five years in Rome was too long a period for Fr. Faria to have remained inactive. It coincided with the tenure of Stefano Borgia (1731-1804) as Secretary of Propaganda Fide. He was known for his dedication to the ideals of indigenous episcopate and vernacular liturgy. The creation of Chinese bishops was actively engaging the attention of Propaganda and names were being discussed from among Chinese priests of the time. This was surely known to Fr. Faria and the admission of his son to the Propaganda college has special significance in the context of the jurisdictional conflicts Propaganda had with the Portuguese *padroado* in the 18th century. It was not a casual decision because ecclesiastical education was available in the Portuguese universities. A doctorate from the Urban University gave access to assignments in the vast missionary space in India or anywhere in the world under Propaganda.

Increasing activity of Propaganda in India as contrasted with the declining Portuguese influence certainly made the adherence to Propaganda more attractive. Mgr. Francisco Ingoli's steadfast patronage and support to Matheus de Castro, the first Propaganda Vicar Apostolic in India, may have conjured up visions of similar success under the dynamic Stefano Borgia and with active British support. Similar successes of the Carmelites in South India had made Padroado jurisdiction of Cranganore archdiocese irrelevant.

This background lends credence to the fact that Fr. Faria rushed to Rome with introductory letters from the Apostolic Nuncio on what Rivara surmises to be a mysterious and secret mission.[19] Fr. Faria knew well the treatment meted out to Goans by the Portuguese owing to their natural contempt for all Eastern peoples, as attested by the Jesuit chronicler Francisco de Sousa.[20] He had sensed the resistance offered to Pombal's directives incorporated in his "Instrucções" and the appointment of Fr. Nazario Caetano Francisco Colaço of Divar as the first ever Goan canon in the Cathedral chapter was merely a sop.[21]

The cryptic comments in *Varthamanapusthakam* (henceforth *VP*) that Fr. Faria lived for some time in Rome and submitted several petitions to the Pope and to the cardinals who were entrusted with the work of evangelisation, and that he returned to Portugal after receiving no favourable reply to work for the good of his country and his community sum up his failure in Rome to sell his plans to the Propaganda.[22]

Fr. Faria had obviously failed in using the Propaganda card. The European lobby had been too strong and the obsession of unsuitability of Indians to be bishops had entrenched itself in Rome so as to make the continuation of the Castro experiment unviable. Reports to this effect were pouring into Rome from vested interests represented by non-Indian missionaries and bishops in India. No counter-move based on hard realities, such as the one of Fr. Faria, could easily succeed. Hence he was forced to revert to the home ground and try the Padroado card in Lisbon.

Very little was known about Fr. Faria's activities, achievements and failures in Lisbon. Documentary evidence must be extant both in Lisbon and Vatican archives to reconstruct the story. The lacuna has been filled to some extent with the publication of the English translation of *Varthamanappusthakam* of the *cathanar* Thommam Paremmakkal (1736-1799).[23] It is the account of the journey from India to Europe between 1773-1778 by Malpam Joseph Cariattil (1742-1786) and Cathanar T. Paremmakkal. They had gone to Rome and also stayed in Lisbon before their return to India in 1786.[24]

The probative value of *VP* lies in its being almost a day-to-day record of happenings in Lisbon, Rome and during journeys. As far as the period covering the stay in Lisbon is concerned, Fr. Faria is the key-figure, given the commanding heights at which he was operating and keen interest he was taking in things Indian. It was a very crucial stage for Fr. Faria, because many Padroado dioceses in the East were vacant, including the archdiocese of Cranganore, following the death of the last Jesuit archbishop D. Salvador dos Reis (1702-1777) and Fr. Cariattil's[25] interest that an Indian prelate be placed at the head of St. Thomas Christians in South India.[26]

The archbishopric of Cranganore was a part of the grand plan that Fr. Faria had envisioned for the East. From his earliest contacts in Lisbon with the Apostolic Nuncio and the influential benedictine Fr. João Baptista de S. Caetano, we gather the single-minded emphasis he had been laying upon involving the Goan clergy in the management of Church affairs in India. This was in tune with the Pombaline directives and backed by Apostolic traditions and practice.[27]

The recall of the archbishop of Goa Fr. Francisco de Assumpção e Brito, a protegé of Pombal, in 1780, was not followed by the appointment of a regular new archbishop. Instead temporary charge of the archdiocese was given to D. Fr. Manuel de Santa Catarina, the then bishop of Cochin, whose inability to have an audience with the Queen in Lisbon prior to his departure to Goa led him to seek the good offices of Fr. Faria to secure it.[28] This unusual pattern of appointment was indicative of a new thinking about filling the "vacancy" as temporary arrangements continued for more than three years up to February 1783 for no cogent reason other than that the step was tentatively preliminary to Fr. Faria's appointment as archbishop of Goa. In fact technically the see of Goa was not vacant, because archbishop Assumpção Brito was still *de jure* its archbishop, since he had neither resigned nor been transferred to any other diocese (he renounced his post only in January 1783). It was by virtue of the brief *Pastoralis Officii* of Gregory XIII that the bishops of Cochin could exercise ordinary jurisdiction in the archdiocese of Goa in the absence of its archbishop. This is corroborated by the fact witnessed by *VP* that Fr. Faria never concealed in Lisbon the clear possibility of his taking over the see of Goa. Accordingly he had plans for appointment of bishops for the vacant suffragan dioceses of the Province.

Cariattil had not succeeded in having the problem of reconciliation of Mar Dyonisius I solved by Propaganda in Rome. He pursued the matter in Lisbon in the context of appointment of an Indian prelate to the see of Cranganore and ended up by his being created its archbishop by the bull *Divina disponente clementia* of December 16, 1782 with nomination of the Padroado. Cariattil had been expressing the vehement opposition of the Christians of Malabar to the appointment of a Goan as archbishop of Cranganore. This was because of the appointment of a Goan Oratorian Fr. Pedro de Figueiredo as Administrator of the archdiocese was regarded as a stepping stone to his elevation as its indigenous archbishop.[29]

Fr. Faria saw in the appointment of Cariattil as archbishop of Cranganore not a setback but a support to his overall plan. *VP* records Fr. Faria as having declared to Cariattil after he had received his appointment from Rome: "I am the Archbishop of Goa. So its is not necessary that Your Excellency should ask Rome for what is necessary for you. It is quite enough if I give it to you. When my nomination arrives we will receive consecration together and will go together to Goa. We will convoke a Provincial Council and will make the necessary laws".[30] Fr. Faria is also quoted as having said that once he became the archbishop of Goa he would nominate some other Goans for other places in India. He seems to have also insisted that either all or none of his nominees should become bishops.[31]

Apparently Fr. Faria was lulled into a sense of self-confidence. In fact he had allocated the dioceses in the East as follows: Cochin to Fr. Caetano Francisco do Couto, who had been its administrator from 1777 to 1779 and had been relieved by D. Manuel de Santa Catarina to accomodate his Portuguese confrére Fr. Jose da Soledad; Mylapore to Fr. Brandão, Fr. Faria's agent in Rome, but subsequently changed to Macau; Malacca to Fr. Alexander, a Franciscan; and finally Mylapore to Fr. José Antonio Gonsalves, who after holding the then prestigious post of parish priest of St. Bartholomew of Chorão had been hand-picked in 1780 to join the staff of Chorão seminary as its professor of philosophy.

This allocation recorded by *VP* provides the clue to the departure of Fr. Couto to Lisbon, followed by Fr. Gonsalves, who resigned his professorship. It disproves also the commonly held view (traceable to Rivara's *Conjuração*) that these two priests went to Portugal on their own, in order to secure their promotion to the episcopate. While Fr. Couto could legitimately be resentful of his summary removal from Cochin, Fr. Gonsalves' talents had been appreciated with his appointment to a seminary run by the religious. The motivation for the departure of Fr. Gonçalves was not known to Rivara.[32], but it is now known to have been at the behest of Fr. Faria who advised him to obtain a doctorate "lest anything should be wanting to him from the point of view of canon law"[33] to ascend the episcopal dignity. It is not unlikely that Fr. Couto was similarly summoned to Lisbon because his close links with Fr. Faria and his stay in Lisbon "in the house of an important lady"[34] are indicative of a well coordinated plan.

It is now known that Fr. Faria was responsible for the decision to have Lazarist priests sent to Goa to be entrusted with the direction of the seminary education.[35] This is corroborated by the earlier mentioned letter of Fr. Faria to the Camara Geral, wherein he states that the king sent two priests of St. Vincent de Paul, accompanied by a lay brother of the same Congregation. He refers to the interest taken by the Crown in the welfare of the Goans by sparing these two priests despite the shortage experienced in Portugal.[36]

The Lazarist Fathers came to Goa in 1779 and the seminary of Chorão was ordered to be handed over to them by the letter of Martinho de Melo e Castro dated March 21, 1779.[37] The actual handing over was formalized in December 1779. It is significant to point out that Fr. José Antonio Gonçalves took over as professor at Chorão seminary from 1780. It is also to be noted that Italian Lazarist Fathers came to Goa.

Along with a thorough overhaul of ecclesiastical education in Goa, Fr. Faria had an ambitious plan of starting in Goa a multilingual printing press to cater to the needs of both Latin and Oriental requirements on the pattern of the Vatican polyglot printing office. Through the Portuguese diplomatic channels he secured from Rome printing types in Latin, Hebrew, Syriac, Chaldean, Greek, Malayalam and Konkani with four compositors. In order to gauge correctly Fr. Faria's determination in obtaining the best Malayalam types we have the witness of *VP* stating that he got them cut in Milan because they were more beautiful than those of the Propaganda.[38]

While an element of over-enthusiasm is clearly discernible in all these moves, it is not clear what was the basis of his anticipating that the was definitely going to be the archbishop of Goa, or what concrete steps he had taken to ensure it. According to *VP* the tide was inexorably turning against Fr. Faria and the Ministers resented his taking undue advantage of his acquaintances in the royal court. The selection of Italian Lazarists and the decision to send priests of the order of St. Camillus (also Italians) are stated to have been particularly resented in the Portuguese government circles.[39]The inevitable backlash followed. The bishop of Cochin was confirmed as archbishop of Goa and those against whom Fr. Faria had passed strictures were appointed bishops, including the Carmelite Fr. Jose da Soledade, who was made bishop of Cochin.

The situation in Goa had changed beyond Fr. Faria's expectations. The enthusiasm shown by him towards the bishop of Cochin, D. Fr. Manuel de S. Catarina in his letter of March 22, 1779 had soured and turned into a bitter hostility. Fr. Faria's hopes that Goans would receive a fair deal at the hands of the bishop of Cochin were belied, as he proved to be a racist. In a letter of the bishop to Martinho de Melo e Castro on March 12, 1785 we have an expression of this: "The natives are undependable for various reasons: Firstly because very few show inclination and aptitude for religious life. The crown should not show too much interest in their admission, because the experience has shown that they are unfit for survival in religious life due to their Asiatic indolence and the inclement weather. Secondly the number of natives should not exceed one third because of the disunion and pride that characterise them. Finally, as a matter of principle, and this is backed by experience, a group of natives will not hold unless they have someone from outside to rule over them."[40]

Fr. Faria's overestimation of his influence in the court precipitated his downfall. His understanding of the principles of equality implied in Pombal's reforms was no longer realistic. The superiority complex of the Portuguese that was so well noticed by Fr. Francisco de Sousa was not in any way watered down by the liberal laws of Pombal. His final written appeal to the crown in Lisbon containing a veiled threat of revolt in Goa was certainly the result of his disillusion and frustrations.[41] However, it gives the clue as to the genesis of the attempted revolt of 1787 in Goa. It was not engineered as commonly believed by Fr. Couto or Fr. Gonçalves out of personal spite for failure to become bishops. Fr. Faria's inspiration for the attempted revolt is to be found in the legitimate reaction caused by Cariattil's elevation as the first ever Indian Padroado archbishop of Cranganore and by rejection of the legitimate claims of Goans for episcopal office, despite "their abilities even to train bishops".[42] This rejection remained until, under political compulsions, two Goans were made bishops in 1955 and 1956 respectively, and that too in the distant regions of West Africa.

It appears to be much more than a mere coincidence that Fr. Couto and Fr. Gonçalves returned to India in May 1786 by the same ship in which archbishop Cariattil travelled from Lisbon on his way to his archdiocese via Goa. That was two and half years after his consecration. It is relevant to record also the rumours of death of Cariattil in Goa four months after his arrival there on September 10, 1786. Poisoning was suspected.[43]

A judicial inquiry instituted by the order of the Governor Francisco da Cunha Menezes (1786-1794) into the details of the attempted revolt revealed Fr. Faria as its guiding spirit. The inquiry was concluded on December 9, 1788. As a result Fr. Faria was arrested in Lisbon. In the meantime his son Fr. José Custodio Faria, Inacio Pinto's son José Antonio Pinto, and others had left for France. Fr. Faria remained boldly behind. More research is needed to shed light on circumstances surrounding his arrest and imprisonment without trial and subsequent developments.

REFERENCES

1. Cunha Rivara, J. H. da, *A Conjuração de 1787 em Goa e varias cousas desse tempo: Memoria Historica*, Nova Goa, 1875.
2. Moraes, G. M., "Contribution of Cunha Rivara to Indian Historiography", *India Past and Present*, I, n. 2 (1984):75-76.
3. *Boletim do Governo*, n. 14, Feb. 17, 1860.
4. *Illustração Goana*, March 1865.
5. Barreto Miranda, J. C., *Quadros Historicos de Goa*, I, Margão, 1863, pp. 87-89; III, Margão, 1865, p. 82.
6. Moniz, E., *O Padre Faria na Historia do Hipnotismo*, Lisboa, 1925.
7. Cunha Rivara, *op. cit.* , p. 13.
8. Moncada, L. Cabral de, *Um 'Iluminista' Portugues do Seculo XVIII: Luis Antonio Verney*, Coimbra, 1941, p. 128.
9. Cunha Rivara, ed., *Cartas de Luis Antonio Verney e Antonio Pereira de Figueiredo aos padres da Congregação do Oratorio de Goa*, Goa, 1858.
10. Moncada, L. Cabral de, *op. cit.* , pp. 135-145.
11. Historical Archives of Goa, Ms. *Monções* n. 159B, fls. 592.
12. *Ibid.* , fl. 558; *Conjuração*, doc. n. 32.
13. Born on Sept. 26, 1723. Son of João Baptista Pinto and Joana de Sousa. Paternal grandson of Pascoal Pinto and Luiza Sequeira. Maternal grandson of Agostinho de Sousa and Lucrecia Maciel of Calangute. He was granted coat of arms by charter of March 14, 1770, registered in the *Registo de Brazões*, No. 1, fls. 122-123v, preserved in the National Archives of Lisbon. His elder brother was also granted another coat of arms. Incidentally, when the charter was issued mentioning that he was descending from "Pintos, Sequeiras, Macieis *deste Reino*" Inacio Pinto refused to accept the honour till the qualification "of this kingdom", suggesting Portuguese ancestry, was

removed! *cf. Conjuração*, doc. pp. 149-150.
It was disclosed in the 1787 conspiracy plans that Inacio Pinto had been selected to head the proposed independent state of Goa, and it is undeniable that the secret confabulations were held at his palatial mansion at Candolim. Yet the Portuguese authorities did not dare to summon him as a witness, but his two sons were arrested. Fr. Joao Baptista Pinto was sent to prison in Lisbon and returned in 1807, and Manuel Caetano Pinto, a military officer, was quartered publicly. Since that day the cornices of the facade of the Pinto mansion were painted black as a mark of mourning and protest. Inacio Pinto died on Feb. 16, 1797.

14. Historical Archives of Goa, Ms. *Monções* 159B, fl. 525v.
15. Teixeira de Aragão, ed., *Descrição Geral e Historica das Moedas*, Porto, 1966, pp. 51-52.
16. Historical Archives of Goa, Ms. *Monções* 159A, fl. 236.
17. *Boletim Eclesiastico da Arquidiocese de Goa*, nn. 5 & 6, May/June 1959, pp. 316-23.
18. *Conjuração*, p. 66.
19. *Ibid.* , p. 70.
20. Sousa, Francisco de, *Oriente Conquistado*, II, Bombaim, 1886, p. 336.
21. *Conjuração*, docs. p. 149.
22. Cathanar Thommam Paremmakkal, *The Varthamanappusthakam*, ed. & trans. Placid J. Podipara, Roma, 1971, p. 103.
23. Before Podipara translated it, *Varthamanapusthakkam* was available in Malayalam published by Luka Matthai Plathottathil, St. Mary's Press, Athirampuzha, Kerala.
24. Moraes, G. M., "Padre Caetano Vitorino de Faria, a would-be archbishop of Goa", *Boletim do Instituto Menezes Braganza*, n. 96, 1971, pp. 291-319. Dr. Moraes used some passages of the *varthamanapusthakkam* translated for him by Fr. Mundadan.
25. Joseph Cariattil was born at Alangat (Kerala) on May 5, 1742 in a family called Puducherri. From the seminary of Alangat he was sent by the Carmelites to Propaganda Urban college in Rome. There he was ordained and took a doctorate in Philosophy and Theology in 1766. On return he taught at Alangat seminary. Accompanied by Fr. Thommam Paremmakkal, a priest of Padroado jurisdiction of Cranganore, he left for Europe with the aim of achieving the reunion of Mar Dyonisius I. His mission failed, but instead he found himself made archbishop of Cranganore, but had to abandon his Syro-Chaldean rite and adopt Latin rite. He did not reach his archdiocese as he died in Goa. There is obituary entry in the Goa cathedral parish records. *cf. A VIDA*, n. 6207 of February 19, 1960; *O Oriente Portuguez*, VII, 1910, p. 240. Cariattil's mortal remains were exhumed and carried to Kerala in 1960. *Cf. A VIDA*, February 17, 1961.
26. Mundadan, A. M., *Indian Christians' Search for Identity and Struggle for Autonomy*, Bangalore, 1984, pp. 144-51.
27. *Conjuração*, p. 68.
28. *Ibid.* , p. 70.
29. *Varthamanapusthakkam*, p. 104.
30. *Ibid.* , p. 213.
31. *Ibid.* , p. 216.
32. *Conjuração*, p. 56.
33. *Varthamanapusthakkam*, p. 195.
34. *Ibid.* , p. 220.
35. *Ibid.* , p. 193.

36. Historical Archives of Goa, Ms. *Monções* 159B, fl. 503.
37. *O Oriente Portuguez*, 1915, p. 108.
38. *Varthamanapusthakkam*, p. 196.
39. *Loc. cit.*
40. Meersman, A., *Annual Reports of the Portuguese Franciscans in India (1713-1833)*, Lisboa, 1972, p. 34, n. 125.
41. *Varthamanapusthakkam*, p. 229.
42. *Conjuração*, docs. p. 61.
43. *Varthamanapusthakkam*, p. 243-44, n. 3; F. X. da Costa, "D. Jose Cariatti envenenado?", *Boletim Eclesiastico da Arquidiocese de Goa*, Dec. 1945, pp. 253-55.

14

FREEDOM STRUGGLE AND GOLD ECONOMY

S. K. Mhamai

Goa was in a chaotic state from late 1940's till its liberation in 1961. This state of affairs had its repercussions and bad consequences for free India on the economic front. The gold-smuggling on a big scale was one phenomenon, and it needs to be studied more thoroughly for its implications of the nature suggested in this brief and preliminary essay on the subject. Ironically, the Portuguese authorities who were involved in suppressing political opposition of lightest nature, did not seem to have taken any serious steps to curb the illicit trade in gold across its Goan borders.

There are no documents relating to gold smuggling prior to 1950, but there is much documentary evidence for the decade that follows. It seems to have been an opportune period for those engaged in gold smuggling. Some of the political opponents of the Portuguese also took advantage of the economic disturbance under the guise of freedom-struggle. It was rumoured that some of those arrested on the border by the Indian police for involvement in this illicit trade were immediately released on being told that they were political sufferers. This is a matter for deeper investigation. The love for freedom on one hand and the lust for gold on the other made it easier for some to carry on a relentless struggle against the Portuguese. There were also some among the merchant community who were totally dissatisfied with the political developments in Goa. They feared that their trading in gold might end once Goa was liberated.[1]

From 1954 the illicit trade in gold seems to have increased considerably. That was the period of the economic blockade imposed on Goa by the Government of India. The Portuguese authorities were under pressure to accept Indian currency on par with its own *escudo*, and the trading community agreed to cooperate with the Government only if it were allowed to import gold against this currency. This indirectly encouraged gold smuggling.

So far no serious attempt has been made to throw light on this *contrabando*. All that I have attempted here is to provide some stray evidence for a very brief period of 1950-51, but with the hope that it will motivate some other researchers with greater competence to pursue the theme. Many more details for this research will be available once all crime records of the corresponding phase of the Portuguese regime are centralised and made available to the researchers in the near future. They are presently still lying in the various individual court archives. It is also learnt that important files throwing light on this subject are also lying in the Secretariat.

In addition to the original material from the Goa Historical Archives, I have utilised excerpts from the contemporary newspapers. The veracity of these reports may require cross-checking with other forms of extant evidence, but they do help to come to at least a provisional reconstruction of the history of *contrabando*.

To begin with we have a report from the *Times of India* dated 16-3-1950 referring to a seizure of 540 tolas of gold. It wrote:"About 540 tolas of gold valued at over Rs. 60, 000 were discovered on the person of 11 passengers from a coastal steamer from Marmagoa, Portuguese India Port. Custom authorities described this as 'the biggest haul' and said a gold cylinder was among the 49 1/2 bars of gold seized at Karwar".

The illicit re-export of gold as reported in the *Sunday Statesman* of 30-7-1950 gives us some idea of the gold traffic between Macao and Goa. It reported that a recent news survey issued by the I. M. F.

gave interesting details, quoted from the New York source, of the role that Goa reportedly played in 'channeling' gold from China to India. Previously, it said, the Portuguese colony handled the bulk of gold shipments into Macao for re-export to China. This traffic seems to have been reversed, at least up to June, presumably because of the anxiety of wealthy Chinese to transfer their assets out of the communist reach. Macao now received gold from China via Hong-Kong and sent it, via Bangkok or direct to Goa, whence the illicit re-export was effected. The traffic is said to be very profitable as the Macao cross-rate moved between $37 and $39. 5, while in Goa, because of high Bombay prices, more than $45 is obtainable (after deducting transport and insurance charges).

The *Indian News Chronicle* of 23-8-1950 reported a landing of gold in Goa from Kuwait. It says that gold bullion valued at Rs. 9, 30, 000 has just been landed in Goa after a secret passage by air from Kuwait in the Persian Gulf. The metal weighing 880 lbs. was carried by a British chartered flying boat. An official of the Aquilla Company, owner of the sea plane, stated that they do not know who sent the gold nor for whom it was really intended!

Another sensational piece of news could be read in the *Times of India* of 23-1-1951. It reported that the central excise authorities on the Karwar-Goa border have detected gold-smuggling in stomachs. A party of 11 persons, who were suspected of smuggling gold were detained at Majali and brought to the Hubli civil hospital for medical check-up. An X-ray of the suspected revealed the presence of gold in the stomach of three persons. The same newspaper referred to another recent case of a goldsmith who had eluded the central excise authorities with gold in his stomach, but who died from "intestinal obstruction".

The *Times of India* also reported the seizure of gold from certain people on board the ship "Sabarmati". Five persons, including three women, had taken up lodgings in Bombay on arrival from Karwar. They were outwitted by the officers of the Rummaging Division and Opium Intelligence of the Customs and 190 tolas of gold, valued at more than Rs. 20,000 were discovered. Following information received by Mr. M. A. Rangaswamy, Assistant Collector of Customs, that some people on board the "Sabarmati", arriving from Mangalore via Goa were smuggling gold into the city, Customs officers led by Inspectors D. Leither and John Goes swooped on the ship on berthing. Scores of other officers took up positions in various places where the passengers had their accommodation. Officers searching the passengers' baggage at the dock could not find any contraband. On suspicion three women passengers were followed by Customs officers M. M. Baria and S. N. Pendharkar up to a hotel in Charni Road. There the women were joined by two others passengers. Later all the passengers proceeded to a nearby hotel, closely trailed by the police, and registered themselves as members of the same family. As they were preparing to settle down in their rooms for the day, the officers raided the hotel, subjecting the concerned women to a close examination. Nineteen gold bars of ten tolas each were recovered from their persons. An experienced Customs officer said that in his 30 years of service he had never come across a case in which the gold was concealed in such an ingenious way.

Another report of the *Times of India* dated 7-2-1951 states that the Customs preventive staff had a busy time during the week-end intercepting smuggling activities in Bombay port. Besides the big haul of gold seized at the airport, the preventive officer Mr. Pendharker is reported to have seized five bars of gold worth approximately Rs. 5,000 from one Mahabaleshwar Appa Narvekar who had arrived from Panjim.

The same daily reported on 17-3-1951 a seizure of gold from the possession of parsi priests. Gold worth Rs. 2, 12, 000 was involved, and it had connection with the activities of a Bulsar gang minting counterfeit coins. All the police check *nakas* had been alerted to be on the look out for persons who might be leaving with counterfeit coins, but the police instead seized the gold from the priests, who claimed to have just returned from Daman in Portuguese jurisdiction. The police recovered from them 1, 900 tolas of the precious metal in 10-tola slabs, concealed in ingeniously made jackets that they were wearing. Both had third class railway tickets from Bulsar to Bombay. This was the biggest gold haul ever made in the Surat District till date.

The *Indian News Chronicle* of 23-11-1951 reported large scale gold smuggling between Goa and Karwar. It said that the customs staff along the 62 mile land frontier between Karwar and the Portuguese territory of Goa is to be strengthened and strict vigil maintained both along the land border and the sea coast to foil attempts to smuggle gold from Goa into India. A considerable amount of gold is known to be finding its way into India through jungle paths in this frontier. Small country crafts were also employed to land the the precious metal along the Karwar coast. Mr. A. S. Kyte, the Collector of the Central Excise and Customs (Bombay) stated that the authorities were planning to employ motor launches to chase suspected boats and defeat smugglers' efforts to take advantage of the extensive coastline. A new instrument for detecting gold was also being commissioned to trap the smugglers.

In yet another report of the *Times of India* dated 8-12-1951 the Finance Minister congratulates the Customs authorities. To quote:" Indian Minister of State for Finance has been quick to congratulate the Bombay customs on their recent haul of Rs. 25 lakhs worth of smuggled gold". The report further says that between India and the Portuguese possession of Goa is a straggling land and sea frontier and between these two areas a two-way illicit traffic has developed, gold and imported commodities being smuggled into Bombay State.

One could find many more newspaper reports throwing light on this subject. Gold came into Goa from the Gulf, Macao and Moçambique and was smuggled into India by a variety of illegal ways. Useful information may be found also in the files of the *Repartição do Gabinete* preserved in the Historical Archives of Goa.[2] To give an idea of this official type of information we have an interesting report to show that in 1950 about 10, 69, 227 tolas of gold were imported into Goa. The document provides the dates and quantities imported. There is also a report indicating the names of the persons from whom bullion was seized by the Indian customs authorities from 1st January 1950 to 26th October 1951.

Goa being a Portuguese colony the Goan traders had close connections with some of the foreigners who had settled in Goa either because of their trade involvement or for other reasons. These foreigners were acting as agents or partners of some of the Goan traders. There is correspondence to show that foreigners like Antonio Shayo of Macao, Fauzi el Hose of Lebanon, and some Goans well known for gold trade were importing kilos of gold into Goa. In 1950 only the above mentioned two foreigners and two other locals had imported 1, 122. 312 kgs. of gold.

Not only some Goans and the foreigners settled in Goa, but also many top business tycoons from Bombay were involved in this traffic. The gold recovered from motor trucks owned by the top Bombay businessmen shows the in involvement of Bombay traders in this illicit gold trade.

There is sizable correspondence that throws light on gold legally imported by many into Goa and then systematically transferred to the Indian Union. A letter dated 13th March 1950 and addressed to the Portuguese authorities states that large quantities of gold have been imported into Goa by a special plane from Macau, and that this gold is being smuggled into India. It further states that in the absence of many more customs posts around Goa, the illegal entry of gold into India cannot obviously be prevented effectively. Besides those involved and mentioned above, also the Portuguese customs guards were in the trade.

The Indian authorities were in constant touch with the Portuguese authorities at Goa to prevent large scale import of gold into Goa and its smuggling. A meeting was once arranged and held between the Portuguese Minister and representatives of the Government of India to check smuggling in gold and other precious articles like watches and diamonds. Measures were discussed to restrict import of gold into Goa that was absolutely necessary for legitimate local consumption. The Portuguese authorities were of the opinion that the amount of gold imported was not excessive in view of the well-known jewelry work and manufacture of articles and images for the religious worship. However, the desire of the Portuguese authorities in checking the contraband activities through Goa was made clear to their Indian counterparts. Diplomatic pressure was brought to bear upon the Portuguese authorities to put their desire into practice. In effect, the new imports of gold were suspended for sometime. The Portuguese authorities also intensified their vigilance to avoid contraband, specially against the Arabs who were the principal gold traders.

Further, on the request of Government of India inspection was carried out in private houses, on board ships, principally in those arriving from the Persian Gulf, and also in the luggage, clothing and other places of concealment of persons entering or leaving Goa. Night patrols were also started at sea within the territorial waters by motorboats of the naval services. These measures helped to check smuggling to some extent. Gold worth 91, 335 grammes (=7. 831 tolas) valued at approximately Rs. 783, 219 was seized. This was just a fraction of the big flow of gold in Goa. The political situation in Goa was extremely fluid during this period, and whatever measures were adopted were aimed at easing the growing tension. The Government of India was appreciative of the measures adopted, but it also expressed its dissatisfaction with the continuation of the imports of gold into Goa and its illicit traffic.

Apprehending danger for the Indian currency structure as gold smuggling continued, the Government of India continued its requests to the Portuguese authorities to check the growing menace of gold smuggling and offered its assistance in any way the Portuguese Government might be in need of.

REFERENCES

1. Antonio Furtado, "How the Smuggling Works", *Free Goa*, I, n. 17, June 1954.
2. Goa Historical Archives: *Repartição do Gabinete*, Files 288, 1262, 3526, 3604.

15

SOME AREAS OF RESEARCH IN GOAN LEGAL HISTORY

Carmo D'Souza

Introduction

In this brief essay I shall try to discuss some probable areas where legal research could be undertaken in Goa's legal history. Goan legal history is important as Goa was one of the first places in our country or in the East to have experienced the full impact of the western jurisprudence in the modern times. The new colonial era with its new juridical concepts is intrinsically connected with the Goan legal history. The history of Goa is inseparable from the history of maritime activity of the colonial era in the fifteenth and sixteenth centuries. New legal concepts had to be developed to sustain the colonial activities and interests, and one can find them in Goan legal history. Goan legal history differs from the British system followed in the Indian legal history. The Portuguese followed the Continental Civil Law, whereas the Anglo-American jurisprudence found its way in India under the British Raj. The Indian legal history remains an incomplete book as long as the Goan legal history remains obscure or does not find its rightful place in it. Finally, the Goan legal history could become a nucleus of the legal histories of other colonies held by Portugal.

Constitutional Law

Portugal had a rich experience in constitutional movement which began as early as 1822. There were the Constitution of 1822, the Constitutional Charter of 1826, the Constitution of 1838, the Constitution of 1911, the Constitution of 1933, besides several other amendments. These various constitutional enactments were applicable to the State of India and had their impact on the life in this State. The constitutional ideas developed and got themselves deeply entrenched in the mentality of the Goan intelligentsia. This is one of the good fields for further research.

Constitutional Law had its impact on the Goan politics and thinking. Many periodicals carried the titles involving references to the constitutional movement. It is possible to undertake research in this field, combining the legal aspect with the socio-political aspect. Quite some material by way of constitutional theories, legal writing, newspaper reports and articles could be gathered and analysed to find the socio-political orientation that resulted from the constitutional impact on the intelligentsia. Many politicians in Goa used and borrowed constitutional concepts to forcefully prove their point or to vindicate their stand. Constitution was not just a mere legal document. It was an ideology, and expression of certain ideals of right and justice.

Constitutional Law can also be studied from a legal angle. The impact of the Constitution on law-making, the effect of the Constitution on case law, and so on. Many laws enacted in the State of India claimed in their preamble power under certain articles of the Constitution, or were enacted to give effect to some article/articles of the Constitution. Many a court decisions were based on the grounds of unconstitutionality. So Constitutional Law could be studied from diverse angles, combining together legal and other materials. A few hypothetical questions may be asked to which perhaps no single or definite answers can be given. What would be the course of the legal history of Goa, if Constitutional Law was not applied to Goa? What was the legal effect of the proclamation of the Constitutional Law on the tendency towards uniformity of legal system in Goa as in Portugal? Has the Constitution hampered or helped the march towards the liberation of Goa, and at which stages? What was the impact of the guarantees and liberties enshrined in the Constitution? Was the Constitutional Law responsible for the idea of a single citizenship for colonial inhabitants too?

As for the sources that could be tapped for the study of the above raised issues there are important series of the *Boletim Official* and the *Diario do Governo*. Besides, there are Government publications of the Constitutional Law, such as the *Carta Constitutional da Monarquia Portuguesa* (1880).

Electoral Law

Electoral Law can be classified into two groups: (a) Electoral Laws which tended to be uniform with the electoral system in Portugal, and these were the result of elections to the central institutions like the Parliament, and (b) Electoral Laws which were enacted specially for the State of India. These two sets of laws show different trends.

Electoral laws can be studied from the legal point of view, for their contents and for their implications. It is to be noted that the electoral system varied from period to period, and depending on the political changes used differing types of systems to assess representation and to determine qualifying requirements for the electors and the candidates. One can use history to interpret the differing legal trends. It is also possible to make a study of the *de facto* impact of the election system by using statistics available in the *Boletim Official*.

A few probing questions can be asked regarding the electoral system that prevailed in Goa. Was an electorate involving the masses ever prescribed *de jure* or *de facto* in Goa? Did the elections involve the media? When did the women get a right to vote, and what were the prescribed requirements? Which class interests were better catered by the electoral system? How did the requirements of educational qualifications, or economic subsistence, or tax payments reduce the number of voters, and what was its impact on the elections as a whole? Did election go always as per Government wishes? It is not possible to describe the electoral system prevalent in Goa as a farce, even though it was restricted to a small number of voters, without a serious study of this subject. The study should take care of the psychological and political factors found in the social milieu of the time. It was also believed in some international circles that the elections were a farce in India till the defeat of the Congress in 1977 and its victory little later proved the contrary. Could we apply this parallel to the legal history of Goa?

Parliamentary Representation

The Portuguese *Cortes* had representatives from Goa during the period of Constitutional Monarchy. The deputies began to be sent to Portugal to represent Goa from 1820s. There were a number of decrees issued to govern the parliamentary representation. It is possible to conduct research on these decrees, correlating it to the *de facto* position. Statistics are available regarding the number of elections held, regarding the electorates and the deputies elected from the State of India. It is possible to obtain the break-down of the parliamentarians in terms of their ethnicity, namely as Asians or Europeans (*Ed.* or Eurasians?). One could also look out for Goans who may have represented any electoral circles in Portugal. The whole issue could be covered under the following four categories: (1) European parliamentarians who contested from circles in Goa but were never domiciled in Goa; (2) European parliamentarians who contested from circles in Goa but were at some time domiciled in Goa; (3) Asian parliamentarians who represented Goan circles; (4) Asian parliamentarians who represented electoral circles of Portugal, if any. Yet another interesting point is to study the ratio of parliamentarians allocated to State of India, as against the provinces of Portugal, and as against the number allocated to other Portuguese colonies. It appears that the State of India was favourably placed specially in the nineteenth century when compared with the African colonies.

Codification

In the second quarter of the 20th century the era of Codes began to dawn in Portugal. By Codes one means the important Codes which are the backbone of the Civil Law system, such as the Civil, Penal, Civil Procedural, Penal Procedural, Civil Registration, Administrative Codes, and such others. Portugal's experiences with the

Code began early under the influence of French and other Continental European systems, and the process of codification was transferred to Goa. One can study this process of codification and its impact on the State of India. The Codes were transferred with modifications, and it is important to analyse what called for such modifications. It is necessary to study the functioning of the Codes in Portuguese India. In fact Codes such as the Administrative Code had to make many allowances to fit in the old traditional structures prevalent in Goa.

A number of questions can be raised on this area. Did the Codes contribute towards the process of uniformity of law in Portugal and in India? What special modifications were introduced in India and why? What radical change was introduced in penology? Did the Commercial Code take into account the commercial practices prevailing in India? Why was the Civil Registration Code adapted to the non-Christian population in Goa? What difficulties were faced during the experimental stages of functioning of the various Codes?

Criminology

The penal system was reformed often in the 19th century and thereafter. These changes require a systematic study. The study can cover a statistical study of criminal activity region-wise or globally. A comparative study too may be undertaken for various periods, such as the republican period, or the dictatorship period, or the post-liberation period. The capital punishment and deportation in the 19th century could also provide much material for an interesting study. One could answer questions like: When was the last death sentence carried out and under which code of justice? What effects did the exile have on the cultural mind of the Hindus? Did the cold relations between India and Portugal in 1950's enhance the criminal activity in Goa? Are there any factors peculiar to Goa that explain the nature and intensity or lack of intensity of criminal activity in Goa?

The High Court

The High Court made a dynamic contribution in settling disputes and in the law-making process in Portuguese India for over four centuries. It would be worthwhile delving on the decisions of the High Court over the centuries. Many a decision, specially in the 16th and 17th centuries, had international repercussions in the eastern half of the world, which even involved sovereign or quasi-sovereign countries. Interestingly, the transfer of Bombay to the English, figured in the High Court of Goa. The *de jure* right of the British for Bombay was acknowledged, but still the Government of Goa was reluctant to hand it over to the successor of Abraham Shipman, as the latter had died before the transfer procedures could be completed. The High Court was of the opinion that Humphrey Cook had the same powers as Shipman. This is just one historical instance, but one could find many other cases of engaging interest. By way of sources one can consult the records of the *Relação* in the Historical Archives of Goa. There are also the *Acordãos da Relação de Nova Goa*, and the *Archivo da Relação de Goa* published by Jose Ignacio de Abranches. The *Boletim Official* also contains many decisions of the High Court.

Hindu Customary Law

It is possible to gather glimpses of Hindu jurisprudence from the *Foral* of 1526, the *Bandos* of the mid-18th century in favour of the inhabitants of the New Conquests, the partial codification of 1824, the codification of 1853, and the codification of 1880. The above laws give the prevailing system, but very much influenced by the Portuguese jurisprudence. In this field the study has to be correlated to the Hindu jurisprudence in the neighbouring areas. Hence, expert knowledge of the Hindu jurisprudence is necessary to be able to analyse the laws and to carry out meaningful research. Some basic information can be read in *Direito Hindu e Mahometano* by Luis Cunha Gonsalves, and compilations of legal enactments are available in print due to praiseworthy efforts of the administrator-historian F. N. Xavier in his *Collecção das leis peculiares das communidades* and in *Collecção dos Bandos*.

Tribunal Militar and the Freedom Struggle

The records of the Military Court are now available in the Historical Archives of Goa and they constitute a very valuable source-material for tracing back the history of Goa's freedom struggle. A study of this material from the legal point of view could shed much light on the nature of the charges levelled by the Portuguese authorities and on the defence approach of the freedom fighters and their sympathisers.

Village Communities

This can be the most important topic in Goa's legal history. Much work has been done, but more remains to be done. Village communities had a very intrinsic, important and essential role in the administration of villages, and until the 19th century they even exercised judicial functions. A thorough study of this aspect is desirable. Besides, a number of laws were promulgated concerning the village communities in the last hundred years. There is for instance the *regimento* of 1871, the decree of 1880, the codes of 1904, 1933 and 1961. All this legislation beginning with the *foral* of 1526 can form the basis of a legal study of the village communities.

The Senate

The Senate of Goa, instituted as early as 1511, enjoyed various privileges, and it was an important organ in the administration of the Goa city. The Senate enacted legal provisions called *posturas*. These can provide much material for a legal study, as they give us an idea of the law-making process in the city of Goa and determine pressures that were clamouring for legal recognition in that society. The area of research could be expanded by joining municipal institutions to the Senate, as they have a historical link and are a part in the developmental chain. The *posturas* of the 19th and early 20th century regulated a lot of activities, such as building, sanitation, vehicles, travel, etc. which today are activities governed by independent codes or regulations. Good amount of documentation on the subject is available in published form in Viriato de Albuquerque's *O Senado de Goa*. Also Cunha Rivara published some relevant material in one fascicle of his *Archivo Portuguez-Oriental*.

Confraternities and Mazanias

Confrarias and *mazanias*, the managing committees or associations attached to the churches and temples were regulated by laws enacted specially for them from time to time. Thus the confraternities were regulated by sets of laws formulated in 1897 and 1932, besides many others. The *mazanias* had their own regulations including the one of 1886. In addition there were a number of Statutes enacted by the individual temples and confraternities and published in the *Boletim Official*. The Statutes covered such issues as foundation of the association, rules for membership, cults and religious services, duties of the members, employees, and servants of the temples and churches. The Statutes were approved by the government, and hence created legal rights and duties. A study of this area can reveal a lot about the socio-religious aspect of the community concerned.

Peace Treaties

The legal implications of peace treaties, their clause by clause analysis, their impact on socio-cultural structures can be a good subject for research. Questions can be asked about: (1) What type of clauses were frequently used in peace treaties? (2) What pressures do the clauses reveal? (3) Why were clauses favouring the missionary activity introduced in the peace treaties? (4) Why did cartazes figure prominently in peace treaties? (5) What could be considered as the period of duration of a peace treaty, even though they were signed as valid in perpetuity? (6) Did the peace treaties give the Portuguese a legal right to interfere with sovereign rulers under the pretext that they had violated a clause of the treaty? (7) What trade restrictions were imposed by the peace treaties? The publications of Cunha Rivara and Bragança Pereira contain useful material for this study. However, Biker's multi-volume *Colleção de tratados e concertos de pazes* is a must for any researcher in the field. Goa Historical Archives have more material, particularly in the collection of *Monções do Reino* and *Reis Vizinhos*.

Cartazes

The legal value of *cartazes*, their acceptance by the neighbouring sovereigns, are some areas that required exploration. The kind of questions one could ask are: (1) Whether the *cartazes* gave rise to any future legal concept in a modified form, or did the concept end with them. (2) What was the reaction of the native princes towards the *cartaz* system? (3) Who were the *cartazes* issuing authorities? (4) Was the *cartaz* system a Portuguese rationalisation of plunder and piracy? (5) How did the system work during the Pombaline era? (6) Could the unilateral imposition of the system bind the international community? (7) How did the entry of other European powers in the Indian waters affect the *cartaz* system?

BIBLIOGRAPHICAL NOTE

The readers will find detailed bibliographical references and more details regarding the published and unpublished source material covered in this article in T. R. de Souza's *Medieval Goa*, New Delhi: Concept Publishing Co., 1979, pp. 188-213, 294-309, and B. S. Shastry's *Studies in Indo-Portuguese History*, Bangalore: IBH Prakashana, 1981, pp. 26-37; "Judicial documents in Historical Archives of Goa", *II Seminario Internacional de Historia Indo-Portuguesa*, Lisboa, 1985, pp. 911-19.

16

DR. LOHIA AND GOA'S FREEDOM STRUGGLE

Sushila Sawant Mendes

Introductory Remarks

This is an attempt to throw light on the genesis, the development and the impact of the 1946 Civil Disobedience Movement, with emphasis on the role played by Dr. Ram Manohar Lohia. It was he who ignited the first spark of Goa's freedom movement during his visit to Goa in June 1946. However, while we concentrate on his role, it is important to remember that several others made their own contribution, and quite a few of these may never figure in a "WHO'S WHO" of the freedom fighters.

Before 1946: A Bio-Sketch

Born on the 23rd March, 1910 at Akbarpur (U. P.), Ram Manohar Lohia inherited from his father Hiralal, an active Congressman, his feelings of nationalism and a strong hatred for foreign rule. At the very early age of 10 he took part in organizing a strike in his school on the occasion of the death of Lokmanya Tilak. His brilliant academic career culminated in 1939 with a doctoral dissertation submitted to the Berlin University on "Salt and Satyagraha".[1] As an angry young man of 22 years, he was physically thrown out from the assembly of the League of Nations, where he was present as an observer and when he blew a whistle as a sign of protest during the address of the Maharaja of Bikaner on behalf of India. Today Lohia is more remembered as one of the founders of the Socialist movement in India, having taken an active part in the formation of the Congress Socialist Party in India in 1934. Two years later he was the Secretary of the Congress Foreign Department and during this period published booklets like "On the Struggle for Civil LIberties", "Government of the foreign contractors", "*Swaraj kya aur kaise ?*". He was arrested more than twenty times by the British, Portuguese, Nepalese, and by the Indian authorities after Independence. An indefatigable champion of civil liberty he argued his own *habeas corpus* petitions and was often successful.[2] When he was tortured and handcuffed in Allahabad, he remarked: "When we have recourse to weapons we become weak of heart".[3] On his release after two years of rigorous imprisonment, he immediately wrote another booklet entitled "The Mystery of Sir Stafford Cripps"[4] vehemently opposing the mission. Lohia was a leading figure in the 1942 rebellion and was instrumental in setting up the underground radio. For this he was arrested on 20th May, 1944 and was tortured in Lahore Fort Prison and kept awake for ten consecutive days. Soon after his release on 24th April, 1946 he addressed a group of students at the Calcutta University. He spoke on the Cabinet Mission as an achievement of people's determination.[5]

On 9th June of the same year Lohia left for Goa at the request of his friend Dr. Julião Menezes from Assolna to study the conditions in Goa under pretext of rest to recover from his long imprisonment.[6] Dr. Menezes was the founder of the Gomantak Praja Mandal and the editor of its organ, the weekly *Gomantak*. Among those who came to see them off at the V. T. (Bombay) were Mrs. and Mrs. Joseph Ferrão (Divar) and Mr. and Mrs. Louis Mendes (Velim). Lohia had taken a keen interest in Goan affairs throughout his public career in India. As early as 1938 he had asserted in an issue of *Gomantak* that "Goa is a part of us and cannot allow her movements for freedom and unity to be suppressed with such wanton ferocity".

Political Conditions in Goa prior to 1946:

The Portuguese continued to rule in Goa, not because the local people wanted them. The banner of revolt was raised only a few years after the conquest in the early 16th century. Beginning with the 1583 revolt of the inhabitants of Cuncolim (Salcete) till the Rane uprising of 1912 one can list at least 40 revolts. They all prove beyond doubt the dissatisfaction of the local population towards the alien rule.[7]

The period from 1820s to 1920s is regarded as a liberal phase. Till 1910 Portugal was a monarchy and was then replaced with a Republic. Goans were given representation in the Portuguese Parliament. All citizens, Hindus and Christians were guaranteed individual liberty as per provisions of the Civil Code. All this was struck down on one sweep when Salazar came in with his dictatorship in 1928, with his Constitution of 1933, and his so-called *Acto Colonial*, which denied all freedoms and liberties to the citizens of Goa. Only those who accepted *União Nacional* were politically acceptable, or the youth that joined its *Mocidade Portuguesa*. To organize a public meeting was an offence and to address one a crime. Speeches and writings came under censorship and a breach of these restrictions meant long terms of imprisonment and deportation. The Church was taken into confidence to promote the imperialist designs of the State. Such a situation had sought to demoralise, depoliticise and denationalize the common run of the Goans.[8]

In this context T. B. Cunha pioneered the establishment of the Goa Congress Committee in 1928.[9] Its affiliation was discontinued in 1934. The Committee that existed after that was often criticised in the *Gomantak* as a Jesuit dominated pro-Portuguese committee.[10] Some eminent Goans continued the struggle in Bombay. On 25th January, 1946, the Gomantak Praja Party declared Goa's independence day and published its manifesto.[11]

Lohia in Goa:

The news of his arrival in Goa on the evening of 10th June, 1946 spread quickly by word of mouth and many went to visit Dr. Lohia at the residence of Dr. Menezes in Assolna village. Among the visitors were Mr. Purshottam Kakodkar and Mr. Vasant Kare, members of the Goa Seva Sangh, Mr. Dionisio Ribeiro, Dr. Antonio Sequeira, editor of *A Voz da India*, and Evagrio Jorge, the acting editor of *O*

Heraldo).[12] Some others closely associated were Mr. Laxmikant Bhembre, Advocate Jose Inacio de Loyola and Vincente João Figueiredo. This association helped Dr. Lohia to get a first hand knowledge of the political situation in Goa, and a decision was taken on the 13th June to launch a direct action against the repressive laws in force. While some were advocating for more time to organize people, Dr. Lohia explained that in a land where civil liberties were so rigidly controlled, organisation would have to be the result of the direct action.[13] The Civil Disobedience movement was to begin on the 18th June with a public meeting addressed by Dr. Lohia. Mr. Purshottam Kakodkar, whose Goa Sevak Sangh had signed with blood to cooperate with Dr. Lohia in the movement took charge of the arrangements.

Evagrio Jorge wrote an editorial article on June 14th on the proposed action, and the next day Dr. Lohia and Dr. Menezes stayed at the Palace Hotel in Marmagoa in order to avoid arrest. The same evening they met a group of Hindu students of the *Vidyarthi Sangh* who invited them to Panjim. On the morning of the 16th a large number of friends and admirers gathered at the residence of Mr. Jaginlal Shah to hear Dr. Lohia. Mr Vinaica Coissoro and Dr. Menezes also spoke on this occasion. A crowd of over a thousand was overflowing into the street.

On 18th June Dr. Lohia and Dr. Menezes came to Margao from Marmagoa and were taken to Hotel Republica where they were met by Adv. José Inacio de Loyola, Baki Bab Borkar and Dr. L. Bhembre. Large crowds surged into Margão ignoring the rains. At exactly 4 o'clock in the afternoon the great leader alighted from a *victoria* near the *capela de batalhão* (now the Church of Our Lady of Grace). The Captain José F. de Miranda, the administrator of Salcete, instructed them to go back. Some Goans came forward with garlands ignoring the Captain's pointed revolver.[14] Dr. Lohia said "point it to me" and proceeded to make a speech, defying the orders of the Portuguese that required permission to do so. Dr. Lohia had concluded his speech with:"People of Gomantak think freely, speak freely, write freely and act to build up organized strength". He and Dr. Menezes were arrested by the Portuguese authorities that were taken aback by such an unusual act of defiance. Many other young men and women were also arrested. Slogans of "Jai Hind" resounded in Margão. Outside the Margão police station the crowd swelled with every passing minute and the police shamelessly requested Dr. Lohia to pacify the crowd. That same night Dr. Lohia and Dr. Menezes were taken to Panjim police station.

The Aftermath: A Diary of Events:

19th June, 1946

The commercial and business establishments were closed in Goa as a mark of solidarity with the movement. The *hartal* extended to most of the villages too. In the evening Dr. Menezes, Tiru Vaidya, Venkatesh Verenkar, Nilakantha Karapurkar and Das Borkar were released. A long procession shouting slogans halted in front of the Panjim police station in the afternoon demanding the release of Dr. Lohia. The police resorted to thrashing the people with belts, and eight persons were injured in this operation, including Kum. Sashi Bandodkar and Kum. Ratan Khaunte. A number of others, including Dr. S. Manpat, E. Jorge, Mr. J. M. Shah, Das Borkar, Vinayak Mayenkar and Mr. Laxmikant Bhembre were detained and later released.[15] Similar demonstrations were held in Ponda, Mapusa and Margão. Lohia was taken to Anmod and as the road to Castle Rock was unpassable the police car had to return to Panjim late in the night.

20th June, 1946

The commercial establishments reopened when Dr. Lohia was released at the border at Collem by a police party headed by Lt. Ribeiro. On this morning a procession at Margão *Praça* was addressed among others by T. B. Cunha, Mrs. Bertha Menezes Bragança, Mr. Venkatesh Vaidya and Mr. Sanches de Souza. This huge rally met in the municipal square which from that day was named "Lohia Maidan". B. Borkar composed some songs on the spur of the moment, e. g. "Dr. Bossa. Dr. Bossa utthun cholunk lag".

21st June, 1946

There was a *prabhat feri* (torch-lit procession) in the morning and a public meeting in the evening. The speakers were Purshottam

Kakodkar, Enio Pimenta, Upendra Talavlikar, and Smt. Umabai Shirali. *Vande Mataram* was sung.

22nd June, 1946

A public meeting was held in Ponda in front of the Church. The speakers were P. Kakodkar, E. Jorge, Laxmanrao Sardessai, Upendra Talaulikar, Sanches de Souza and Carlos Pires. A huge demonstration was also organized at Vasco da Gama. It started from the Jai Hind Maidan (now Tilak Maidan) and marched through the main road. At one stage it was attacked by the black troops. Among those who spoke on this occasion were Mr. D. A. Deshpande and Mr. Gerald Pereira.[16]

23rd June, 1946

A flag hoisting ceremony was held at Margão in the verandah of the *communidade* house. A meeting was held in Chinchinim to explain the movement to the local people. Among the speakers were Armando S. Pereira, L. Bhembre, Cristovão Furtado and Jose Mario Furtado.[17] Another meeting was also held at the residence of Dr. Jose Inacio de Loyola Furtado. The so-called loyalists who were against the continuation of the movement held a meeting at the residence of Vicente João Figueiredo.

Public meetings, demonstrations and rallies were organized almost every day at some place or the other.

30th June, 1946 and after

At a meeting in Margão where Bertha de Menezes Braganza spoke armed African soldiers were sent to cordon the area. The meeting was scuttled, but slogan-shouting could not be stopped. Tristão was badly injured when he refused to say "Viva Portugal" as ordered.

In the months that followed many more meetings were organized in Mapusa, Bicholim, Mardol, Carmona, Zambaulim, Cuncolim and Chandor. The meeting at Chandor on 10th July coincided with the funeral of Luis Menezes Braganza. Small girls sang *Vande Mataram*.

Several speeches were made, and at one stage when the name of Salazar was mentioned, the police captain ordered his force to disperse the crowd.[18]

On 8th July Dr. Lohia issued a press statement in Bombay. It stated among other things: "Action and organization must go together.... Goa may be a minor pimple but it is a pimple that disfigures the face of Hindustan.... " The next few days were marked by a series of arrests: T. B. Cunha was arrested on 12th July and sent to Fort Aguada after a summary trial by a military court. He was accused of having participated in a flag hoisting ceremony, wearing uniform of the Indian National Congress and shouting Jai Hind. For these breaches of law he was sentenced for 8 years of rigorous imprisonment.

Bhaskar Bhandari was arrested on 13th July. On 18th a great *prabhat feri* was organized in Margão, converging on the Lohia Maidan at 4 in the afternoon to protest against the arrests and to defy the orders banning the meetings of more than three persons. A similar meeting was held at Mapusa and those arrested were Shirkant Sahukar, Prabhakar Dalal, Mukund Gaunkar and Shivaji Dakerkar. Most of the leaders like P. Kakodkar and E. Jorge were forced to go underground. Despite police repression meetings continued to be held during the first half of August in Margao, Sanvordem, Kakoda and Zambaulim. Within the next few days P. Kakodkar was arrested and also sentenced to 9 years of R. I.

Gandhiji was writing in *Harijan* on 11th August, 1946: "Though the politics of Dr. Lohia probably differs from mine, he has commanded my admiration for having gone to Goa.... "

LONDA CONFERENCE AND DR. LOHIA'S SECOND VISIT

On August 18th hundreds of Goan workers went to Londa. Dr. Lohia had been busy with a political movement in Nepal, and he deputed his colleague Ashoka Mehta to attend the conference. Two trends were noticeable at Londa: One pleaded for direct action, while the other felt the necessity of waiting and seeking the assistance of the Government of India.[19] The differences were resolved and the National Congress (Goa) came into existence. Some of the main stalwarts present were Dr. Rama Hegdo, Lakshimikant Bembro, Dr. Naraina Bembro, E. Jorge, Nilkant Karapurkar. On the 18th September L. Bembro offered satyagraha and was sentenced to 4 years R. I., and on that day Dr. Lohia announced his second visit to Goa. He criticised the military tax of Rs. 42 which every Goan male had to pay. On 28th September he entered Goa and was arrested at the railway station in Collem. He was accompanied by George Vaz who avoided arrest by intermingling with some Jesuit priests in the same train. That day the police *lathi*-charged a crowd of over 5, 000 in Margao. Dr. Lohia was put into solitary confinement in Aguada jail.

In a letter addressed to the Chief Justice of Goa Dr. Lohia demanded an apology from the Portuguese Government for his illegal imprisonment as he had not violated any Goan law. But he had to remain in solitary confinement till October 2. Gandhiji reacted to this event in *Harijan*: "Dr. Lohia is not a little man and the injury done to him is injury done to our countrymen in Goa. "[20] The Portuguese released Dr. Lohia in the presence of the British consul in Goa on the border with a ban on his re-entry for the next five years. Protest meetings were held at Quepem, Ponda, Bicholim, Margão, Canacona during the days following the release. Mr. P. P. Shirodkar was arrested and sent to Aguada for reporting on Dr. Lohia's arrest in the Free Press Journal.

BELGAUM MEETING AND ITS FOLLOW-UP

After his release Dr. Lohia's activity was restricted to the neighbouring areas. A meeting was held at the residence of Dr. D. G. Naik at Tilakwadi in Belgaum. This was attended by two hundred Goan workers. Prominent among these were George Vaz, Manohar Prabhudesai, and K. Hegdo Desai. National leaders like Nanasaheb Gore, Kamlatai Chatopadhya, Ashok Mehta, Achut Patwardhan.

Dr. Narain Bhembre objected that organization in Goa will suffer if direct action was used again. Dr. Lohia recommended formation of fighting committees and start satyagraha in phases on the 8th, 18th, and 28th of each month in each taluka. As a result the first committee under Dr. R. Hegde offered satyagraha in Margao on 18th October and was arrested. This was followed by Manohar Sardesai in Chawdi on 18th November, by George Vaz in Sanquelim, by E. Jorge in Cuncolim, by Dr. N. Bhembre in Quepem, by L. Sardesai in Panjim, by Venkatesh Vernekar in Ponda, and by Vinayak Mayenkar in Bicholim. All of them were either sentenced to R. I. or deported.

From Belgaum Dr. Lohia carried his flame of protest against the Portuguese to Karwar, Ratnagiri, Kolhapur, Sawantwadi,

Khanapur, Londa, Castlerock and Nandgad. Also at Halyal, Yellapur, and Kumta Lohia addressed huge meetings attended by peasants. At Mangalli, a border village of Goa, Dr. Lohia broke the ban and entered Goan territory. The people of Goa were attending the various meetings enthusiastically despite the armed guards posted at the frontiers. Secret paths over hills and through forests were used.

At a meeting at Ankola on the way from Karwar to Kolhapur nearly fifteen thousand people were present. More meetings were held at Gadhigalanj, Satarda, Arondah and Banda. At all these meetings volunteers came forward to offer satyagraha in Goa and also promised to collect funds for the organizational activity. Dr. Lohia also addressed mass meetings at Vengurla, Shiroda, Kankavali, Kudal and Amboli. He advocated a **praja raj**(=people's government) of the masses, but the Portuguese had begun calling the upsurge a *movimento da rua*.

In November 1946, in an open letter to the people of Goa he answered the question: "What are we fighting for?" To create a new Goa where every single Goan is a happy citizen, who tries to acquire the dignity of full democracy and is willing to live and die for a free Hindustan.... The Hindu Muslim division does not weaken this area."[21] He was against any act of sabotage, as it would kill the movement or limit it to a small number. He wanted it to be a peaceful movement so that every adult Goan could participate in it. His satyagraha movement included mass resistance, peasant morchas, picketing of drink shops, campaings against stamp, revenue and lotteries, and setting up of propaganda units and also panchayats in each village. He also suggested constructive work after liberation. This could take the form of building parks and resorts, setting up of large and small industries and making agriculture a cooperative task. He concluded saying that "five lakh of full democrats can shake the Portuguese into submission. Get arrested, get beaten, suffer bullets, but take your morchas and demonstrations and refuse to pay taxes...."

POLITICAL ACTIVITY IN BOMBAY

Although Dr. Lohia did not re-enter Goa till 1961 he continued to keep contact with the Goan freedom struggle. The *Bombay Chronicle* dated 9th January, 1947 reports a public meeting under the auspices of National Congress (Goa) in Jinnah Hall, at Vithalbhai Patel Road where many Goans lived. The meeting was presided by Adv. S. D'Silva and attended by about 1, 500 people. Dr. Lohia appealed to Goan youth to provide an army of 5, 000 satyagrahis to defy in batches the repressive laws of the Portuguese. Borkar, Kakodkar and D'Sa sang poems on "Goa's Struggle". Gold ornaments donated by Mrs. Shanta Borkar, Miss Ratan Shirodkar, and Mr. Wamanrao Desai were auctioned by Dr. Lohia and a sum of Rs. 1, 300 was collected.[22] From 13th January onwards a 12-day training camp was organized at Khanapur in Belgaum for the satyagrahis.

On 18th June 1947 a public meeting was held at the same Jinnah Hall to mark the first anniversary of the civil liberties movement. It was presided by S. K. Patil. The *National Standard* of 19th June referred to it as the Goan *kranti* day. On 21st June a Goan political conference was held at Sunderbai Hall (Bombay) and it passed the "Quit Goa" resolution. Mrs. K. Chattopadhyay was the main speaker. On 27th July at a meeting of the Goan political workers in the Cruzo studio, C. C. I. premises, Bombay, Dr. Lohia spelled out a four point programme: 1. To uplift the backward sections of Goans; 2. Education for all those engaged as cooks, butlers and tailors; 3. Formation of a representative organization to coordinate the constructive activities; 4. A volunteer organization to work out these plans.[23]

At a meeting of over 2, 000 Goans at the Cama Oriental Hall, Bombay, when a new executive of the National Congress (Goa) was elected, Dr. Lohia reiterated: "We demand complete destruction of Portuguese rule in Goa.... the arrests of over 500 persons during the last year in the struggle for freedom was only a beginning".[24] However, on 8th August "Goa Day" was celebrated in the Sunderbai Hall (Bombay) with non-cooperation of some members of the National Congress (Goa).[25]

On 7th December, 1947 at a meeting of the National Congress (Goa) in the Gujarati Forbes Hall (Bombay) a resolution passed by Dr. J. Menezes reaffirmed the faith of the struggling Goans in the leadership of M. Gandhi and Dr. Lohia "who represent the spirit of freedom".[26] On 19th January, 1948 Dr. Lohia addressed an extraordinary meeting of the National Congress (Goa) at Forbes Hall, asking the Goan workers to take up serious constructive work among the people.[27]

On June 1, 1948 a press statement issued by Dr. Lohia criticised the United Nations and its Human Rights Commission which had refused to take note of the strangulation of human freedom in Goa.

The last recorded date showing Dr. Lohia's link with the struggle of Goa is 8th January, 1959. In a report of George Vaz, General Secretary of Goan People's Party, to the *Sunday Chronicle*, he makes reference to Dr. Lohia condemning one Dr. Ubaldo Mascarenhas (President of the 2nd Goan political conference held in Goa some days earlier). This goes to show that despite his involvement in freedom struggles elsewhere in the country he did not sever his links with the Goan cause after 1950. Goans will always remember him as the catalyst who lit the flame of the freedom struggle in Goa and brought to the forefront countless patriots, who casting aside their personal considerations became the torch-bearers of Goa's freedom.

REFERENCES

1. Mehrotra, N. C. *Lohia -- a study*, New Delhi: Atmaram Publishers, 1978, pp. 1-6.
2. Lohia, R. M., *Wheel of History*, New Delhi: Ram Manohar Lohia Samata, 1955, p. 1.
3. Lohia, R. M., "Dr. Lohia's statement in Court", *Harijan*, X (25 August, 1940), p. 93.
4. Lohia, R. M., *The Mystery of Sir Stafford Cripps*, Bombay: Padma Publications, 1942, p. 11.
5. Kelkar, I., *Lohia Sidhanta Aur Kaun?*, Hyderabad, 1963, p. 113.
6. Lohia, R. M., *Action in Goa* (henceforth referred to as *LAG*), Bombay:

August Publication House, 1947, p. 30.

7. Rao, R. P., *Portuguese Rule in Goa: 1510-1961*, New York:Asia Publishing House, 1963, p. 60.
8. Cunha, T. B., *Denationalization of Goans*, Bombay:Goa Congress Committee, 1940, p. 4.
9. Cunha, T. B., *Goa's Freedom Struggle*, Bombay:T. B. Cunha Memorial Committee.
10. Menezes, J., "The Goa Congress Committee: A Hoax", *Gomantak*, I, n. 29 (Bombay, 3 Feb., 1940), p. 2.
11. Menezes, J., "The Manifesto of the Gomantak Praja Party", *Gomantak*, I, n. 40 (Bombay, 21 Sept., 1946), p. 1.
12. Jorge, E., *Goa's Awakening: Reminiscences of the 1946 Civil Disobedience Movement (= JGAR)*, Panaji:Silver Jubilee Celebrations Committee, 1971, p. 10.
13. *Loc. cit.*
14. Neurekar, V., "Dr. Ram M. Lohia", *The Navhind Times*, Panaji (19 Dec., 1986) p. 5.
15. Menezes, J., *Goa's Freedom Struggle*, Bombay, 1947, pp. 56-57.
16. Pereira, G., *Viva 18th June Movement*, Panaji: Goa State Committee C. P. I., 1971, pp. 22-30.
17. Lohia, R. M., "O movimento de 18 de Junho", *Gomantak*, X, n. 25 (Bombay:19 Feb., 1949)p. 1.
18. *Ibid.*, X, n. 26, 5 March 1949, p. 3.
19. Mascarenhas, L., "Goan Freedom Movement outside Goa", *Goa Wins Freedom*, Panaji, 1986, pp. 123-137.
20. Gandhi, K., "The arrest of Dr. Lohia", *Harijan*, X, 20 Oct., 1946, p. 361.
21. *LAG*, pp. 48-72.
22. *Goa's Freedom Struggle vis-a-vis Maharashtra, 1946-1960*, Vol. VIII, Part I: Bombay, Gazzetteer Department, Govt. of Maharashtra, 1978, pp. 84-86.
23. Menezes, J., "Lohia's Plan of ACtion", *Gomantak*, IX, n. 6, 2 Aug., 1947, p.1.
24. Menezes, J., "Mass Meeting of National Congress (Goa)", *Gomantak*, IX, n. 21, 15 Nov., 1947, pp. 1-2.
25. Dessai, W., "Communists-Socialist combine to wreck Goan Unity", *Gomantak*, X, n. 4, 14 Aug., 1948, p. 3.
26. Menezes, J., "What National Congress (Goa) Stands For", *Gomantak*, IX, n. 26, 13 Dec., 1947, p. 1.
27. Cf. *supra* n. 22, p. 110.

17

QUALITY OF LIFE IN COLONIAL GOA: ITS HYGIENIC EXPRESSION (19TH-20TH CENTURIES)

Fatima Gracias

Introduction

This is an attempt to provide some idea of the quality of life in Goa during the last century and a half of the Portuguese rule in Goa. This is sought to be expressed through what may be considered as one important indicator: Health.

I have selected this theme as it is closely connected with my larger research, and I felt that I could put down some of my preliminary findings in order to elicit comments and suggestions. Besides, health and hygiene has become an important budget-item of the public exchequer, and as much as 13% is being spent on it annually. One could ask whether this represents an important change in quality of life, and if it does mean a change for the better.

The geographic extension covered by the period of this study is the entire State of Goa as we have it today.

Population

The population of Goa in 1810 was estimated as 1, 22, 944 for the

Old Conquests and 69, 675 for the New Conquests.[1] In 1850 it is recorded as 2, 41, 932 for the Old Conquests and 1, 20, 812 for the New Conquests.[2] The population increased steadily up to the third census of 1910. A decrease was noted in the subsequent period. The decrease of 3. 55% was attributed to emigration, epidemics and certain economic conditions. Ilhas taluka was most densely populated, but by the end of the 19th century Bardez had emerged as the most densely inhabited. This density decreased after 1931 due to emigration flow.[3]Emigration had its impact on the home population also due to transmission of infectious diseases. Several epidemics broke out in the beginning of the present century. Among these was the epidemic of influenza that broke out in 1918 and the mortality it caused was very high. Its effects were felt all over Goa, and particularly in Bardez which had more contacts with British India, where many diseases existed in endemic form. T. B. was little known in Goa before the 20th century, but in the second half of this century a sudden growth of this disease was noted.

During the decade from 1940-1950 no increase in population was noticed in relation to the previous census. In early 1950's many people left their land on account of the economic blockade, because their family-earners in India could not remit money to Goa freely. At the same time the blockade gave an impetus to the development of ore extraction. The emergence of mining brought about a shift of population to the mining areas of Sanguem, Bicholim, Quepem, and Satari. The population of these talukas saw an increase of 44. 6%, 26. 95%, 27. 41% and 17. 05% respectively. A corresponding increase of population was also experience in Marmagoa port region.[4] Around 1961 there were 5, 89, 997 people in Goa, including 3, 30, 219 in the Old Conquests, and the remaining in the New Conquests. This appears almost doubled in the 1981 census.[5]

Economic Conditions

The size of the population and its growth were influenced by economic conditions of life that were based predominantly on agriculture. Paddy cultivation was the main occupation of the people. Lands usually belonged to the village communities or to the landlords who employed wage labour.

In the coastal region fishing was an important occupation. In addition to these occupations there was toddy-tapping, carpentry, and other artisanal works. Some lived on their rents, and quite a few exercised professions of law, medicine and business. The census of 1900 lists nearly 100 occupations. Goa did not have any major industry under the Portuguese. The traditional artisans produced enough for their living and there were no incentives to produce more.

The staple produce of Goa was rice which depended on the vagaries of the monsoons. Agriculture received little or no encouragement from the Government. Due to lack of agricultural products every year at least twenty lakhs of rupees were spent on cereals and vegetables.[6] During the second decade of this century nearly two and half lakh rupees were spent annually on rice imports.[7] Despite this fact the cultivation of coconuts received more attention than that of cereals and vegetables.

Coconut plantation was considered useful because of the export demand and because of the dependence of Goans upon many palm products for habitation and food.[8] However, during the first two decades of this century the prices of coconuts suffered a decline, owing probably to overcultivation. In 1893 coconuts worth Rs. 995, 137 were exported as compared to Rs. 308, 269 in 1903.[9]

The main exports of Goa were coconuts, bettlenuts, salted-fish, fire-wood and salt. This last item was one of the most important income earners and its export was always on the rise. In 1916 salt valued at Rs. 4, 12, 854 was exported.[10] These exports paid in part for a variety of goods imported, such as rice, cloth, refined sugar, wheat, tobacco, glassware, hardware, fruits and vegetables. The imports were always in excess over exports, causing a great financial drain which had to be replenished by the remittances of the emigrants.

The majority of the population could be called poor, and job opportunities were scarce. Cottineau de Kloguen, who visited Goa during the first half of the 19th century remarked about the economic conditions of the people in Goa. He found few rich families in the colony and no fortunes seem to exceed an annual income of Rs. 2, 000. There would be many with an annual income of five to six-hundred rupees. He observed that quarter of a rupee or half *pardao* was sufficient for a decent maintenance of an individual per day. However, four-fifths of the population were truly poor and miserable.[11]

However, during the second half of the 19th century an important development took place in the rural economy of Goa. It was the replacement of agriculture with emigration as the chief means of subsistence. The state of agriculture could not maintain so many cultivators as there were available. As a result large numbers began to migrate to British India. It appears that Goans first began to work for the British at the time of the British occupation of Goa following the threats of a French invasion of Goa. When the British occupation forces withdrew the Goans followed them to their various camps in Pune, Bombay, Karachi, Madras, Calcutta and Singapore.[12]

In mid 19th century the Portuguese Government opened schools in Bardez and Salcete to meet the needs of the emigrants. Later more schools emerged to meet the growing demand for English education. By an order of July 14, 1899 the Portuguese Government provided grants to English schools in Goa.[13]Goans who received English education found it easier to obtain jobs in British India. Those who could not afford much education trained themselves as cooks, waiters, bakers, tailors, musicians and practised these crafts in British India.

Various events in the 19th and 20th centuries provided an additional impetus to emigration of Goans. The construction of railroad in 1870's made it possible for more people from Salcete to settle in the neighbouring areas of Hubli, Dharwar, Belgaum, Pune and Bombay.

Many Goans migrated to Portuguese and British colonies in Africa to work as doctors, musicians, traders, clerks and tailors. The partition of Africa after 1870's and subsequent opening of its interior created a great demand for people to assist in the administration and in construction works. In 1896-7 over 9, 000 Goans migrated to East Africa. The number rose to over 13, 000 in 1900. However, there was a decline after that owing to the war of Transvaal and the policy of discrimination against the Indian emigrants.[14]

The remittances of emigrants contributed vitally to Goan economy. These remittances enabled the middle class in Bardez and Salcete to keep up a reasonable standard of living. The great depression was not without its impact on Goan economy. The salaries of those working in Goa were very meagre. A school teacher for instance received Rs. 60 per month. There was a dramatic increase in salaries in the last years of the Portuguese regime, and the Government servants were kept contented in order to win their support to the continuation of the Portuguese rule in Goa.[15] In the meantime some serious attempts had been made to explore ore mines after 1945. But it was only from the 50's that ore rush began. In 1961 there were 23 big mine owners who were also exporters. Because of the availability of deposit almost on the surface, open cast mining did not require expensive equipment, and little capital investment went into actual mining operations.[16]

Goa had some commercial towns where all kinds of goods, both local and foreign were available for sale. In 1961 there were only a few industrial units, including rice and flour mills, oil crushers, a powerloom, cashewnut processing, brick manufacture, ice manufacture, soap factories, a carbonic gas plant, a match factory, and some cottage industries for handicrafts. All units were privately owned. The Portuguese did little to create a public sector or encourage capital development.

Hygienic Expressions

1. **Water Supply**:

Protected water which is essential for diet and maintenance of health was not readily available in Goa during major part of the Portuguese regime. No efforts were made to supply water to the people by means of pipes. Throughout this period majority of people had to be contented with the natural sources of water supply, namely rains, rivers, springs and wells. Even the famous Golden Goa had no facility of running water during its heydays. The first attempt to provide the city of Goa with potable running water was made in 1535. It was planned to bring the water from the spring of Our Lady of the Mount.[17] Colonial politics also killed another proposal in 1601. It was proposed to start a limited project to direct the waters of

Timmayya's tank which lay above Trindade to the city below. The plan was aimed at mitigating water shortage during the summer months.[18]

Most wells were privately owned, built in the courtyards of houses, and sometimes close to toilets. Water from these wells was often unfit for human consumption as it contained chlorides, nitrites and decomposed organic matter.

The peculiar habits of the natives gave rise to sources of contamination. Thus, when a native went to the well, he did so to wash as well as to drink. Water was drawn with copper or mud vessels with the help of dirty ropes. Some wells also served to wash cattle. The filthy water then percolated back into the well.

In areas situated along the river banks, particularly in the New Conquests, people consumed dangerous water from the rivers. Even today in remote areas people drink water from the rivers in the absence of better alternative.

Panjim, the capital town of Goa, till the end of the last century depended on water of two springs. However, the majority of its population used contaminated water from wells. Orders were issued to prevent people from bathing around the wells, but these orders were hardly observed. Perhaps the only factor that saved the people in the midst of such a situation was the natural immunisation. The Portuguese made no efforts to provide potable water and thereby to improve the health and hygiene of the territory.

In 1907 the Government earmarked 620000$000 to start a scheme of water supply in Panjim when it was realized that lack of water affected food, hygiene and growth of population. Mortality was exceeding birth-rate in Panjim during this period.[19] In 1914 Panjim had one hundred wells of potable water and others with contaminated water.

The attitude of the people was also responsible for the state of affairs. They were uncooperative and suspicious of any change introduced. When, for instance, wells were opened, springs cleaned and reservoirs built to tap water in the Sanguem taluka, the people still preferred to use water from the rivers, rather than draw it from the wells. In order to attract them to the wells, pumps were set in many wells, but these stopped working due to carelessness.[20]

Water supply was a serious problem in Goa during the months of April and May. Lack of pure water was responsible for many diseases, such as typhoid, cholera, gastro-enteritis. As late as 1950 only a small section of the population had access to protected water supply with pipes in Ilhas and Marmagoa talukas. In Panjim two hundred and six houses, and in Marmagoa fifty one houses received tap water.[21] In 1956 the Government approved a plan to provide tap water to several villages in Goa.

Mortality rate was high among children below the age of five, and this was largely due to infectious diseases like gastro-enterites, scabies and diseases of the eyes like trachoma, all related to water. Typhoid and cholera are water-borne diseases. Untreated water raised the risk of these infections. In the post-colonial water the situation has improved considerably as far as water supply is considered in absolute terms, but it appears to be far from satisfactory in terms of growing population and other uses that were far restricted earlier.

2. Nutrition

The prevailing economic conditions of life were responsible for the level of nutrition. Majority of our people before 1961 lived on agriculture and remittances from across the borders. Most lived in chronic economic stress and as such they could not afford to spend much on their food. Cereals, certain kinds of fruits and vegetables were not easily and cheaply available. They had to be imported from elsewhere in India and abroad. As a result this important component of diet was largely missing. Banana was consumed by the majority of the population and other traditional seasonal fruits. Oranges, grapes and apples were imported and only the upper classes could afford them. Goa could definitely grow more vegetables, but there was no incentive in this direction. Most people had no habit of drinking milk and eating milk products as they were expensive.[22] Eggs too were expensive due to the fact that poultry farms had not developed in Goa.

The diet of the middle class was poor in animal protein and contained few dairy products. The diet of the humbler groups was poor in quantity as well as quality. To overcome the deficiency of fruits and vegetables the people consumed rice in large quantity. This provided only carbohydrates and very little protein. It was consumed for breakfast in the form of canjee, and then for lunch and dinner. It was also used in preparing varieties of snacks and sweetmeats. The Hindus had their rice milled raw and they cooked it without salt. The Christians milled their rice after boiling the paddy, and this way it lost 75% of vitamin B2. The washing of rice before cooking took away also some iron and phosporus.[23]

The dietary habits of the Christians changed on conversion. Beef and pork entered their diet, specially of the upper classes. These changes were largely influenced by the Inquisition, which in 1736 for instance forbade Christians from eating boiled rice without salt as done by the Hindus.[24] Many Portuguese culinary habits were absorbed by the Christians, including the use of salt and vinegar for preservation or meats. The Hindus consumed only mutton and chicken, and that too on rare occasions. The Muslims ate mutton, beef and chicken. Fish was an important daily item of diet, and so also the coconut. Wheat and millet were not easily available in Goa, and as such were not much used. Wheat was used mainly for bread. The *kunbis* consumed large quantity of nachini, and pulses also were consumed only by a certain sector of the population.

The commercial treaty of December 26th, 1878 with British India brought further changes in the diet of the Goans. Before this treaty majority of the people had never heard of coffee or tea or chocolate with milk or without milk. Sugar started replacing juggery. In 1880 sugar worth Rs. 84, 895 was imported for local consumption and by 1892 the amount spent was Rs. 1, 57, 383.[25] The demand for sugar almost destroyed the juggery industry.

The diet of the majority was insufficient and faulty due to lack of proteins, calcium, iron and certain vitamins. The main cause of undernourishment and malnutrition was poverty, and in particular the low productivity of man and land in agriculture. Additional causes of malnutrition were storage difficulties and certain popular preferences and irrational food habits sanctioned by religion. Faulty nutrition was to a large extent responsible for many diseases prevailing in the State, such as beriberi, anemia, goitre, pellagra and scurvy. Of greater significance was the fact that malnutrition led to "hidden hunger" -- a chronic debility that impairs people's labour input and decreases their resistance to diseases. The most vulnerable parties were the pregnant women, infants and children. Malnutrition was one of the main causes of infant mortality in Goa. Statistics show that more than 28% of the deaths during the early decades of this century were registered among children below five years of age. During the years 1938-40 and 1948-50 the mortality rate up to one year compared to general death rate was equal to 21% and 22% respectively.[26] Poor diet had its effects on the height and weight of the poorer children as compared to the children of the richer classes.

This situation has improved due to better economic conditions and greater awareness of nutrition. People now are more conscious about their diet. Education and legislation has done much for this change. Abundant supplies of medicine, multiplication of hospitals are desirable and essential, but they are not sufficient. Most essential for the prevention of the disease is a higher standard of health, a better physique and a greater power of resistance to infections. This can be attained only through an adequate nutrition.

3. **Infant Mortality**

Something has already been said about this earlier. It needs more detailed consideration because it is a sensitive index of health conditions of a place. Infant mortality was high during the early centuries of Portuguese rule in Goa and this situation had not changed till about forty years ago.

Infants of the low-income groups were breast-fed up to 36 months, but the milk was inadequate. The child had to depend completely on it, because no supplementary food was there, excepting water mixed with juggery that was administered to clean the intestines. The water used was often not boiled and it was fed with the help of a piece of cloth dipped in water and then squeezed into the mouth of the child. Children under five were most susceptible to the ill effects of malnutrition. Many suffered of diarrhea caused by variety of bacterial and viral agents present in water. But diarrhea was also a direct result of acute malnutrition. In addition heavy toll of infants resulted from the dreadful conditions under which deliveries took place, ignorance of the mothers, and infectious diseases.

Until a few decades back most births in Goa took place at home, attended by a village *dai* (midwife) with no formal training. It was almost a hereditary skill or rather lack of skill that was greatly responsible for high infant mortality. According to certain cultural traditions among the Hindus the actual event of birth was regarded as ritually impure. Hence the deliveries were to be conducted by women of low caste. These had little knowledge of hygiene and even less of obstetric science. In the New Conquests very few doctors were available. In 1908 the Sanguem taluka with an area of 815 sq. kms. had only one doctor.[27] Poverty and lack of transport did not allow people in need to seek help of trained doctors. Hence, they had to be contented with the *daias* and quacks.

Many newly born were prone to death by tetanus caused by infection of the umbilical stump which was often cut with unsterilised instruments. It was one of the most common causes of infant mortality. In 1913 about 22% of deaths among infants were caused by this. That explains why traditionally *sotvi* was known as curse of Durga Devi.[28] In an inquiry carried out in 1943 among 36 families of school-going children from Panjim primary school, it was found that 11% of children died before school-going age. This percentage rose to 12% in 1951.[29]

As a result of improved ante-natal and intra-natal care, plus increasing availability of medicine, establishment of maternity homes in rural areas, expansion of education and means of transport, mortality incidence among infants has declined in the last few decades. The situation of Goa in this regard is better than elsewhere in the country.

4. Personal Care

Despite all we have said we read in early accounts, such as the one of Linschotten, a Dutch traveller in Goa in the late 16th century, that he was greatly impressed by personal cleanliness in Goa, specially of the womenfolk.[30] Another visitor of the early 17th century, namely Pyrard de Laval, remarks that unlike people of Africa in India people were free of body odour.[31] The Hindus had their bath everyday before lunch. Leaves of caju or mango tree were used as tooth brushes. Bettle was chewed to keep teeth strong and to prevent bad breath. In rural and coastal areas people were fond of swimming in the rivers and sea.

To protect themselves against excessive heat people often wore light white clothes which they changed often. Lower classes wore only *langoti* (loin cloth passing between thighs and held behind with a cord or metal chain tied around the waist). At home the lower class men usually slept almost naked. Children moved around naked up to the age of seven as it was considered a healthy habit. Only later boys wore shirts and pants and girls wore *gagra* and *choli*. The dress habits had changed considerably among the Christians who had been influenced to adopt more westernized styles of dress, which did not always suit the local climatic conditions.

5. Housing and Waste Disposal

Housing standards varied from class to class. The upper classes lived in spacious houses of stone and mud. However, some rooms were permanently closed preventing light and air. Store rooms were breeding ground for rats. There were two-storeyed houses, but they were few in the Old Conquests. Hindu houses were different from those of the Catholic gentry. Hindu houses were low with small windows, wooden grills and a courtyard inside. Kitchens were situated at the back of the houses beyond sleeping area and close to the well and toilets.

Despite abundance of space in rural areas, the houses of humbler classes were overcrowded. This along with inadequate sleeping arrangements helped the spread of transmittable diseases. Furthermore the roofs made of thatch or palm-leaves were leaky, and the floors smeared with cow-dung helped breeding of fleas. Till the second half of the 19th century some Church floors were covered with cow-dung.

Houses had no proper toilets for a long time. Sanitary arrangements were generally bad and constituted a major health hazard. Facilities for disposal of waste were primitive. Many used the river banks, open fields, hills and streets to answer the calls of nature. Dr. Fryer, an English traveller who visited Goa in the 17th century refers to a curious habit of throwing excreta on the roof tops for the birds to do the clearing.[32] In some cases the courtyards were used for ablutions and these often became breeding grounds for mosquitoes causing malaria.

The upper class people in the city of Panjim made use of pots which were emptied by night-soil carriers (*bonguis*) brought from British India and employed to empty the waste pans in the rivers.[33] This practice still continues in some areas of the capital town. In 1863 some individuals from Panjim had put forward suggestions to improve the sanitary conditions in the city. Very often people tended to keep the night-soil in the house the whole day as they had no one to carry it to the river. It was suggested that one hundred blacks be brought from Angola to do the job.[34] The use of pigs was regarded dangerous for health, because the pigs were later consumed by people. No action followed on the part of the government due to alleged lack of finance. In the absence of better alternative the Medical Board suggested that all excreta should be disinfected. Separate pots for solid and liquid excreta were to be distributed among the poor and night-soil carriers employed to carry the excreta within twenty-four hours. However, not much improvement followed and epidemics continued to take a heavy toll of life year after year.

Situation has improved over the years, but there is much to be desired. Panjim is the only city of Goa with sewage system. There are hardly any public toilets, and people have to still depend on open spaces and river banks and hill sides. Sun, rains, pigs and birds destroy great part of filth. But for these natural friends it would be difficult to live in many parts of Goa.

6. Epidemics

Poor hygienic conditions, malnutrition, impure water supply, bad drainage and refuse disposal system favoured frequent epidemics during the colonial times. They occurred at regular intervals even after inoculation was introduced. Probably the improved means of communication with British India and emigration were also responsible for the frequency.

Cholera was widely prevalent during this period. The first outbreak was in 1818. Deaths due to cholera increased in the third quarter of the 19th century. Another disease which was common and dreaded was smallpox. It appeared in epidemic form in 1870, 1872, 1884, 1888-1892, 1894 and 1897. There were also all kinds of fevers. Among them typhoid and malaria had become endemic in certain talukas like Canacona, Sanguem and Ilhas.

The 20th century began with outbreak of plague, cholera, smallpox and fevers. Cholera raged throughout Portuguese India. In 1900 at least 400 people died of cholera in Salcete[35]. From there it rapidly spread to Ilhas, Ponda, Bicholim, Bardez, Pernem, Sanguem and Quepem. Around the same time plague broke out in Ilhas. It was of virulent nature and normally struck the poor people who slept on humid floors. Despite the measures adopted rats carried the disease far and wide.[36]

Between 1910-1914 at least 35% of deaths in Sanguem taluka were caused by malaria. Dense and humid forests of the area, combined with poor hygiene were largely responsible for this. However, little was done to change the situation till the last ten years of the Portuguese rule.[37]

Smallpox too broke out in many areas in the beginning of the century. In 1918 a fearful epidemic of influenza killed thousands of people all over Goa. It coincided with acute shortage of food provisions in Goa.[38]

Meningitis in epidemic form appeared at Velim and Assolna in Salcete. It struck children and seems to have been brought from Africa. From Salcete it spread to Quepem.[38]

In 1933 several epidemics affected many parts of Goa. They were typhoid, dysentery, whooping cough, smallpox, cholera and chicken -pox. It is believed that cholera was brought by some pilgrim returning from Pandharpur.[39]

Cholera ceased to be common by 1945 due to regular inoculations. But if these diseases continued to visit Goa, it was often due to merchants, sailors and pilgrims.

7. Health Services

Soon after the Portuguese captured Goa they introduced western system of medicine and it was only available to the ruling urban class. However, the European doctors who came to Goa were few and inexperienced in tropical problems. Besides Goa did not attract the cream of Portuguese medical profession. At the same time the colonial rulers created conditions that led to the destruction and the decay of the existing health practices, particularly the ayurvedic medicine that prevailed in Goa at the time of the Portuguese arrival. Even so, till late 17th century some 30 *panditos* (native medicine men) were in the service of the city municipality and they were also in demand in the religious convents and of the high civil authorities.[40]

Seeking help of quacks, such *curandeiros*, *herbolarios*, *feiticeiros*, *sangradores* was common in villages as well as in the urban areas. The therapeutic knowledge of these medicine men was inherited one and they had no formal education.

The Portuguese introduced formal education in medicine as early as 1842, when a medical school was opened. It was set up along the lines of similar schools in France and Portugal. However, the facilities provided were limited and the best teachers did not find incentives to teach there. But despite these limitations the achievements were quite commendable. Eight to ten doctors graduated from this school annually as general practitioners.

In 1895 a *delegado de saúde* (health officer) was created for every taluka. But they could barely meet the needs of the population. For instance, Embarbacem with 26, 000 inhabitants had only one doctor.[41] This situation did not improve till the beginning of this century. Out of 186 doctors, 178 practised in the Old Conquests and only 8 in the New Conquests. In 1921 Sanguem had two doctors for a population of about 20, 000, whilst Satari during the same period had one doctor for 17, 313 inhabitants.[42]

Male nurses often practised as doctors and prescribed medicine to the patients. In Goa for a long time there was shortage of trained nurses and it stemmed from several factors in addition to lack of training facilities and scarcity of girls with sufficient general education. In Goa girls from higher classes hardly ever joined this profession. Work outside home was regarded as unsuitable for any woman of other than the lower classes. Fortunately this attitude changed in course of time.

Dentists were few in Goa, and most of those who practised this profession had only rudimentary knowledge of dentistry. Generally people lived without proper dental care.

A course in pharmacy was started in the medical school. In 1852 about 16 students joined this course, but these diploma holders preferred to work in Government hospitals in urban areas or to be in charge of chemist shops. During early period there was a great shortage of pharmacists in the New Conquests.

Hospitals in the 19th century were mainly situated in urban areas to cater to the needs of urban population. In Ilhas taluka there was one attached to the Medical School and another run by the Holy House of Mercy (*Santa Casa de Misericórdia*). There was also a military hospital. In 1862 Rev. Antonio João Miranda established a 10-bed *hospicio* in Margão for the poor with the help of donations. Special hospitals were set up during the first forty years of this century by the Government and its agencies to provide care to lepers, T. B. patients and mentally ill people. There were also some isolation hospitals for the victims of various epidemics. By 1928 Goa had four full-fledged hospitals, including the Central Hospital with 62 beds for curative medicine. Later the Government set up rural hospitals in Sanguem, Quepem and Valpoi.

During the above period health services were looked after by a Director. He was assisted by five doctors, two pharmacists, the teaching staff, and by 16 health officers (*delegados de saúde*). In 1945 the health services were separated from the Medical School.

Since the liberation the medical scene has changed, the number of trained doctors has increased, and almost every village has a health centre where medical aid is available free of charge to the poor people. Several small clinics have been set up in rural areas by the Government and private doctors.

8. Preventive Medicine

During the colonial period the health services were dominated mainly by curative activities, and preventive aspects were confined to providing environmental sanitation, water supply and immunization coverage to particular areas, usually urban areas inhabited by the ruling class. For the rest of the population anti-epidemic measures were adopted only when there were outbreaks of serious epidemics.

Cholera inoculation was introduced in Goa in 1927. It was made compulsory for those entering Goa from British India. The natives believed that cholera was a curse of Durga Devi when she was not given due recognition. In order to pacify her they resorted to sacrifices rather than to medicines and other rational means of controlling the disease.

Repeated attacks of smallpox during second half of the 19th century forced the State to make vaccination compulsory in 1883. But the vaccination campaign does not seem to have succeeded. Chief among the factors responsible for this failure was the difficulty of keeping lymph potent for a long enough period to make it possible to dispatch it to remote areas and to use it in time. There were also faulty techniques of vaccination. The officials were also reluctant to assert their authority in a field where people's attitude and behaviour pattern were closely entwined with religion and tradition. The vaccinators were also poorly paid.

Smallpox vaccination was made compulsory in 1914 to all children seeking admission in Government primary schools[43], and two years later to all ship crews leaving Marmagoa harbour.[44] The epidemic did not disappear till quite after some time, because people often concealed cases of smallpox from the authorities fearing that they would be sent to isolation hospitals in Colem, Reis Magos, Marmagoa and Margao. The concealment was never complete because the uneducated people believed that *neem* leaves hung at the entrance of the room prevented the spread of the disease and had a beneficial effect on the patient.

The first anti-malarial campaign on war footing was launched in Old Goa in late 1940's. Several wells were closed down, marshy areas were filled up, D. D. T. was sprayed and quinine tablets were distributed to the inhabitants. Large sums were spent to improve the sanitary conditions of the old city. Before the introduction of preventive measures nearly 60, 000 people died of malaria in Goa every year. In early 1950's two doctors were deputed to the Malaria Institute in New Delhi to receive training in malaria control. On their return they were posted in Sanguem and Canacona. The eradication programme was then extended to Quepem. Malaria seems to have made a come-back and that too in the capital town of Goa.[45]

Concluding Remarks

The colonial policy was greatly responsible for the state of affairs in Goa. Lack of enforcement authority and lethargic attitude on the part of the State was responsible for poor health conditions in the territory. Health services and health care were dependent on political decisions of the rulers. Policy decisions regarding resource-allocation, manpower-training and availability of health services were taken at the political level. Colonialism, like every other form of government, had its own politics of health.

During the post-colonial era the situation has improved due to greater awareness among the people regarding hygiene. This has happened through spread of literacy, improvement in economic conditions, better transport and communications. The rapid decline of many older diseases can be ascribed to the application of new medical technology and changed attitudes and habits of the people. Powerful drugs have revolutionized the treatment of a number of infectious diseases, and inoculation drives have been successful. These could be counted as some of the blessings of the liberation. However, it is difficult to conclude that we do not have serious health and hygiene problems anymore. New dangers are caused by changed circumstances resulting from the so-called "development".

Industrialization, new work-conditions, emigration, rapid growth of population, have in many ways reduced the positive impact of the improvements made in the area of health and hygiene.

REFERENCES

1. Fonseca, J. N. da, *An historical and archaeological sketch of the city of Goa*, Bombay, 1878, p. 8.
2. *Statistical Report on the Portuguese Settlements in India*, ed. Captain Kol, in *Selections from the Records of the Bombay Government*, No. X, New Series, Bombay 1855, p. 328.
3. Almeida, J. C., *Some Demographic Aspects of Goa, Daman and Diu*, Panjim, 1975, p. 169.
4. *Ibid.* . p. 188.
5. Census of India 1981, Series 29, Goa, Daman and Diu, p. 52.
6. Fernandes, F. X. Ernesto, *India Portuguesa: Estudos Economicos Sociaes*, Bastora, 1905, p. 53.
7. Miranda, J. A. de Piedade, "Balanço comercial: A nossa exportação e importação", 5o. Congresso Provincial, Nova Goa, 1922, p. 55.
8. Souza, T. R. de, *Medieval Goa*, New Delhi, 1979, p. 53.
9. Fernandes, *op. cit.* , p. 55.
10. Miranda, *op. cit.* , p. 57.
11. Cottineau, D., *An historical sketch of Goa*, Madras, 1831, p. 117.
12. Pinto, J. B., *Goan emigration*, Goa, n. d., p. 1.
13. Fernandes, *op. cit.* , p. 71.
14. Khan Haward, R., "An urban minority: The Goan Christian Community in Karachi", *The City in South Asia*, eds. K. Ballhatchet and J. Harrison, London, 1980, p. 299.
15. D'Souza, G. B., *Goan Society in Transition*, Bombay, 1975, p. 195.
16. Angle, P. S., *Goa: An Economic Review*, Panjim, 1983, p. 43.
17. Albuquerque, V. A. C. B. de, *Senado de Goa: Memoria Historico- Archaeologica*, Nova Goa, 1909, p. 444.
18. Souza, T. R. de, *op. cit.* , p. 268.
19. Boletim Oficial, N. 39, 17th May 1907.
20. "Fomento do Concelho de Sanguem: A report", *Arquivos da Escola Medica Cirurgica de Goa*, 1937, p. 1687.
21. Census 1950, Goa, pp. 139, 175.
22. Almeida, *Aspects of the Agricultural Activity in Goa, Daman and Diu*, Panjim, 1967, p. 289.
23. Pacheco Figueiredo, J. M. de, "A alimentação na India Portuguesa", offprint of *Anais do Instituto de Medicina Tropical*, Sept. 1953, p. 1244.
24. Braganca Pereira, A. B. de, *Etnografia da India Portuguesa*, II, Bastora, 1940, p. 378.
25. Fernandes, *op. cit.* , pp. 202-203.
26. Pacheco Figueiredo, *op. cit.* , p. 1270.
27. *Arquivos da Escola Medica Cirurgica de Nova Goa*, Bastora, 1930, p. 583.
28. *Archivo Medico da India*, I, n. 5, 1854, p. 100.
29. Pacheco Figueiredo, *op. cit.* , p. 1211.
30. Burnell and Tiele, eds., *The voyages of John Huyghen van Linschoten to the East Indies*, II, London, 1885, p. 184.
31. Basto Magalhães, ed., *Viagem de Francisco Pyrard de Laval*, Porto, 1944, p. 51.
32. Fryer, J., *New Account of East India and Persia*, II, London, 1912, p. 152.

33. de Melo, Froilano, "Le service de sante en l'Inde Portugaise, 1927-1928", *Arquivo da Escola Medica Cirurgica de Nova Goa*, Bastora, 1930, p. 673.
34. *Jornal da Pharmacia e Sciencias Medicas*, Nova Goa, Março 1863, p. 2.
35. Silva Correia, G. da, *Nosografia da India Portuguesa*, Nova Goa, 1921, p. 225.
36. Silva, F. A. W. da, *Relatorio sobre a epidemia de peste*, Nova Goa, 1902.
37. Oral information from Dr. P. A. Borker and Dr F. da Silva. They were the ones sent to Delhi for training in malaria-control methods.
38. *Vidiaprassaran*, Ponda, 17th August 1919, p. 2.
39. "Relatorio de servicos de saude", *Boletim Geral de Medicina*, 1934, p. 63.
40. Souza, T. R. de, *op. cit.* , p. 159.
41. Fernandes, *op. cit.* , p. 110.
42. *Arquivos da Escola Medica Cirurgica de Nova Goa*, 1930, p. 583.
43. "Hospicio do Sagrado Coração de Maria", *Anuario da India Portuguesa*, Nova Goa, 1930, p. 198. This hospital in Margão had its foundation stone blessed on 13th May 1867.
44. Historical Archives of Goa: Ms. 10550, fl. 5.
45. *Ibid.*, fl. 81.
46. *Herald*, Panjim, 27th May 1988, p. 3, cols. 4 & 5.

18

SOURCE MATERIAL FOR LATIN AMERICA IN GOA (WITH SPECIAL REFERENCE TO BRAZIL)

Archana Kakodkar

This is an attempt at cataloguing the source material on Latin America available in the libraries and archives of Goa.

We know that following the historic journey of Vasco da Gama in 1498, another Portuguese navigator Pedro Alvares Cabral set out in 1500, seeking a westward route to India and he was accidentally washed ashore the Brazilian coast. This opened the way for long term contacts between India and Latin America. Though we are still unsure about the details of the Indo-Latin American commercial exchange which lasted till the middle of the 19th century, it is estimated that they were of great volume.[1]This can be examined with the help of the documents existing in the libraries and archives in Goa.

I. The relevant records from the Goa Historical Archives are found in the following three series:

1. *Monções do Reino*, 456 volumes.

2. *Provisões dos vicereis*, 3 volumes.

3. *Ordens Regias*, 86 volumes.

1. The documents from the *Monções do Reino* can be grouped under the following headings:

a. Establishment of Indian weavers' colony in the captaincy of Para (Brazil).
b. Cultivation of spices and Indian drugs in Brazil. Commercial Relations between Brazil and Estado da India.
c. Brazilian troops in Goa.
d. Insurrection in Pernambuco (Brazil).
e. Miscellaneous documents.

a. *Establishment of Indian Weavers' Colony in Para*

By the royal letter of 12th March 1588 the viceroy of India was ordered that persons who could spin and weave cotton should be sent to Brazil, as there was a great quantity of cotton available on the coast of Para. Married couples were to be preferred. There is no evidence to prove whether the viceroy was able to satisfy the royal desire, as it was unlike that an Indian weaver would go to Brazil in those times. On 21st March 1750 the government of Portuguese India received new orders from the royal court to make arrangement to gather married couples from India from among those who would weave and print cotton muslins and handkerchiefs, preferably from south India. These families were to be transported to Bahia, from where they could go to Para. Along with these weavers cotton manufacturing machinery, like looms, wheels, and colour ingredients for dyeing cloth, were also to be sent. The instruction also mentioned a "raiz de ruinas" (=root of ruins?) available in Marastrao(?).

It is interesting to note the terms which the home government in Portugal was offering to these workmen to settle down in Para of Brazil: (1) Ten *patacas* would be paid to each person, old or young, of both sexes, to prepare for the voyage. The payment would be made to the head of the family; (2) The weaving looms, paints, and other tools which they would bring along would be purchased at the cost of the State; (3) The government would meet the travel expenses of those coming from Coromandel to Goa. They were to be treated with all care all along their travel to Goa and further to

Brazil; (4) Those wishing to travel from Coromandel by land to Goa would receive the amount of money required for the travel against a personal guarantee; (5) They were to be looked after well during their stay in Goa and also in Brazil for a period of three years at the cost of the State; (6) On arrival in Para they would be free to choose any island in that River or in that of Amazonas. They would be given any island, even if one chosen was already occupied by others, excepting the big Island Joannes; (7) The island they decided to choose would become their property to be enjoyed by them and their descendants. It would be divided among the settler families equally; (8) In the said island no other settlers other than the families from Coromandel and their descendants will be allowed, excepting those they may invite to help them in cultivation; (9) Every family will receive a good quantity of paddy seed, cereals and fruits for their food, as well as appliances required for cultivation, fishing and activities connected with settlement; (10) They will be allowed to keep their customs without any constraints, but they will not be permitted anything against the Faith and good manners; (11) Once established, they will enact their own statutes for their administration, police, as needed by their community, and these laws will be respected after receiving approval from the crown; (12) The heads of these families and their descendants will be entitled to hold any job and honours without any opposition due to caste and will be reputed among themselves as equals without distinction of castes; (13) These families will come accompanied by a missionary of the Madure mission, and he will assist them also in their settlement; (14) They could go to the city of Para or any other place as their trade or other business may require, but they were not to leave the State; (15) For the greater benefit of these families and their descendants no entry or exit tax would be levied on *xitas* (=cotton prints) manufactured in the crown domains; (16) Once the number of settlers grows, they will be given more land, provided they continued their craft; (17) If more families chose to come from India and preferred to settle in the mainland rather than in the island, they would be allowed to do so freely. A district could be assigned to them and divided among the new settler families; (18) The captaincy of ports of Para, where these families are to be transported has an extension of 700 leagues (2100 miles) or more, and corresponding breadth, and along its whole length it is crossed by the river Amazonas, which is the biggest of the whole world. Within a short distance from the city of Para there are other big rivers containing innumerable islands, small and big. Nearer the sea there is one of 100 leagues in length, known as Joanes. The soil of the mainland and the islands is fertile, and the waters abound in fish and tortoises, which provides food without much work. There is plenty of rice growing naturally, and so also many varieties of cereals and fruits, specially cocoa. Cotton seeds grow in abundance and without cultivation, and there are many plants producing dyes and colours. The climate is very much like that of the Indian peninsula, but cooler, even though closer to the equinox, and it is healthy. It is in all aspects a lovely country that needs inhabitants knowing how to avail of its wealth.

On 30th January, 1751, the viceroy Marquis of Tavora wrote to the Secretary of State that all the endeavours made by him to send families of Indian weavers and painters were fruitless, because "the Indians have a great reluctance to leave their country".[2]

b. *Cultivation of Cinnamon, Pepper and Other Indian Drugs*

When in 1677 D. Pedro de Almeida was appointed viceroy, the king ordered him to dispatch to Brazil in every monsoon the slips and seeds of some fruit yielding trees from India, and he mentioned particularly the cinnamon, cloves, pepper, nutmegs and ginger.

In January 1680 two boxes filled with mud and containing stems of pepper plants, plus 10 vases with 30 stems of cinnamon were shipped to Brazil in the war-ship "Nossa Senhora de Conceição".

During the monsoon of 1690 Fr. João de Brito arrived from Lisbon, and he was asked by the king of arrange experienced men to work in the cultivation and plantation of cinnamon and pepper. They were to be sent to Bahia. Apparently the Governor, D. Rodrigo da Costa had already sent two men for the purpose. However, even in 1695 the viceroy of India was receiving instructions to send to Bahia some Sinhalese cultivators from Ceylon. Two ways of doing this had been suggested: The first is through a Goan priest named Joseph Vaz, a very pious man, who goes about in Ceylon disguised and doing the work of God among the Christians there. The said priest could be asked to look out for some cinnamon planters among his Christians. The other way would be to request the captains of the vessels sailing from Goa to the coast of Coromandel, Bengal or Macau to arrange on their return journey via Ceylon to contact the Christians (who remain faithful to the crown of Portugal) and get them to send the required planters for Brazil. However, this second alternative is regarded as less viable and slow as it would take at least one year for the vessels to return.

Strict secrecy was recommended in carrying out these orders, in order that the Dutch might not get suspicious and stop the execution of the plan. This risk could be avoided by depending on the aforementioned priest, who could guide the planters to the Fishery coast, and from there they could be easily and in less time brought to Goa. Whatever the choice of means adopted, the planters were to be assured of good treatment.

In January 1706 the viceroy Caetano de Melo de Castro sent Fr. João de Assunção to Bahia to help the execution of the scheme of cinnamon cultivation.

In January 1718 25 boxes of pepper plants were dispatched from Goa to Brazil along with soil of the place of origin.

It was not possible for the Indian authorities to obtain the seed of the fine cinnamon trees of Ceylon on account of a heavy tax imposed by the Dutch on the export of cinnamon from that island.

The king of Portugal continued his requests through the second half of the 18th century for spice plants to be sent to Bahia. In 1750 the viceroy Marquis of Alorna was instructed to take along with him to Bahia some Goan Christian peasants ("canarins") who were experienced in the cultivation of palm-trees.

In 1790 a parcel of cinnamon and pepper trees was sent to Brazil. The Governor of Bahia wrote to the viceroy of India on this occasion that if he continued sending more parcels and instruction on how best to plant them and extract the bark of cinnamon, the plantation could grow to become a commercial venture.

In December 1811 the governor of Goa sent to Brazil in response to royal wishes some mango saplings of "afonsa" and "fernandina" varieties.[3]

c. *Commercial Relations*

A royal decree of 9th March 1672 conceded freedom of trade in textiles, spices, and slaves to all Portuguese living in the kingdom, Brazil or any other colony. This was to be effective from March 1673.

The government of Bahia was insisting in 1690 that there should be commercial relations between Brazil and the ports of the Estado da India, particularly with Moçambique. It was proposed among other things that (1) 3 vessels could go every year from Bahia, Pernambuco and Rio de Janeiro to Moçambique, Goa and other cities of the East; (2) India could be helped militarily by soldiers from Brazil rather than Portugal; (3) Vessels from Brazil could carry "gerebitas", sugar, tobacco, "pau violeta", and sacaranda; (4) they could transport from Moambique and Goa all the provisions they may require.

The authorities of the "India House" in Lisbon were of the opinion that these proposals were not beneficial. The same opinion was expressed by the experienced persons in Goa at a meeting on 10th November 1700.

Among the articles of India sold in Brazil textiles occupied an important place. They bore many different designations like "de negro", "de Damão", "de Diu", "de Surate", "de Balagate", depending obviously on the source of their manufacture and origin. They were collected from Goa.

On the 30th April 1790 the governor in Goa, Francisco da Cunha e Menezes was informing the Secretary of State that some indigo had arrived from Brazil and that it found a very profitable acceptance in the markets of Surat. He expressed his opinion that this item could become an important branch of commerce with India. The item that had a great demand in Goa, mainly since 1766, was the leaf-tobacco coming from Bahia. It is known that 30 bales of that tobacco were brought to Goa in 1773 by an agency house of Anselmo Jose de Cruz and Policarpo Jose Machado. The export of tobacco from Bahia to India in 1780 was 262 bales. over 275 bales were sent in 1785, and 314 bales in 1789. Tobacco was being sent also in the form of rolls and powder weighed in *arrobas* and pounds. In 1802 Goa received 264 bales, in 1807 200 bales, in 1821 323 barrels. It was expected that the Estado da India should pay for the imports of tobacco with saltpetre. About two thousand quintals of saltpetre per year were desired.[4]

d. *Troops from Brazil*

The government of Bahia suggested to the home government in 1699 that it would be more economical and practical to send soldiers to India from Brazil. Businessmen in Brazil were prepared to send people to India without any cost to the royal exchequer. In return they were to be allowed free trade from the ports of Bahia, Pernambuco and Rio de Janeiro.

It is known from the proceedings of the State Council in Goa dated 14th October 1702 that the crown had ordered that India should be helped with troops from Brazil. The archives in Goa contains documentation pertaining to numerous soldiers and officers from Brazil serving in India from the 17th to the 19th centuries.

Captain Artur de Sa of great fame in Portuguese India in the second quarter of the 17th century came from Rio de Janeiro. He rose to become captain-general of St. Tomé of Mylapore (1653). Unfortunately the Goa archives do not seem to hold documents relating to the illustrious Brazilian woman Maria Ursula de Abreu e Lencastre, born in Rio de Janeiro, and who served in Portuguese India with the disguise of a male soldier, calling herself Baltazar do Couto Cardozo. She served courageously in the campaigns against the Bhosles of Sawantvadi (1705-1706).[5]

e. *Insurrection in Pernambuco*

The governor of Pernambuco was deposed by a revolutionary government installed in that captaincy, and he reached Lisbon on 25th March 1817. As a consequence of this the king declared that all the ports of Pernambuco were in a state of blockade and the governor of India received orders to sequester vessels that may belong to the Pernambucan merchants who were sentenced in the inquest. These were: Bento Jose de Costa, Jose de Oliveira Ramos, Jose Joaquim Jorge, Antonio Marques da Costa Soares, Antonio de Silva, Jose Joaquim Jorge Gonsalves, Joaquim Antonio Gonsalves da Oliveira, Joaquim Jose Mendes, Domingos Jose Martins and Manuel Jose Martins Ribeiro.[6]

f. *Miscellaneous Information*

It is evident from a petition of Srinivas Naique, a Hindu merchant from Panjim that he had bought one negro to be sent to Rio de Janeiro in 1828.

The viceroy of India was writing to the crown on 20th January 1718 requesting that a frigate built in Brazil be sent to India. He says that the Brazilian wood will last longer than the wood used for shipbuilding in Europe.

The Government of India was informed by the Viscount of Anandia in a letter written from Rio de Janeiro on 7th July 1808 that a Supreme Military Council was established in that State with royal seal on the opening of the ports of Brazil for the purpose of trade to the foreign vessels.

The king announced in a letter written from Rio de Janeiro on 3rd September 1817 and addressed to the viceory of India, count of Rio Pardo that the royal prince D. Pedro de Alcantara was married. The inhabitants of the *Estado da India* could celebrate "with the festive demonstrations of joy and gaiety used on such occasions".[7]

2. *Provisões dos vicereis (1602-1621)*

A small but useful collection of documents (3 vols) relating to trade and navigation. The bulk of the documents cover the years 1599-1609 and 1621. The pagination is very erratic. The first volume is in a bad state of preservation, but contains some original documents concerning the illegal voyage of D. Rodrigo de Cordara from China (Macao) to Peru.[8]

3. *Ordens Régias (1630-1864)*

This series runs into 86 volumes. Vol. 3, fls. 385-409 contains transcripts of documents pertaining to the Pernambuco rising against the Dutch and the resultant hostilities in Brazil (1645-1646). The volume also includes information on trade with Zambesi and transplantation of spices to Brazil. They are documents of the late 17th century.[9]

II. *Documents at the Xavier Centre of Historical Research, Goa*

The private business records of the the Mhamai agency house that was involved in coastal and international trade during the late 18th and early 19the centuries are preserved at the Xavier Centre of Historical Research (Porvorim, Goa). These manuscript papers are written in old Kannada script, Modi (Marathi), Portuguese, French, Gujarati, and English. There are even a couple of Persian records. The documents in European languages have been classified under the following categories: (1) Incoming correspondence;(2) *Borradores* or drafts of outgoing correspondence; (3) Books of accounts of farmed revenues and commercial transactions; (4) Copies of judicial processes.

These records constitute an example of indigenous sources for Indo-Portuguese and Indo-Brazilian historiography. It may take some years before this collection is fully classified and made available to the researchers, but quite a few papers have already been used by some scholars. There is a letter in this collection written from Rio de Janeiro by Domingos Gomes Loureiro and sons on 17th May 1809 to Mhamai brothers. It says that the revolution that brought the royal family from Portugal to Brazil, shifting thereby the entire direction of the Portuguese commerce, had moved them to establish their agency house in Rio de Janeiro, and that they would take care with utmost zeal of any business that may be entrusted to them by the Mhamai brothers and other Indian businessmen. Their ship "Rainha dos Anjos" was going to visit the ports that were formerly closed to businessmen of Brazil, and they hoped that the revolution would be very useful to the Asian merchants as the goods from Malabar would be specially in demand.[10]

REFERENCES

1. Jadeja, D. P. *India and Latin America: Partners in Progress*, New Delhi: Asian Publications, 1988.
2. Historical Archives of Goa (=HAG), *Monções do Reino*, No. 3-A, fls. 289-289v; No. 123-B, fls. 581-2, 641, 643v.
3. *Ibid.*, , No. 45, fls. 68, 72, 76, 120, 121; No. 55-B, fls. 319, 348-9; No. 59, fl. 320; No. 68, fl. 234; No. 70, fl. 29; No. 80, fl. 319; No. 88, fl. 31; No. 123-B, fl. 694; No. 129-B, fl. 718; No. 131-B, fl. 520; No. 133-B, fl. 332; No. 171-B, fl. 578; No. 172-B, fl. 831; No. 175, fl. 232; No. 181-A, fl. 79; No. 191-C, fls. 539-40.
4. *Ibid.*, No. 6-A, fl. 114; No. 37, fl. 194; No. 60, fl. 74; No. 63, fls. 418-22, 428-49; No. 64, fls. 160-68, 174; No. 71, fl. 87; No. 103-A, fl. 130; No. 115, fls. 45, 48; No. 132, fl. 224; No. 151, fls. 157; No. 159-C, fls. 683-4; No. 163-B, fl. 585; No. 164-A, fls. 151-2, 187; No. 164-G, fls. 1982-3; No. 166, fls. 337, 375-6; No. 178-D, f. 1086; No. 169-B, fl. 672; No. 170-C, fl. 897; No. 171-B, fl. 566; No. 172-B, fls. 742, 750, 833; No. 181-B, fl. 577; No. 187-B, fls. 550, 557; No. 189, fls. 33, 39; No. 199-B, fls. 428, 431.
5. *Ibid.*, No. 64, fl. 170; No. 164-G, fls. 992-4, 1974-79, 1986, 1988, 1990, 1998, 2000, 2002, 2004, 2006, 2008; No. 171-B, fls. 568-72, 817-18; No. 181-B, fl. 537; No. 199-B, fls. 430, 450.
6. *Ibid.*, No. 196-A, fls. 7-10, 13.
7. *Ibid.*, No. 83, fl. 321; No. 189, fl. 32; NO. 196, fl. 47; No. 199, fl. 398.
8. Boxer, C. R., "Glimpses of Goa Archives", *Bulletin of the School of Oriental and African Studies*, London, 1952.
9. *Loc. cit.*
10. De Souza, T. R., "Mhamai House Records: Indigenous Sources for Indo-Portuguese Historiography", *Indian Archives*, New Delhi, Jan-June, 1982, Vol. 31, No. 1.

N. B. For more details on the topic covered in this essay the readers are referred to author's research on *Bibliographical survey of source material for Latin American studies in selected libraries in Goa* (Unpublished dissertation submitted to the Bombay University for Master's Degree in Library Science, 1986)

INDEX